AMONG THE TREES

AMONG THE TREES

HAYWARD GALLERY
PUBLISHING

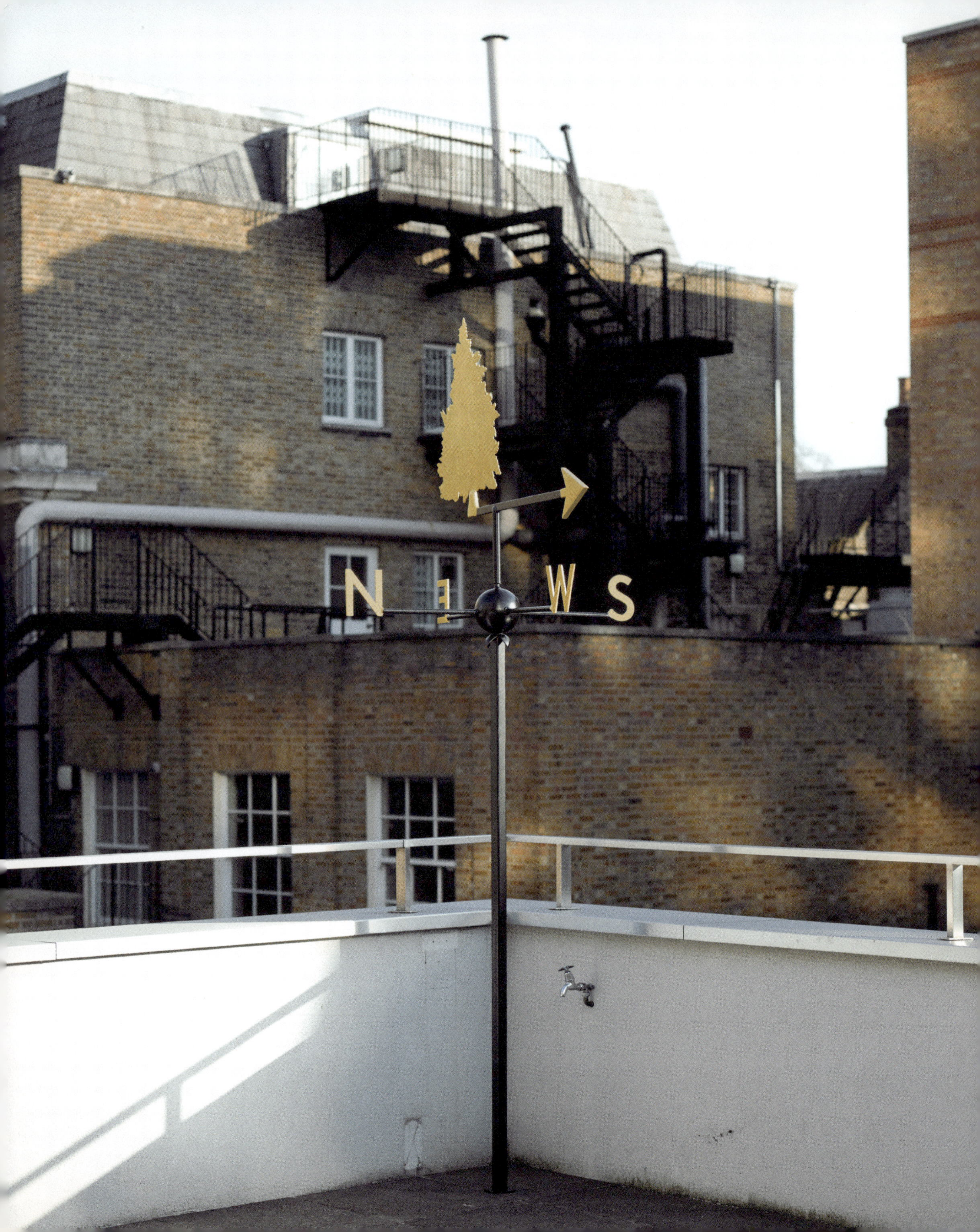
N
W
S

Virginia Overton
Untitled (Juniper), 2014

FOREWORD

Approximately 50 years ago, coinciding with the rise of the modern environmental movement, the subject of trees emerged as a motif in works by some of the most adventurous and influential artists of the time. In the years since, this engagement with trees has grown into a rich vein of contemporary art to which artists working in diverse media and different parts of the world have contributed. While their art draws on the visually arresting character of trees – including their complex spatial and architectural forms – it conveys much more than mere descriptive facts. Instead, their work invites us to reimagine our relationships with trees and forests as both symbols and living organisms that have helped to shape human civilisation and continue to play an indispensable role in our lives and imaginations.

Among the Trees gathers together works by more than 30 artists who reconfigure traditional genres and develop new ways of representing trees in order to shift our conventional perceptions and understanding. It surveys a remarkably expansive artistic terrain, encompassing a wide range of approaches and media whilst reflecting on myriad aspects of its universally recognised, yet still little-understood subject. Trees provide a point of departure for artists concerned with upending our anthropomorphic perspectives or with confronting us with images that conjure alternative measures of time. Still other artists explore the blurring lines between our concept of nature and culture or seek to prompt reflection on forests as systems characterised by complexity, growth and connectivity, chiming with recent scientific discoveries about the 'wood wide web' – the network of underground roots, fungi and bacteria that connects forest organisms in symbiotic relationships.

Most of the works included here do not explicitly raise ecological concerns, yet many almost inevitably bring to mind the vulnerability and precarity of trees and forests in what has been called the Anthropocene era. According to a 2015 study published in the journal *Nature*, approximately 46 per cent of the world's forests have disappeared since humans began chopping down trees. At present rates of deforestation, there will be no more trees on the planet in 600 years. It is my hope that *Among the Trees* can provide an inspiring range of perspectives and instil a renewed sense of appreciation for the crucial place that trees occupy in our shared world.

It has been a true pleasure and privilege to work with the many artists in this exhibition, and our thanks go first and foremost to them. They have enriched us all by making artworks that provocatively enlarge our sense of the conceptual and aesthetic boundaries of the role that trees play in our imaginative and physical worlds.

It would not have been possible to realise this exhibition without the generosity of the many lenders involved, including individual collectors, galleries, foundations and the studios of the participating artists. We extend to them our gratitude for making these artworks available to the public through their inclusion in this exhibition. I also wish to acknowledge our deep appreciation for the help provided by supporters of the exhibition, including Gagosian, Gallery Hyundai, Lisson Gallery, Pace Gallery, Pro Helvetia and Sadie Coles HQ.

We are very grateful to the authors Jeffrey Kastner and Matteo Pasquinelli for contributing essays to this book that brilliantly illuminate the artworks in the exhibition as well as their larger social and art historical contexts. Lucy Biddle, Marie-Charlotte Carrier, Phoebe Cripps, Katie Guggenheim and Helen Luckett contributed exemplary short texts on the individual artists in the exhibition. Hayward Art Publisher Alice Nightingale and Publishing Project Manager Diana Adell did a superb job supervising all aspects of this publication. It was a delight, as always, to work with designer Melanie Mues, who has fashioned the playfully thoughtful design of this book.

As with any exhibition of this scale, numerous people provided substantial help and assistance. On the Hayward Gallery team, I would like to single out for mention Assistant Curators Phoebe Cripps and Katie Guggenheim, who managed the many challenges posed by a large international exhibition with ingenuity and exacting thoroughness, and who received brilliant support from Curatorial Assistant Marie-Charlotte Carrier. Exhibitions Interpretation Manager Lucy Biddle developed the interpretative materials for the exhibition with great care and thoughtfulness. A special thanks goes also to the sterling work of Installation Manager Juliane Heynert, Senior Technician William Clifford, Senior Registrar Imogen Winter, Assistant Registrar Alice Peters and Exhibition Bookings and Indemnity Co-ordinator Alison Maun, without whom this exhibition would never have come together. In her role as Hayward General Manager Aoife Leach has provided invaluable support across many different areas.

Finally, my gratitude goes to Southbank Centre CEO Elaine Bedell, as well as Southbank Centre's Board of Governors and Arts Council England for their enthusiastic support.

Ralph Rugoff
Director, Hayward Gallery

THE AGE OF TREES

Ralph Rugoff

This era should clearly be the Age of Trees.
—Jimmie Durham[1]

Life as we know it would be unimaginable without trees. One of the oldest life forms on earth – having evolved approximately 380 million years ago – trees produce a substantial portion of the oxygen in the air we breathe. They have furnished us with fuel for cooking, warmth and smelting; with sustenance in the form of fruits and nuts; with shelter from sun and rain. They have also provided timber for constructing buildings of every kind and furniture to go in them, as well as ships, bridges, railway sleepers, paper, musical instruments, etc. Their gravity-defying architecture has been a major source of inspiration for our buildings. Now scientists have confirmed that they also positively affect our mood (something poets and naturalists have long known). In brief, it would be difficult to overestimate the indispensable and intimate role that trees have played in the evolution of human civilisation.

Testifying to the almost universal recognition of their importance, trees have appeared as cultural icons in mythologies and religions across the world. Historically in both Eastern and Western societies they have inspired the mystical symbol of the *arbor vitae*, or tree of life. From the Bodhi tree under which Buddha became enlightened to the Garden of Eden's Tree of Knowledge and the Norse Yggdrasil, they have served as symbols connoting transmission and abundance, regeneration and also mortality. In our everyday phrases we find reflections of our long-standing connection with arboreal life: we speak of having roots, of activities bearing fruit, of branches of government. We trace our lineage in family trees. We also make use of dendritic structures as a model for

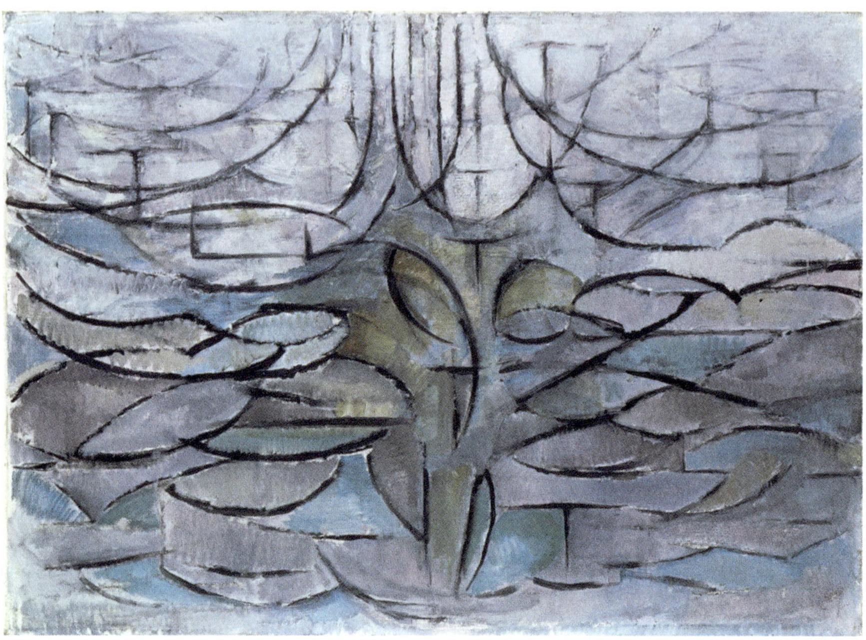

Fig. 1
Piet Mondrian
Flowering Apple Tree, 1912

thought and decision-making, including for artificial intelligence.[2] And trees have been embraced as vital emblems of national character: the oak was once the symbol of the Royal Navy and British state, whilst Germany's primeval forests were seen as an integral component of its national identity.

Yet despite the tree's widespread use as a multivalent symbol, it has been relegated to the background throughout much of Western art history over the past 500 years. From Michelangelo to Rodin, for example, we find no great sculptures of trees, and while a handful of painters occasionally took up this subject as the focus of a particular work, trees were generally depicted as secondary elements of scenery, the backdrop for a portrait or a generic feature of a landscape. And then in the course of twentieth-century modernism, they essentially disappeared from view. This vanishing act was famously staged in a series of celebrated paintings by Piet Mondrian, in which the Dutch artist rendered his subject in progressively abstract terms. Moving from his expressionistic, yet still conventionally legible *Red Tree* in 1908 to the cubist-influenced *Flowering Apple Tree* of 1912 (fig. 1), Mondrian gradually abstracted his subject until it was merely a schematic trace in a field comprised of horizontal and vertical lines. From the viewpoint of modern progressive artists engaged with an aesthetic of reductive formalism, the tree could be discarded as an obsolete motif; it was linked to traditional landscapes, after all, that had no cultural relevance in a society defined by the churning rush and spectacle of urban modernity. In neither painting nor sculpture from the 'high' modernist period do we find examples of influential artworks that depict individual trees; and whilst some well-known photographers in this period, such as Alfred Stieglitz, occasionally took up the subject, the works they produced generally looked backwards towards Romantic genres of the nineteenth century.

It was not until the late 1960s that the tree re-emerged as a motif employed in conceptually advanced and adventurous artworks. It is probably no coincidence that this was also a time of growing social awareness about the damaging impact of industrial chemicals and pollution on the natural environment. In any case, over the course of the past half century artists have repeatedly revisited this subject in works that map out an expansive and varied artistic territory. While it highlights the complex and visually rich architecture of trees, the best of this work is not concerned with conveying mere descriptive facts; instead it has taken up the task of reimagining our conventional imagery in order to open up new ways of thinking about our complex relationship with arboreal life.

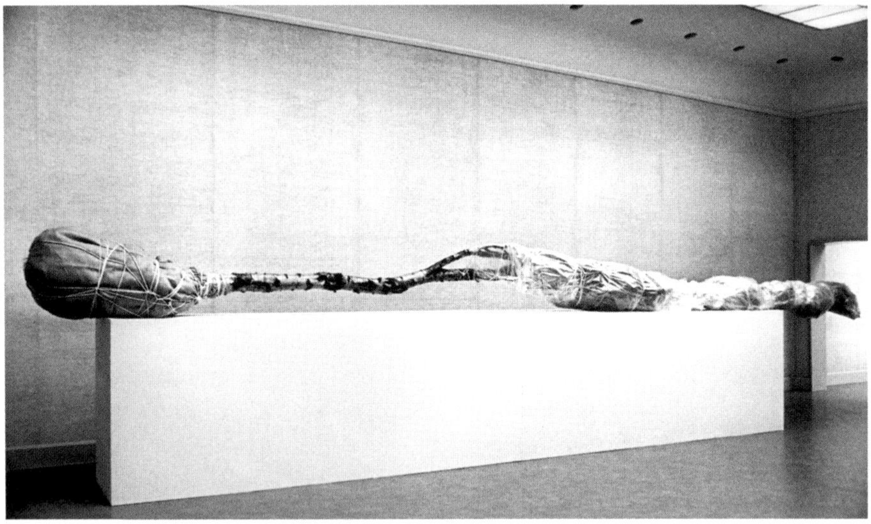

Fig. 2
Christo
Wrapped Tree, 1966

Dead Trees

What are the roots that clutch, what branches grow
Out of this stony rubbish?
— 'The Waste Land', T.S. Eliot[3]

On its publication in 1962 Rachel Carson's groundbreaking exposé *Silent Spring* brought widespread attention to the deadly environmental consequences of chemical pesticides and pollutants. Eventually translated into 30 languages, the book helped to catalyse the rise of the modern environmental movement. Later that decade – at roughly the same time that a burgeoning international counterculture was embracing 'return to nature' lifestyles – several highly publicised environmental disasters, including major oil spills off the coasts of both the United Kingdom and the United States, helped to spur growing public consciousness around ecological concerns. In the early 1970s, the founding of activist groups in North America like Greenpeace and Ecology Action signalled a heightened seriousness about protecting the environment, which was shortly echoed by the establishment of Europe's first green political parties.

This changing cultural context explains, at least in part, why trees re-emerged in the late 1960s as the subject of complex, thought-provoking works of contemporary art. The potential meanings they could evoke had dramatically shifted: rather than innocent figures in a picturesque conception of landscape, trees could now conceivably be cast as victims of an unchecked industrial assault upon the environment. Christo was among the pioneers in exploring this new symbolic territory: included in his 1966 exhibition at the Stedelijk Van Abbemuseum (Eindhoven), his *Wrapped Tree* (fig. 2) sculpture consisted of a skeletal birch with its branches tightly bound by polyethylene sheets and rope, and its roots covered in jute fabric. Whilst its appearance recalled the manner in which trees are routinely packed for transport in commercial nurseries, Christo's work seemed to veer towards a more anthropomorphic reference. Displayed horizontally, *Wrapped Tree* extended beyond the head and foot of its sleek white plinth, suggesting an ungainly corpse laid out upon a too-short mortuary slab. One writer described this work and its later iterations as conjuring 'mummified corpses [...] [which] appeared to be precious objects but also looked harrowed, weak, suffering and old'.[4] Beyond its associations with everyday practices of preserving, packaging and shrouding, Christo's sculpture implicitly questioned the pervasive and morbid commodification of both nature and art in Western societies.

Three years later, Robert Smithson, who once dismissed galleries and museums as 'mausoleums for art', contributed the disconcerting sculpture *Dead Tree* (1969) to the *Prospect 69* exhibition at the Düsseldorf Kunsthalle (fig. 3). In the lexicon of Smithson's art, *Dead Tree* was a 'site/non-site' work: the artist relocated a roughly 13-metre-high tree, including its rootstock, from its original 'site' in nearby Langfeld (Germany) and installed it in the 'non-site' of the Kunsthalle's exhibition space. Smithson positioned the tree horizontally on the floor of a spacious gallery, making visible the morphological mirroring of its crown and roots. He also interspersed a dozen rectangular mirrors around the tree, thereby introducing images of visitors into the work (particularly their feet) and setting up illusionary sight lines that ricocheted in all directions. With its still-leafy branches, *Dead Tree* was clearly a specimen that had only recently been alive. Within the gallery's container-like environment, it confronted visitors with an image and experience of something drastically deracinated, denatured and displaced. Given

Fig. 3
Robert Smithson
Dead Tree, 1969

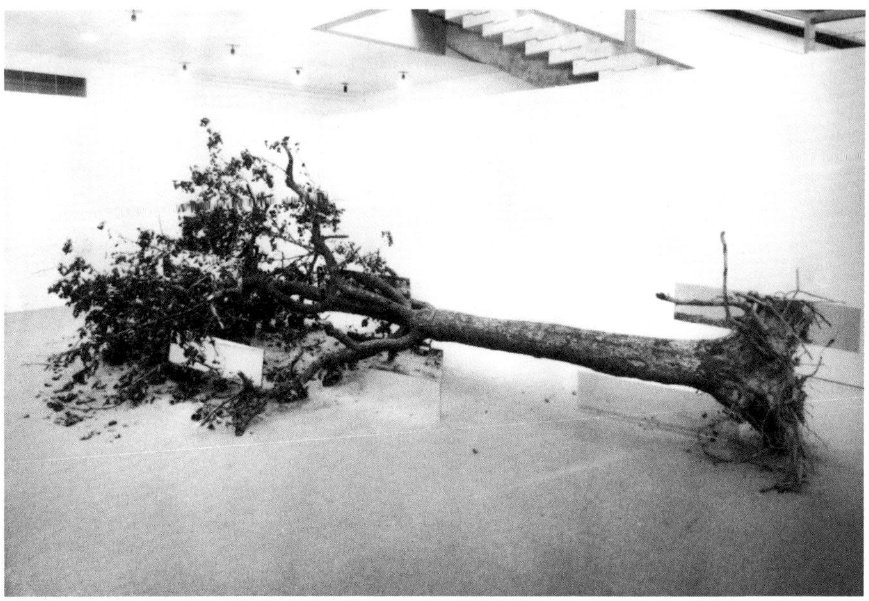

the fact that the Vietnam War was then raging (with the US military napalming huge swathes of jungle forests), it seems significant that the American artist titled this work after a line in the 'Burial of the Dead' section of T.S. Eliot's poem 'The Waste Land' (1922) that evokes the spiritual desolation of a post-war society.[5]

Borrowing a page from Marcel Duchamp, these works by Christo and Smithson essentially employed the tree as the central element of an 'assisted readymade.' Duchamp's readymades, however, had made use only of industrially produced articles; in treating an organic life form as a readymade, Christo and Smithson inevitably introduced the idea of death into the equation. Their works seemed to comprise a kind of literal, and desublimated, sculptural iteration of *nature morte*; rather than suggesting a still life, each work instead conjured a sense of a *stilled life*. Although neither evinces any direct ecological critique, both works underscore their institutional framing in ways that suggest a link between the destruction of a tree and the larger cultural arena. (Christo's later proposals and projects that involved wrapping trees on city streets, made with his collaborating partner Jeanne-Claude, would strike a more directly ecological note in focusing attention on the health and care of urban trees).[6]

Working in Italy at roughly the same time, Giuseppe Penone took a very different approach in his initial works made with trees. Begun in 1968, his *Alpi Marittime (Maritime Alps)* series of black-and-white photographs recorded his interventions and actions with trees in the forested foothills of Piedmont. In contrast to Christo and Smithson, Penone interacted with living trees in these works, modifying their growth in some instances through the use of wire bonds or in another case by embedding an iron cast of his hand in a tree trunk. Existing outside the gallery environment, these projects were either short-lived or designed to change over time, often using a tree's growth as a driver of formal or structural evolution. That same year, Penone made *Albero di 8 metri (8-metre Tree),* a type of sculpture that he has continued to develop in various iterations ever since and which stands as a landmark in his pioneering body of arboreal artworks (fig. 4). For *Albero di 8 metri*, he essentially reverse-engineered a machine-cut beam, carving back the wood along the outer growth rings in the timber to uncover the shape of the tree at an earlier stage of its development. (This kind of 'excavation' is possible because trees grow outwards, adding new living tissue on the outside of, and on top of, the previous year's growth.) Conflating organic growth and man-made construction, hand-carving and machine-assisted labour, *Albero di 8 metri* cannily embodied the tensions between tradition and modernity that characterised northern Italy's post-war transition to an industrialised economy. At the same time, Penone's approach seemingly aligned the form-making work of the artist with the growth of matter in nature.

All of these groundbreaking works from the late 1960s made use of the tree as sculptural material in ways that questioned or destabilised its identity as a 'natural' object. Paradoxical, ambiguous and multi-layered, each of these works engages the viewer in a process of re-examining the semantic boundaries that separate our notions of culture and nature. In this respect, they all share characteristics linked to a number of 'movements' of the time, including conceptual art but also nouveau réalisme in France (a tendency with which Christo was initially associated), and arte povera in Italy (with which Penone was closely identified). Common to all of these tendencies was a recognition that art generates meanings by playing with cultural and social codes and conventions, and a corollary rejection of the idea that artistic expression reflects the artist's inner experience.

Decentring the Anthropomorphic Gaze

> *Man is an inverted tree, and a tree is an inverted man.*
> — Aristotle[7]

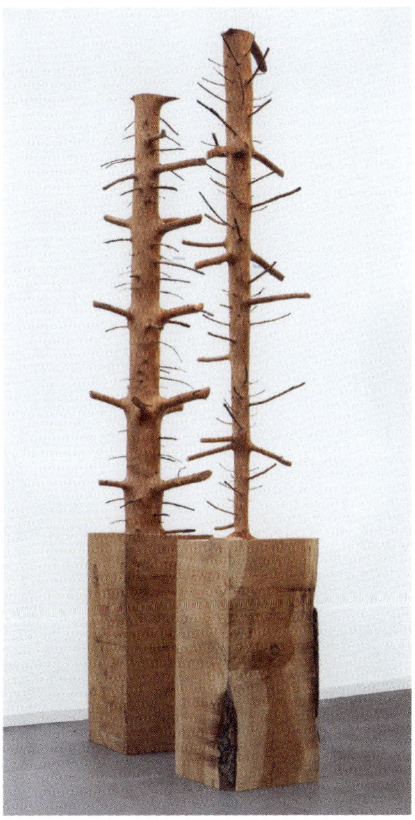

Fig. 4
Giuseppe Penone
Albero di 8 metri (8-metre Tree), 2000

Much of the most interesting art from the past 50 years that explores our relationship with trees and forests has taken up this more rhetorical orientation. Even when employing forms associated with documentary traditions, these works typically focus on questioning values embedded in established visual tropes and historical genres. Exemplifying this approach, Rodney Graham made a number of works in the late 1970s that sought to subvert Romantic traditions of landscape art, in which the natural environment is treated allegorically as a reflection of human emotions and mental states. Graham's *75 Polaroids* (1976) consists of seemingly random snapshots of a forest taken at night with the camera's flash as the only source of illumination. It is a work which, as Jeff Wall has written, is 'perfectly negative in relation to the lyrical landscape tradition [...] It reinvents the tradition, cutting away all pipe-dreams about inner landscape.'[8]

Three years later, Graham constructed a shed-sized camera obscura on his family's farm in British Columbia (Canada), with its pinhole lens facing a solitary tree; on entering the space, viewers saw a luminous inverted image of the tree projected on the back wall. Graham's *Camera Obscura* (1979), as in the manner of many land art projects in that era, also included a gallery exhibition in which he presented an architectural model of the viewing device and a photographic print of the inverted tree image (fig. 5). Conflating concerns about the architecture of optics and cultural frameworks that skew our perception of 'nature', this work led to the artist's ongoing photographic series, begun in the 1980s, featuring upside-down images of solitary trees (pp. 72–73).

Literally turning tradition on its head, these pictures derail, with a kind of deadpan absurdity, the Romantic pictorial trope in which an isolated tree is treated anthropomorphically as a figure in a landscape. Whilst they also allude to the inverted images produced by the optics of both the human eye and the camera obscura, Graham's compositions have an immediate visual impact on viewers. As the artist has commented, the inverted image 'creates a kind of obscurity. It's always disturbing to look at something upside down.'[9] Disrupting the legibility of the familiar object that they portray, these large-scale pictures conjure a hallucinatory mirror world in which branches have become roots and the ground has dissolved into sky.

The philosopher Maurice Merleau-Ponty has suggested that 'to turn an object upside down is to deprive it of its meanings'.[10] Yet in negating one set of meanings, Graham's uncannily defamiliarised images of trees – which provoke a more sustained and nuanced scrutiny due to their novelty – derail our anthropomorphic tendencies to open up other possible readings of their subject. Graham's topsy-turvy arboreal portraits find an antecedent, which the artist himself has cited, in Robert Smithson's 1969 series of photographs that depict small individual trees buried upside down by the artist in three different locations (p. 71). With their thorny crowns of roots suggesting a distorted mirror image of a canopy of branches, Smithson's *Upside Down Tree* pictures trigger a disorienting double take. On one level, they seem to record a kind of violent act: one art historian relates them to St Peter's martyrdom on an inverted cross.[11] More to the point is the disarming way in which they forcibly undercut our usual identification with the vertical orientation of trees. Underscoring the anti-anthropomorphic thrust of these images, Smithson maintained that flies were attracted to his upside-down trees due to their riddle-like character. 'The trees are dedicated to the flies...' he wrote, adding: '*Why should flies be without art?*'[12]

Whilst trees and forests have been enduring subjects of photography going back to the mid nineteenth century, a number of artists in the past decade have made works that raise questions about the camera's ability to accurately depict them. Eija-Liisa Ahtila's six-screen video installation *Horizontal – Vaakasuora* (2011) presents a cinematic portrait of a 30-metre-high spruce tree (pp. 74–75), but like Graham's photographs it invites us to confront a familiar image from an unsettling vantage point. Recorded in six segments that are projected horizontally in the gallery to create a joined-up image of a giant tree laid out on its side, *Horizontal – Vaakasuora* forces viewers to recalibrate their perceptual orientation. Rather than reflecting an arbitrary aesthetic decision, the work's multi-screen format points to the limits of the recording apparatus itself: due to the aspect ratio of the video frame, it is impossible to create a portrait image that would capture the full size and height of the tree. (One could shoot it from a distance, of course, but the result would then be a landscape, rather than a picture of an individual tree.) Ahtila's solution was to create a composite, stitching together footage of consecutive segments of the tree, which were shot straight on by an elevated camera. But since most exhibition spaces do not have 30-metre-high ceilings, the only way to squeeze this image into a gallery is by showing it sideways. *Horizontal – Vaakasuora*, in other words, makes it evident that the actual

Fig. 5
Rodney Graham
Camera Obscura, 1979

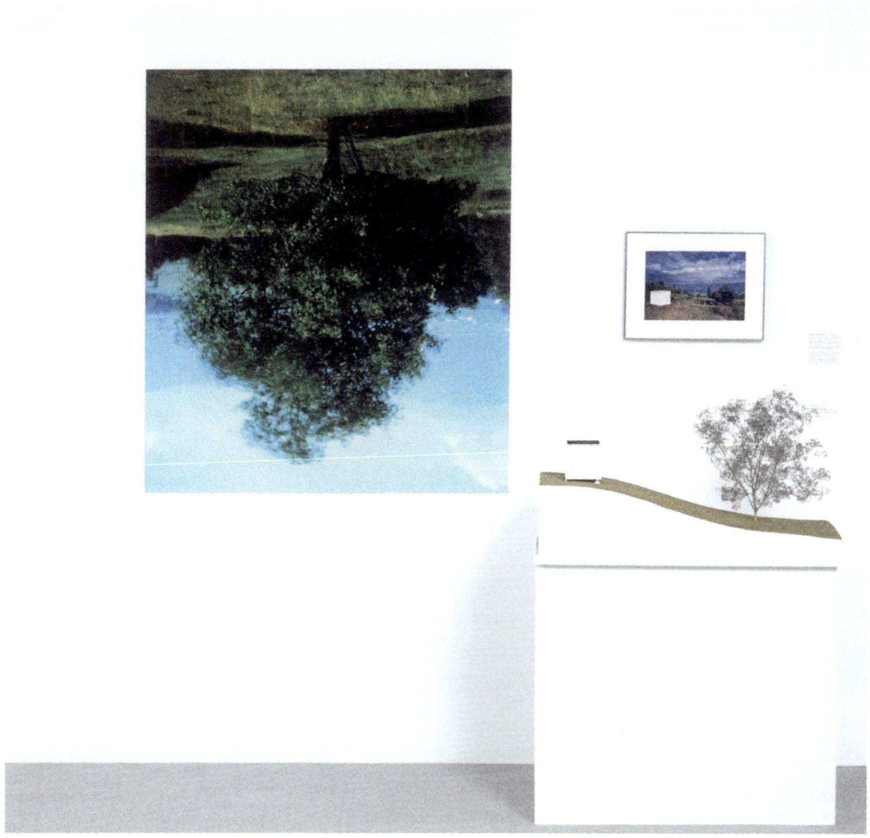

tree it depicts exceeds both our architectural as well as optical framing devices. Indeed, one of the most remarkable aspects of this work is that even as it engages us in a mesmerisingly intimate encounter with a highly detailed image of a tree, it simultaneously compels us to acknowledge how its subject ultimately eludes the means we have for representing it. In this regard, the artist cites her work's connection to the ideas of pioneering bio-philosopher Jakob von Uexküll, who maintained that different living organisms inhabit different, yet coexisting, spatial and temporal zones.[13]

Not surprisingly, one of Sigmund Freud's key images of the uncanny relates to the experience of being lost in a forest – a narrative motif also associated with countless fairy tales and horror movies.[14] Dense groupings of trees frustrate our desire for clean lines of sight; they subvert our efforts to orient ourselves and seem to entrap us. Environmental writer Barry Lopez has argued that they also defy our capacity to accurately represent their collective complexity, insisting that 'the woods defeat the viewfinder, drawing paper, they cannot be framed.'[15] Indeed, even the fractal architecture of a single tree seems to stretch the limits of our visual apprehension with its intricate layers of interlacing branches and thousands of leaves (a mature oak in summer, for instance, can have over 200,000 leaves).

A number of contemporary artists have made work that draws on these dendritic characteristics to engage us in a process of looking that mirrors the intricate spatiality of their subjects. Thomas Struth's *New Pictures from Paradise* – a series of large colour photographs, first exhibited in 1999, that depict rainforests and jungles in different parts of the world – make use of an all-over composition that mirrors their subject (pp. 54–57). Unlike in classical landscape imagery, there is no foreground, vista and horizon in these pictures. Instead most of these images confront the viewer with a dense, almost depthless surface of trees, branches and leaves. Struth has said that he 'wanted to make photographs in which everything was so complex and detailed that you could look at them forever and never see everything'.[16] With their decentred, non-hierarchical compositions, which invite the viewer's gaze to wander aimlessly across the picture plane, Struth's jungle photographs suggest a model of vision that defies what one critic has called 'the immanent anthropocentrism of the central perspective'.[17]

In moving away from what could be considered anthropomorphic framing, Struth's photographs engineer a type of viewing experience that has been associated with abstract painting. This link is explicitly picked up in works by a number of contemporary painters in which trees prominently feature. In his painting *The Architect's Home in the Ravine* (1991), which depicts a view looking down at a modernist home through a forest, Peter Doig contrasts the building's rationalised, rectilinear structure with the irregularity of the woods (pp. 50–51). But Doig has also covered the entire surface of the picture with a white lattice work of overlapping branch-like lines that loosely suggest dendritic structures. This overlay wreaks havoc with our sense of distance and depth, and sends one's gaze skidding around the composition much as if we were encountering an abstract field painting.

In works by several other artists that seemingly present us with pictures of trees, we likewise unexpectedly encounter intersections with abstract art. Toba Khedoori's meticulously rendered drawings and paintings of intricately entangled branches and leaves veer between flatness and illusory space (pp. 62–65). Seeming to float in some undefined dimension, Khedoori's images conjure a different sense of the term abstraction, as they seem to have been removed (or 'abstracted') from any kind of grounding context. In focusing solely on the complex architecture and materiality of trees, these works solicit a slow scanning process that derails our habitual speed-reading of imagery and, like much abstract painting, brings our attention to the act of looking itself. Robert Longo – who has described himself as 'an abstract painter working representationally' – has dedicated a series of dramatic charcoal drawings to the fractal forms of large trees that specifically invoke abstract expressionism.[18] The artist's 2014 *Medusa (Banyan Tree, Homage to J. Mitchell and J. Pollock)*, which depicts a sprawling banyan tree with quasi-photographic precision and at cinematic scale, namechecks in its title two leading abstract expressionists, Joan Mitchell and Jackson Pollock, underscoring the link between the decentred compositions in their paintings and the epic dendritic structures featured in this drawing.

By pointedly linking depictions of trees to abstract compositional strategies, these artists ask us to reconsider our assumptions about the relationship between organic and culturally produced structures. In this regard their work calls to mind a rhetorical question poised by Smithson in which the artist underlined the connection between nature and abstract art. 'What are the lattices and grids of pure abstraction, if not renderings of a reduced order of nature?' he asked, adding that 'there is no escaping nature through abstract representation, abstraction brings one closer to physical structures within nature itself.'[19]

Mixed Environments and Hybrid Specimens

The Anthropocene, a term generally attributed to atmospheric chemist Paul Crutzen and biologist Eugene Stoermer, defines this geological era as one in which human activities and industrial pollutants are significantly altering aspects of our climate and physical environment; though not universally embraced, its use has been adopted by an increasing number of scientists and authors in recent years. In a corollary development over the past several decades, a group of leading philosophers and ecological thinkers, from Bruno Latour and Donna Haraway to Timothy Morton, have rejected our traditional concept of 'nature'; rather than an autonomous entity that exists as something separate from us, they have instead proposed ways of envisioning our environment as an interaction of human and natural systems. During roughly this same period, a number of artists began exploring how arboreal life coexists within social and industrial as well as organic systems and structures; their work suggestively outlines the extent to which trees are shaped by our historical, economic and social frameworks.

In 1997, Zoe Leonard made a sculpture that eerily evokes this state of affairs. The artist took apart a tree that had been struck by lightning and then reconstructed it, Frankenstein-style, with steel plates and metal rods holding the various limbs and branches in place. The resulting artwork, *Tree*, conflates our categories of nature and culture; it mimics the form of a living tree but simultaneously appears as a slightly monstrous composite that reflects a history of mechanical intervention. Leonard went on the following year to further elaborate her concern with 'altered nature': using a deadpan documentary style, she photographed New York street trees that had changed shape by growing into or swallowing up parts of the chain-link fences and metal bars meant to contain them (pp. 136–37). These ambiguous pictures depict 'mutant' trees – in other words, trees that have evolved by adapting to the very physical structures built to isolate and separate them, and that reflect our desire to keep nature in its place.

Far from construing trees as emblems of rooted stability, a number of current artworks recast them in ways that underscore our increasing uncertainty about how we define our relationship to the natural world. Combining cuts of wood from different types of cultivated trees and fragments of industrial machinery, Jimmie Durham's 2012 series of sculptural assemblages summons thoughts of a factory-style forest as well as the industrial harvesting in Italy of young olive trees (among others) which are routinely destroyed in the process (p. 83). Pascale Marthine Tayou's *Plastic Tree* sculptures comprise yet another example of an explicit nature/culture hybrid; made with branches that are festooned with gaily coloured plastic bags, they allude to the familiar urban sight of litter-bedecked trees, a cross-over 'species' that can appear disarmingly decorative (p. 112).

Artworks such as these open up new ways of imagining the myriad roles that trees play in our lives and the different forms they can assume. Other artists adumbrate a shape-shifting conception of arboreal identity. Giuseppe Penone has explained the motivation of his work as deriving from the stimulus he finds in 'the imaginative quality of every door, table, window, or board – all of which contain the image of a tree'.[20] Not dissimilarly, William Kentridge's large drawings of arboreal species native to South Africa, executed in Indian ink on found pages of old books and encyclopedias, are informed by the artist's notion of how trees are caught up in the flux of human affairs, including capitalist economies (pp. 118–19). 'It's easier to draw a table,' he has noted, 'if you understand that table as an intermediary stage between the tree, the factory, its moment in the room in front of you and its future... '[21] In the eyes of artists like Penone and Kentridge, the life of trees encompasses not just their 'natural' existence, but also their material metamorphoses that are engineered by humans.

◈◈◈

In an essay first published in 1994, Jeff Wall observed that we rarely find isolated trees in urban environments. The reason for this, he maintained, is deeply ideological. 'The lone tree is the great ancient symbol of the mortal individual, rooted in the totality of nature yet suffering its solitary destiny. In an epoch when the totality of nature begins to suffer mortally', he argued, 'a tree standing self-consciously alone in the city would, better than any other monument or form of propaganda, evoke the environmental tragedy which implicates our economy, our culture of cities, and our social order.'[22]

As if echoing Wall's remark, Yto Barrada made a series of tragicomic photographs in the 2000s that portray solitary palm trees sandwiched between Tangier's vacant lots and its modernist apartment buildings (pp. 138–39). Surrounded by rubble and concrete, and dwarfed by the architectural structures around them, these orphaned trees evince the forlorn status of weeds. They are landscaping accidents, incidents of unintended decor that call attention to the absence of ornamentation in their surroundings. The comical element in these pictures springs from how out of place these specimens look amidst a cityscape defined by a modernist predilection for straight lines and hard edges, and a disdain for organic form.

Albeit in a very different manner, some of Robert Adams's modestly scaled black-and-white photographs from the mid 1970s and 1980s convey a similar sense of trees marginalised within man-made environments. Part of his series of pictures that chronicle the rapidly expanding suburbs of central Colorado at this time, these photographs focus on single trees existing within new commercial and residential developments. *Fort Collins, Colorado* (1976) presents a nocturnal scene featuring a small tree at the end of a brightly lit, empty parking lot, looking like a forest relic abandoned in a vacuum of artifice (p. 143). In *Longmont, Colorado* (1976), another night-time scene, Adams focuses on the truncated shadow of a tree that graces the garage door of a suburban split-level home, the dark outline of its leafy branches lending a ghostly beauty to an otherwise lifeless setting (p. 142).

These photographs by Barrada and Adams seemingly reflect societies in which a sense of connection to trees has been largely lost. Adams, who spent much of the 1990s making photographs of 'clear-cut' forests in the northwestern United States, has spoken of making pictures to counter the 'cultivated blindness' that enables people to remain indifferent to the widespread decimation of ancient forests.[23] Taking up this concern at a moment when industrial deforestation across the world has itself become a significant source of carbon dioxide emissions contributing to global warming, a number of artists have produced work that responds to the precarity of arboreal life today. Few works have conjured this situation with the haunting melancholy of Roxy Paine's installation *Desolation Row* (2016), which telescopes a view of a burned forest into an eight-foot-wide diorama featuring scorched earth, charred logs and what appear to be glowing embers (pp. 92–95). Paine's tableau is especially disconcerting because it draws attention to the deep uncertainty today about the causes of forest fires, which are increasing in both number and severity; whilst fires have always occurred due to natural reasons, in the Anthropocene era a burnt landscape such as this inevitably suggests the scene of a crime, leaving us to wonder about the role played by human agents or by natural systems that are already compromised by global warming.

The tree is a being that memorialises the feats of its existence in its very form.
— Giuseppe Penone[24]

In his 1979 book *The Tree*, novelist (and amateur naturalist) John Fowles remarks that trees create a variety of times: their existence reflects seasonal changes as well as annual cycles of growth, whilst their life spans often far exceed our own. A tree's rings, meanwhile, are essentially organic recording devices that contain information about past climate conditions – including temperature and rainfall – as well as data on events that in some cases date back thousands of years.[25] In approaching trees as a subject, a number of contemporary artists have taken up this matter of mixed temporalities. Contrasting processes of organic decay with the fixity of traditional sculptural materials, Anya Gallaccio's installation *because nothing has changed* (2000) featured a bronze cast of a small apple tree festooned with real fruits that slowly rotted over the course of the work's presentation. These elements were displayed on a plywood floor that had been scorched black, raising the spectre of the sudden and violent transformations to which trees are vulnerable due to the combustibility of wood (see p. 89).

Because they outlive us, trees confront us with the relative transience of our own existence. Sculptures of trees, when made of durable materials, amplify this contrast of temporal horizons. Made over the past decade, Ugo Rondinone's sculptures of ancient olive trees, cast in aluminium from moulds of living specimens, embody what the artist has called 'an experience of a differently calibrated temporality'.[26] The twisted forms of their branches and trunks do not reflect the decisions of the artist, but the impact of wind, rain and climate over long periods, making each sculpture a 'memorial of condensed time'. The artist has uniformly covered the surfaces of these works with matt white enamel paint, yet each of these works is too vivid and specific in its depiction of a particular tree to evoke classically 'timeless' sculpture; instead, Rondinone's casts of trees, which evince a slightly ghostly presence, invite us to recast our sense of mortality within an alternative, more expansive temporal framework (p. 105).

That is certainly also the case with the remarkable series of colour photographs made by Rachel Sussman that document some of the world's most ancient trees (pp. 122–23). Made during the first half of the last decade as part of a larger project aimed at chronicling the oldest living things on earth, Sussman's pictures of trees are framed, in part, as a type of research: each print includes a handwritten caption on its bottom white border that lists the type of tree, its age and location. The extraordinary information these convey is sometimes belied by the less-than-spectacular imagery: one photograph appears to portray a mundane grouping of small green plants that – as we learn upon reading the caption – are in fact the tips of the topmost branches of

Fig. 6
Rachel Sussman
Underground Forest #0707–1333 (13,000 years old; Pretoria, South Africa) DECEASED, 2007

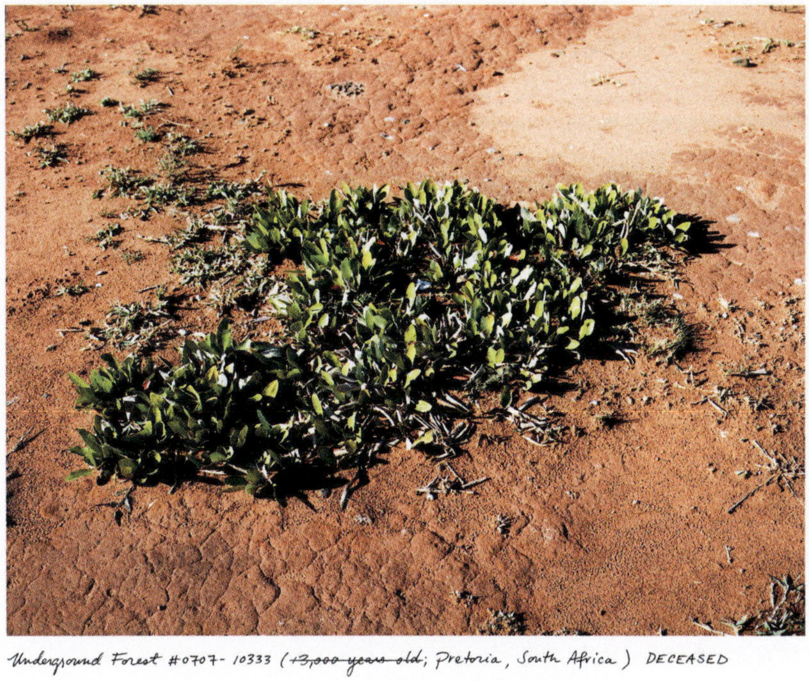

a 13,000-year-old underground baobab forest (fig. 6). (Botanists speculate that this forest, located in Pretoria, South Africa, developed beneath the ground as a way to survive frequent fires in the region.) Like many of Sussman's photographs, this image testifies to an arboreal time zone that is unimaginably vast compared to the measures of human history, but her project also makes clear that despite their capacity for longevity, trees are continually endangered by our civilisations. The underground forest in this picture was destroyed not long after Sussman photographed it, bulldozed as part of the construction of a new road.

As living links to the past, trees have also been cast in contemporary artworks as witnesses of forgotten histories and traumatic events. Using a nineteenth-century photographic process that produces murkily atmospheric prints, Sally Mann has made a series of works depicting woodland sites of Civil War battles, framing prosaic patches of forest in relation to our knowledge of the unspeakable carnage that once took place around them (pp. 134–35). Johanna Calle's series of tree drawings, meanwhile, take as their context the history of land reform in Colombia (pp. 116–17). Ingeniously made using typewritten texts that refer to Colombia's Law of Land Restitution, some of the tree silhouettes in these drawings reference the shape of the native ceiba trees that were historically used by farmers and indigenous people to demarcate their property borders. Working in very distinct ways, artists such as Steve McQueen have made photographic works that reference trees once used for racially motivated lynchings in the United States; in these pictures the tree is transformed into an uncanny historical relic, its seeming innocence belied by the horrific violence for which it was used (pp. 130–31).

◈◈◈

For hundreds of years, artists in the West were guided by the Aristotelian principle that art should strive to represent an idealised, perfected vision of nature. Today that task has been taken up and embraced by advertising and mainstream media. Images of pristine landscapes beckon us in adverts for holiday getaways; SUV commercials take us on drives through majestic and unsullied forests. The ecological equivalent of glamour photography fuels an industry of coffee-table books and calendars, whilst nature programmes on television, produced with ever more dazzling camera work and portraying beguiling visions of untrammelled environments, offer entertainment that is at best one step removed from 'nature porn'. In a world where Disney's jungle cruise ride may be far more appealing to many people than the actual jungle in the Amazon, these seductive images of perfected nature inevitably skew our already-distorted perceptions.

The contemporary artists in *Among the Trees* seek to distance us from the cliched images and stale tropes that inform our conventional understanding of trees and forests and to make us conscious of their constricting hold on our imagination. At the same time their work celebrates the strangeness of trees, as well as their complexity and beauty. It does so, in part, by disrupting the historical conventions and genres as well as the anthropomorphic conceptions and metaphors that have shaped and limited our awareness of our multi-dimensional relationships with trees. Inviting us to consider their subject from complex and multi-layered perspectives, their work provokes us to seek a keener resonance between the physical and cultural landscapes that we inhabit.

Finally it is worth noting that many artists, from Paul Klee to Giuseppe Penone and William Kentridge, have considered the tree's structure as a model of the creative process. Making a related point, artist Gabriel Orozco has remarked on the manner in which a tree grows from a centre in all directions, a process that corresponds to the way that many artists develop the initial seed of an artwork through forking pathways of non-linear thinking, following chains of associations that branch out and link far-flung yet interconnected ideas. And whilst it is shaped by specific and immutable natural laws, the growth of trees always results in the creation of individual forms. Penone compares this organic model of growth with the act of drawing as well as with seeing – the branching architecture of the tree is like a spatialisation of the speculative exploration, the reaching out and probing, that characterises intensive acts of looking. One suspects that this correspondence between dendritic structures and creative thinking and seeing has contributed, at least in part, to the sustained appeal that the subject of trees has held for artists over the past half century.

1 Jimmie Durham, 'Is This Interesting?', *Mousse Magazine*, No. 42 (February – March 2014), moussemagazine.it/jimmie-durham-is-this-interesting-2014/ [accessed 7 October 2019]

2 So-called 'random forests', ensembles of randomised decision trees, are widely used for classification and regression tasks in machine learning and statistics.

3 T.S. Eliot, 'The Waste Land', in *T.S. Eliot: Collected Poems 1909–62* (London: Faber and Faber, 2002), unpaginated

4 Sonja Dümpelmann, *Seeing Trees: A History of Street Trees in New York City and Berlin* (New Haven: Yale University Press, 2019), pp. 192–93

5 Eliot, 'The Waste Land'

6 In an unrealised project initiated in 1966, Christo and Jeanne-Claude proposed to wrap the crowns of about 40 living trees near the Saint Louis Art Museum in Forest Park, Missouri. Two decades later, a version of this work was eventually realised in Augsburg (Germany): the two artists wrapped trees in the street with a layer of synthetic gauze, calling attention to their presence and spatial profile as well as to the labour required to maintain them in urban areas.

7 Aristotle, *On Parts of Animals* (c.350 BC), quoted in Matteo Pasquinelli, 'The Arborescent Mind: The Intelligence of an Inverted Tree', in Carroll Khadija von Zinnenburg (ed.), *Botanical Drift: Protagonists of the Invasive Herbarium* (Berlin: Stenberg Press, 2018), pp. 163–74

8 As Jeff Wall observed, the complete project 'could not be seen as a whole in any one place, and its disunity expressed a sense, well-recognized in the public discourse of the time, of the widening split between city and country, glimpsed against a background of the decay of regional agriculture under the domination of American agribusiness which supports the aimless sub-urbanization of great B.C. [British Columbia] farmland.' See Jeff Wall, 'Into the Forest: Two Sketches for Studies of Rodney Graham's Work', in *Rodney Graham: Works from 1976–1994* (Toronto: Art Gallery of York University, 1994), p. 22

9 Barry Schwabsky, 'Inverted Trees and the Dream of a Book: An Interview with Rodney Graham', *Art on Paper*, Vol. 5, No. 1 (September–October 2000), p. 67

10 Maurice Merleau-Ponty, *Phenomenon of Perception* (1945), trans. Colin Smith (London: Routledge & Kegan Paul, 1962), p. 252, quoted in Yve-Alain Bois and Rosalind Krauss, 'A User's Guide to Entropy', *October*, Vol. 78 (Autumn 1996), p. 43

11 Suzaan Boettger, 'In the Yucatan: Mirroring Presence and Absence', in Cornelia Butler and Eugenie Tsai (eds.), *Robert Smithson* (Berkeley: University of California Press, 2004), p. 204

12 Robert Smithson, 'Incidents of Mirror-Travel in the Yucatan' (1969), in Jack Flam (ed.), *Robert Smithson: The Collected Writings* (Berkeley: University of California Press, 2000), p. 162

13 See Cary Wolfe, 'Eija-Liisa Ahtila', *Bomb Magazine*, Issue 120 (1 July 2012), bombmagazine.org/articles/eija-liisa-ahtila/ [accessed 30 September 2019]

14 Sigmund Freud, *The Uncanny* (1919). See web.mit.edu/allanmc/www/freud1.pdf, p. 10 [accessed 30 September 2019]

15 Barry Lopez, 'Introduction', in John Fowles, *The Tree* (New York: Ecco, 2010)

16 Thomas Struth quoted in Sean O'Hagan, 'Thomas Struth: Photos So Complex "You Could Look at Them Forever"', *Guardian* (3 July 2011), www.theguardian.com/artanddesign/2011/jul/03/thomas-struth-interview-photography-whitechapel [accessed 30 September 2019]

17 Hans Rudolf Reust, 'Paradise Revisited', in *Thomas Struth: New Pictures from Paradise*, exh. cat. (Munich: Schirmer/Mosel Verlag, 2017)

18 Robert Longo quoted in Joe Lloyd, 'Robert Longo: "I'm making artworks out of dust"', *Studio International* (22 September 2017), www.studiointernational.com/index.php/robert-longo-interview-im-making-art-works-out-of-dust [accessed 30 September 2019]

19 Robert Smithson, 'Frederick Law Olmsted and the Dialectical Landscape' (1973), in Smithson, p. 162

20 Giuseppe Penone quoted in Germano Celant, *Giuseppe Penone*, exh. cat. (Bristol: Arnolfini Gallery, 1989), p. 55

21 William Kentridge quoted in Leora Maltz-Leca, *William Kentridge: Process as Metaphor and Other Doubtful Enterprises* (Oakland: University of California Press, 2017), p. 100

22 Wall, p. 20

23 Robert Adams quoted in 'Turning Back: Interview with Robert Adams', *Art21*, art21.org/read/robert-adams-turning-back/ [accessed 30 September 2019]

24 Giuseppe Penone quoted in Elizabeth Mangini, '1000 Words: Giuseppe Penone', *Artforum*, Vol. 49, No. 2 (October 2010), www.artforum.com/print/201008/1000-words-giuseppe-penone-26418 [accessed 7 October 2019]

25 Jim Robbins, 'Chronicle of the Rings: What Tree Rings Tell Us', *New York Times* (30 April 2019), www.nytimes.com/2019/04/30/science/tree-rings-climate.html [accessed 30 September 2019]

26 Ugo Rondinone quoted in the press release for Creative Time's project *Art on the Plaza*, New York (1 February–30 April 2007).

THE FOREST FOR THE TREES

Jeffrey Kastner

Metaphysics? What metaphysics do those trees have?
Only that of being green and lush and of having branches
Which bear fruit in their season, and we think nothing of it.
We hardly even notice them.
But what better metaphysics than theirs,
Which consists in not knowing why they live
And in not knowing that they don't know?
— 'The Keeper of Sheep', Fernando Pessoa[1]

Early on in *Forests: The Shadow of Civilization*, Robert Pogue Harrison's elegantly ranging meditation on the place of the woods in the Western cultural imagination, the scholar considers the deep history of the idea of matter in Greek thought: a notion, he says, which philosophy could long not find a way to speak of 'in any logical fashion'. There were neither 'word[s], images, or categories for undifferentiated matter since form [was understood to be] the condition of our logical access to reality', Harrison continues. 'Yet there is one word that Aristotle could not avoid using when he spoke about the unspeakable – *hyle*. He is the first to give the word its philosophical meaning of "matter". But *hyle* in Greek does not originally mean matter, it means forest. Let us repeat that: *hyle* is the Greek word for forest.'[2]

There is something a little giddy in Harrison's tone here, a sense of wonderment that often suffuses tree-thought; that something so familiar and ubiquitous as a forest could be thought by the philosopher to be an apt expression of the fullness of material existence catalyses a certain joy for Harrison, as it will both for readers starting in on his sweeping study and for viewers encountering the diversity of arboreal engagement seen in the artworks included in *Among the Trees*. Of course, it is precisely the commonplace nature of trees that marks them as candidates to stand in for the fullness of the physical world – we circulate among them like fish in water, so enmeshed in their presence that their constant company begins to register almost as an extension of our own bodies and consciousness. The chasm between what we know about a plant and what a plant might know may seem unbridgeable, but in our recognition of the adjacencies, and contingencies, in our shared terrestrial profusion, there nevertheless exists a kind of kinship: a sense of a common condition, and perhaps a common fate.

A 2015 study estimated that there are more than three trillion trees on earth, and the scale of their proliferation across the centuries as the subjects of philosophical, literary and artistic consideration would seem to be nearly as voluminous.[3] Images of trees, though rare compared with those of animals or humans, can occasionally be found in prehistoric art; vegetal forms often figure as ornamental motifs in Ancient Greek decorative objects, and by the time of the Romans, trees – in many cases, rendered with enough attention to detail that they are identifiable as specific species – begin to proliferate in frescoes (fig. 1).[4] In his *Treatise on Painting*, Leonardo da Vinci urges artists to be especially precise when

Fig. 1
Fresco from Villa Livia, Museo Nazionale Romano, Palazzo Massimo, Rome, c.30–c.20 BC

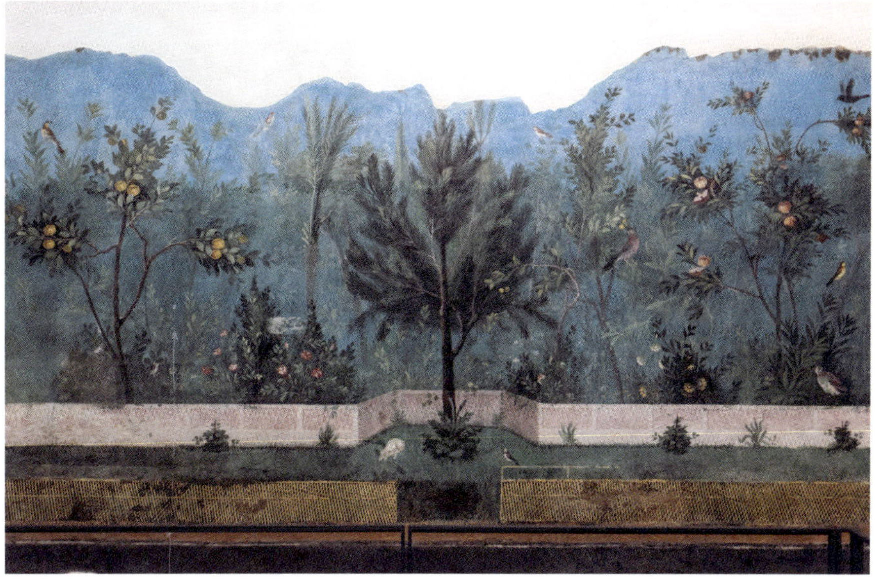

dealing with the particularities of trees as pertains to season and climate; and from the early pure landscapes of the Danube School artists – like Albrecht Altdorfer – in the sixteenth century, and the lavishly pastoral scenes of Claude in the following one, to the flowering of the picturesque aesthetic in the decades around 1800, the form of the tree thoroughly suffuses the history of classical painting.

As the naturalism of the mid nineteenth century made way for the more afigural currents of post-impressionism, expressionism, cubism and beyond, the destabilisation of the tree as physical object similarly complicated its status as immediately identifiable icon of the grandeur and solitude of nature. No longer a serenely aloof figure of surpassing material solidity and temporal duration, the tree was now caught up, as was the world at large, in an atomising net of physical and, increasingly, conceptual deconstructions. The ramifying modernist gaze found endlessly variegated formal and symbolic potential in their existential condition – individual but also clandestinely communal; solid and firmly ingrained, but also always branching and assaying, both above and below; natural factories that transmute common resources into extraordinary efflorescences that become resources for us in their turn; things of the ground and of the sky. And across the twentieth and into our present century, these thickly planted beings, whether understood as objects or as subjects, continued as they have for centuries to be most excellent things with which to think, and to make.

In 1968, the then 21-year-old artist Giuseppe Penone went into the Piedmontese woods outside his childhood home of Garessio, and began to execute a series of experimental sculptural interventions in the

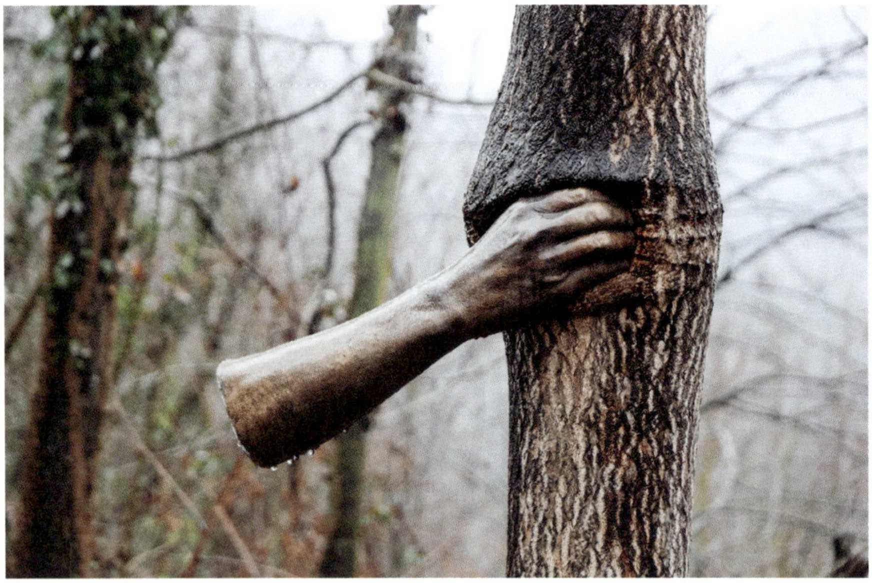

Fig. 2
Giuseppe Penone
Continuerà a crescere tranne che in quel punto (It Will Continue to Grow Except at That Point), 1968–2003

natural world. Among these was *Continuerà a crescere tranne che in quel punto (It Will Continue to Grow Except at That Point)*, a cast steel sculpture of the artist's wrist and hand, its fingers pinching off the thin trunk of a young tree (fig. 2). The sculpture is designed not so much to adorn the tree but to enter into it, the idea being that as the wood worked over time to find its way around the point of impediment where the hand grasps it, it would grow up and eventually over the human form, finally swallowing it within a boll. For Penone – whose practice across the last half century has engaged with trees as consistently as any in contemporary art – the gesture described an ambition for fusion between two natural bodies that would come to widely inform his conceptual outlook. 'I feel the flow of the tree around my hand/ placed against the trunk,' he wrote of the action, which began with his own haptic encounter with the wood. 'The altered sense of time makes what is solid, liquid, and what is liquid, solid. The hand sinks into the tree trunk which, owing to its rapid growth and the plasticity of its matter, is the ideal element for shaping.'[5]

Beyond its personal significance for the artist, Penone's statement also speaks to a larger question very much in play in tree-related artworks, namely what the philosopher Georges Didi-Huberman has described as the fusion of the 'tactile site' and the 'site of thought'.[6] Didi-Huberman introduces the concept in a book-length meditation on Penone's work and ideas surrounding it, but an engagement with the relationship between being-with and thinking-with can be seen as an influence on a range of tree-related artworks. The sense that in order to know trees one must bring them near, put them in sufficient bodily proximity that they begin to give up some of their inner life, is palpable in the work of artists such as Ana Mendieta, for example, where it takes the form of a kind of reciprocal opening up, as the nearness of artist and tree becomes a site not just for contemplation but also for a certain kind of physical and emotional candour on the part of the maker. Across her practice, Mendieta frequently seeks out contact with arboreal bodies. In a documentary image from the 1970s, for example, the artist appears to be either climbing into or emerging out of the hollow trunk of a gnarled tree. The form is also an integral aspect of both her *Silueta* and her *Tree of Life* series; in a memorable photograph of one 1976 action from the latter group, the artist leans against a large rough-barked trunk with her elbows bent and arms upraised, her naked body smeared with chocolate-brown mud like a kind of primeval camouflage (fig. 3). Of course, the very core of Mendieta's practice is expressly about courting bodily ways of knowing the earth. As she wrote in an undated text: 'My art is the way I re-establish the bonds that unite me to the universe [...] [An] African custom which I think [...] is analogous to my work [...] The men from Kimberly [in South Africa] go outside their village to seek their brides. When a man brings his new wife home, the woman brings with her a sack of earth from her homeland and every night she eats a little bit of that earth. The earth will help her make the transition between her homeland and her new home.'[7] For the artist it is, paradoxically perhaps, emphatic nearness to terrestrial realities that serves to unlock the empyrean mysteries of existence.

Just a few years before Mendieta began her *Silueta* series, Gordon Matta-Clark – an artist with what would seem to have been a markedly different psychospiritual outlook than Mendieta, whose work often

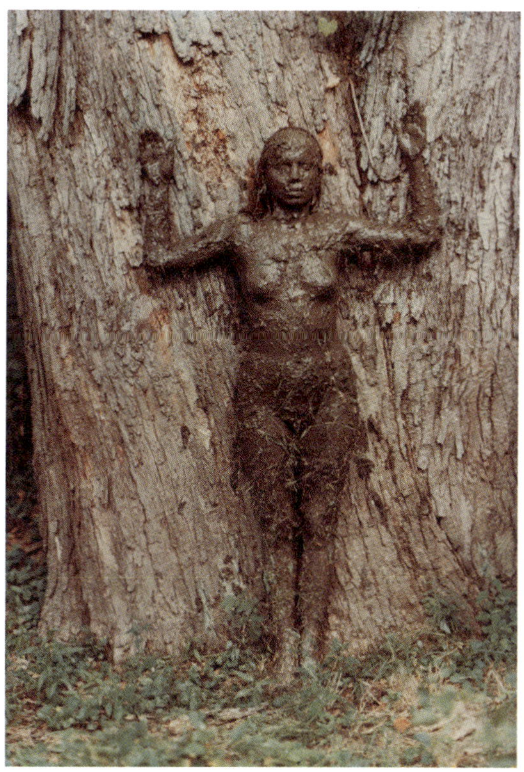

Fig. 3
Ana Mendieta
Tree of Life, 1976

made explicit references to pantheistic ritual – staged his own scene of arboreal intimacy. *Tree Dance* was a temporary sculptural installation created by Matta-Clark on the campus of Vassar College in upstate New York on 1 May 1971 that was designed to host a Judson-style movement performance involving the artist and a number of his friends and colleagues, including Tina Girouard, Carol Gooden, Suzanne Harris, Jene Highstein, Jeffrey Lew and Richard Nonas (fig. 4).[8] Though Matta-Clark had originally intended to occupy the network of ropes, ladders and cocoon-like hung bivouacs he installed in the tree for a week or more, he and his colleagues were only allowed to stay up for one day (although images from the artist's archive show that he did return later that summer and surreptitiously reoccupy one of the nests amid the tree's now leafed-out summer branches.) For the would-be anarchitect, a term picked up by Matta-Clark and his colleagues to describe the group's oblique relationship to conventional modes of building, the tree would become a near-obsessive fixture in the following years. This is especially evident in his *Energy Tree* drawings (1970–74), which Matta-Clark scholar Frances Richard has described as '[t]racking electrical flows through what appear to be the astral bodies of trees', and properly seen in close relation to the tree works that had come before them, as well as cultural symbols such as 'the Tree of Life in Hermetic writings'. She continues:

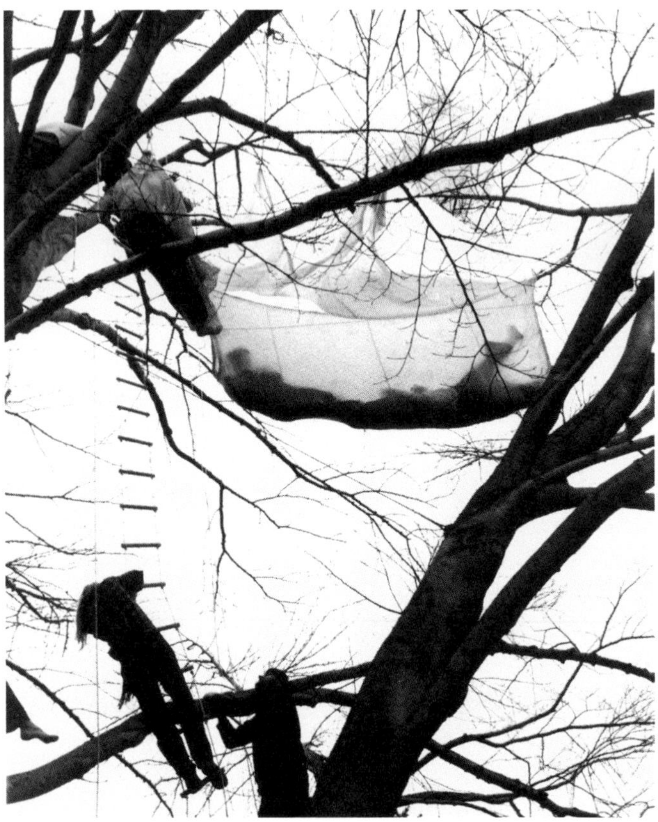

Fig. 4
Gordon Matta-Clark
Tree Dance, 1971

> *Brightly colored trunks, boughs, and foliage entwine to form lattices, helices, Gordian knots. Tree-bodies arc and snake, winding promiscuously into one another and pulsating with strokes of pencil and/or Magic Marker that coalesce in braided streams, explode into particles, and regather in whooshing vortices. In the networks of this energy, organic and inorganic matters fuse: there is a drawing of trees growing through junked cars, and one of trees caged in a chain-link box. Several show trees with hammocks and windmills sprouting out of them.*[9]

There are of course other strategies for founding a physical and conceptual proximity between artist and tree, between artistically mediated tree and viewer. Rather than go to the tree in its domain, to seek out a theatrically natural relationship to it as in the case of Mendieta's site-specific nature works or Matta-Clark's *Tree Dance*, many artists have instead chosen to bring the tree to them, and to the viewer, through a process of spatial and conceptual denaturalisation. (Matta-Clark had already explored this modality in a string of tree-related works produced in the year or so preceding the Vassar project, including *Untitled (Christmas Piece)* of 1969, in which he created an installation at 98 Greene Street Loft – a new performance venue opened by dealers Holly and Horace Solomon – by hanging theatrical lights in a Christmas tree, a holly bush and a flowering peach tree; *Cherry Tree/Time Well*, a durational work begun on New Year's Day 1971, one part of which consisted of a small fruit tree planted under grow lights in the basement of 112 Greene Street – an alternative space founded by the artist with Jeffrey Lew and Alan Saret a few doors down in SoHo; and an untitled performance a few months later in which Matta-Clark suspended himself upside down above a transplanted pine tree on New York's Pier 18.[10]) Such quite literal dis-locations of the entity from its natural state constitute a transformation, if one analogises from a Heideggerian sense of being-in-the-world, from the ready-at-hand (where the tree is in some crucial ways unavailable to us as an object of full contemplation because it is operating in its naturally instrumental way) to the present-at-hand (where it reappears to our conscious attention and becomes newly available for theorising precisely because it is unable to exercise its native function). The tendency that is epitomised by these works – and by other works that aim to dislocate the tree from its natural state through either physical displacement (Robert Smithson) or via photographic reorientations (Rodney Graham, Eija-Liisa Ahtila) – is one that seeks to quite literally overturn the vertical dominion of the arboreal form in order to foster a new clarity of perceptual and affectual understanding. Even when the tree is thus estranged from its comfortably dominant upright posture, it manages to present as nevertheless vibrantly alive, not enervated but rather energised by such attempts to coax out the *res cogitans* that resides inside the *res extensa*.

'We're tired of trees,' write Gilles Deleuze and Félix Guattari in the introduction to *A Thousand Plateaus* (1980), the second of the two books that constitute their groundbreaking study *Capitalism and Schizophrenia*. 'We should stop believing in trees, roots, and radicles. They've made us suffer too much [...] It is odd how the tree has dominated Western reality and all of Western thought, from botany to biology and anatomy, but also gnosiology, theology, ontology, all of philosophy...: the root-foundation, *Grund, racine, fondement*.'[11] In contrast to the hegemony of vertical, arboreal thought, however – a State philosophy, according to the book's translator Brian Massumi, that relies on the 'limitative distribution' and 'hierarchical ranking' of meaning – Deleuze and Guattari do not stray far from the vegetal, famously proposing as a new model instead the rhizome, a spreading, horizontal sort of thinking made up of constantly brachiating multiplicities, a kind of 'nomad thought [that] does not immure itself in the edifice of an ordered interiority; it moves freely in an element of exteriority. It does not repose on identity: it rides difference. It does not respect the artificial division between the three domains of representation, subject, concept, and being; it replaces restrictive analogy with a conductivity that knows no bounds.'[12]

If trees have been ubiquitous across the centuries as symbols of a certain sort of unitary order and purpose, perhaps it is the form of the rhizome with its ecumenical, associative, interconnected means of existence that offers the best sorts of possible models for a future art of trees. Like the 'wood wide web', that largely invisible system of microbes and fungi that undergirds the towering figures of the forests, the deterritorialising power of rhizomatic thought reveals trees not as the solitary beings they have so often been cast as but rather as stations in a kind of global relay, points of irruption where the concealed subterranean work of the unifying network sends out a highly visible message.[13] It is not hard to see how such a metaphysics might also be applied to the forests of humanity in the age of the Anthropocene, where the individual comes to be seen for what she or he is below the surfaces of easy appearance: not a monad but a myriad, reposed not on isolated identities but fed and sustained by hidden matrices. Trees have long provided test cases for the degree to which we are like or not like the things around us, the ways in which nature and culture are in some senses inaccessible to each other but in others fully interleaved. Artists have tried in their multiplicity of ways to bring trees closer – to themselves and to us – in order that we all might better understand them and the larger world of entities they symbolise. Aristotle believed that their matter was a fitting emblem for all matter, that when we encounter one we encounter the other. Perhaps in a world where deep interrelation is increasingly understood to be the crucial truth of existence, these sites of meeting – of touch, of sight, of thought – might finally begin to show themselves for what they are: encounters with ourselves.

1 Fernando Pessoa, 'The Keeper of Sheep', [c.1914] in Richard Zenith (ed. and trans.), *Fernando Pessoa & Co.: Selected Poems*, (New York: Grove Press, 1998), p. 49

2 Robert Pogue Harrison, *Forests: The Shadow of Civilization* (Chicago: University of Chicago Press, 1992), p. 28. Harrison points out that the Latin word for matter, *materia*, also traces its roots back to wood, and also shares 'the same root – yes, root – as the word *mater*, or mother'.

3 Thomas W. Crowther, et al., 'Mapping Tree Density at a Global Scale', *Nature*, Vol. 525, No. 7568 (10 September 2015), www.researchgate.net/profile/Thomas_Crowther/publication/281820435_Crowther_et_al_2015_Nature/links/55f9781408ae07629deb6269.pdf [accessed 19 September 2019]. A highly detailed worldwide tree density map is available for download from Yale University Library, elischolar.library.yale.edu/yale_fes_data/1/ [accessed 19 September 2019].

4 For an engaging summary of this history, see Charles Watkins, *Trees in Art* (London: Reaktion Books, 2018), to which this historical précis is indebted.

5 Giuseppe Penone quoted in Gianfranco Maraniello and Jonathan Watkins (eds.), *Giuseppe Penone: Writings 1968–2008* (Bologna: MAMbo/Birmingham: Ikon Gallery, 2009), p. 27

6 Georges Didi-Huberman, *Being a Skull: Site, Contact, Thought, Sculpture*, trans. Drew S. Burk (Minneapolis: Univocal Publishing, 2016), p. 35. Didi-Huberman describes Penone's work as 'an interrogation of sites'; he introduces the term in question in relation to a 1521 painting of St Jerome by Albrecht Dürer that pictures the theologian resting his head on one hand as he touches a skull on the table before him with the other, but clearly intends it to evoke Penone's relationship to his tree subjects.

7 See Mary Sabbatino, 'A Narrative Biography', in *Ana Mendieta: Blood & Fire* (Paris/New York: Galerie Lelong, 2011), pp. 69–70

8 The Judson Dance Theater, so called because it met in the Judson Memorial Church in New York City's Greenwich Village neighbourhood, was a collective of choreographers, visual artists and composers who worked and performed together in the early 1960s. Influenced by John Cage, Merce Cunningham and Anna Halprin, and including figures such as Trisha Brown, Lucinda Childs, Robert Morris and Yvonne Rainer, the Judson group introduced to choreographic practice new concepts of movement and of contact, both with other bodies and with objects and structures.

9 Frances Richard, *Gordon Matta-Clark: Physical Poetics* (Oakland: University of California Press, 2019), p. 245

10 See Mark Wigley, *Cutting Matta-Clark: The Anarchitecture Investigation* (Zurich: Lars Müller Publishers, 2018), p. 393, and Richard, pp. 106–11. Both scholars identify this period of arboreal engagement as a critical one in the development of Matta-Clark's larger practice; for his part, Wigley says of *Tree Dance* that the artist 'was never able to leave this project behind. It haunted his work.' See Wigley, ibid.

11 Gilles Deleuze and Félix Guattari, *A Thousand Plateaus: Capitalism and Schizophrenia*, trans. Brian Massumi (Minneapolis: University of Minnesota Press, 1987), pp. 15, 18

12 Brian Massumi, 'Translator's Foreword' in Deleuze and Guattari, p. xii

13 There have been numerous scientific papers over the last decade exploring the mycorrhizal networks that proliferate beneath the forest floor and connect what appear to be individual plants. For a wonderfully readable overview of the science, see Robert Macfarlane, 'The Secrets of the Wood Wide Web', *New Yorker* (7 August 2016), newyorker.com/tech/annals-of-technology/the-secrets-of-the-wood-wide-web [accessed 19 September 2019]

THE ARBORESCENT MIND

Matteo Pasquinelli

The aim of this text is to record a spectrum of homologies and resonances across the history of the tree as a symbolic and logic form. The inspiration for this comes from the simple recognition that a plant is found at the centre of ancient cosmologies as much as at the centre of modern epistemologies. The tree form has been adopted to support religious architectures as much as the abstract world of logic. 'We're tired of trees' remarked, though, the French philosophers Gilles Deleuze and Félix Guattari in 1980, especially after reading Julien Pacotte's book *Le Réseau Arborescent, Scheme Primordial de la Pensée (The Arborescent Network, Primordial Diagram of Thought)*. Already in 1936 Pacotte explored the abstract tree form in disciplines such as mathematics, biology and chemistry. He believed that the ramifying network is a 'universal aspect of intimate reality' and 'the very foundation of formal thought'.[1] In any case the enslavement of a natural form says more about political and social structures and hierarchies of human knowledge than about the mind itself. As much as other biomorphic symbols, the tree figure is but a mirror of the human and through the inversion of its branches we discern the society of its time.

1. The Assyrian Sacred Tree

The most famous tree of the Western tradition is of course the Tree of the Knowledge of Good and Evil, sometimes described as the Tree of Life. It appears in the book of Genesis but it was acquired into the Jewish tradition via Assyrian culture during the Babylonian captivity (fig. 1).[2] The Assyrian Sacred Tree was a basic diagram of social order: the tree was the symbol of fertile and prosperous agriculture and the king was depicted beside it protected by the spirit of a winged sun (which was later developed in the iconic Faravahar of Zoroastrianism). Aside from carrying the simple sketch of social organisation (economic, political and spiritual power), this image is said to refer also to a cosmogenesis and to more complex scales of knowledge. In many bas-reliefs the Sumerian tree appears very stylised and abstract, with each branch referring to a specific god. According to a controversial yet suggestive genealogy, the Sefirotic tree of the Kabbalah may have originated in the Sumerian tree via a further abstractification of its elements. The Sumerian gods (Anu, Sin, Ea, Mummu, Samas, Marduk, Istar, Adad, Nabu, Nergal) would have been replaced by a system of abstract faculties (Crown, Wisdom, Understanding, Kindness, Severity, Beauty, Eternity, Splendour, Foundation, Kingship).[3] In order to save the unicity of god (that is to avoid the social disintegration of the chosen people), monotheism had to transform the tree of the many gods into a tree of incorporeal ideas: abstraction was the fruit of a tree.

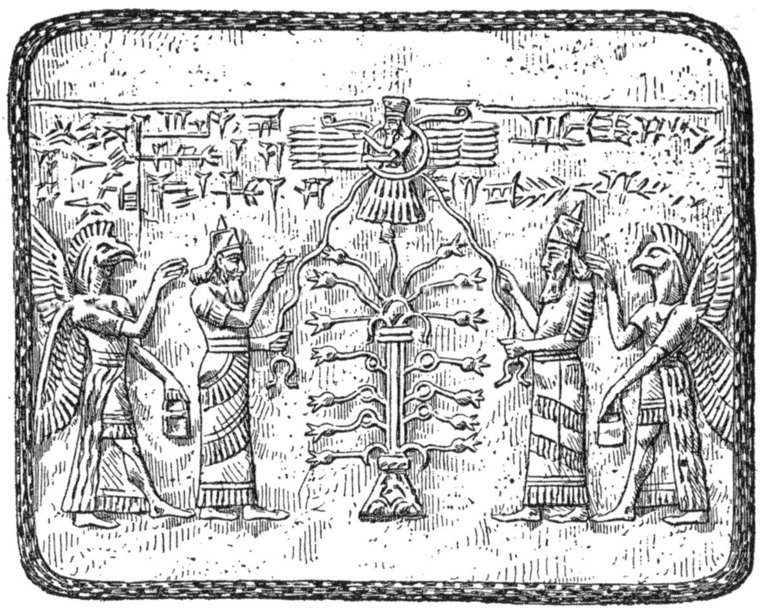

Fig. 1
Worship of the Sacred Tree, Assyrian cylinder, engraving in James Ward, *Historic Ornament*, 1897

In the ancient tree-based cosmologies there was no active space assigned to the human, the man and the woman – like Adam and Eve – being just subjects to the Tree, that is to the religious and political order. A different and indeed more secular tradition of symbolism appears in Ancient Greece, in which the human conquers the tree form and politically turns it upside down. In *Timaeus* (c.360 BC) Plato defined the man as a 'heavenly plant' with its branches on earth and roots in heaven. If the plant absorbs nutrients from the soil, by contrast the human protrudes its roots in the heaven of Ideas. 'Man is an inverted tree, and a tree is an inverted man,' echoed Aristotle in *On the Parts of Animals* and after him repeated many Jewish, Christian and Muslim scholars in the Middle Ages (fig. 2). Traditionally the image of the inverted tree, or *arbor inversa*, signifies that the human is projected towards the spiritual in opposition to the instinct of beasts. The growing roots of the human mind are a vivid metaphor of the ever-growing knowledge of humankind. It is clear that this image represents a political reappropriation of the tree form and almost a statement of independence of the citizen in the age of Athenian democracy, if compared with the oppressive symbolism of the ancient tree of power. The figure of a tree that connects heaven and earth will be subsequently and more famously represented by the cross of Christ, which is the most influential of all abstract trees. The tree of Christianity appears to repeat the reversal of the Judaic Tree of Life: it is no longer the tree of fertility and prosperity but of exile and suffering.

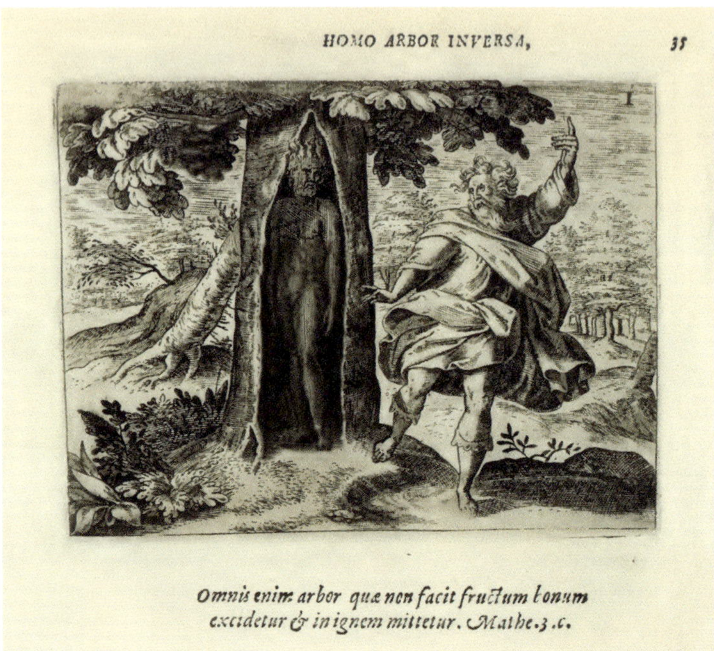

Fig. 2
Gérard de Jode, *The Man as Inverted Tree*, in Laurentius van Goidtsenhoven, *Mikrokosmos: Parvus Mundus*, 1579

3. The Porphyrian Tree

In medieval logic the tree form returns as a scheme of Aristotle's categories, which were in their own way a vision of the cosmos, dividing knowledge and the universe into genera and species that scale down from the highest genus ('universal substance') to the lowest species ('mortal human being', for example). The Porphyrian tree was developed by the Neoplatonic philosopher Porphyry of Tyre in the third century CE under the influence of Plotinus's theory of emanationism. According to emanationism the world is created by the progressive and systematic emanation from the One (God) as a cascade of beings. Porphyry gave to this 'scale of being' the form of a logic tree (fig. 3), which had a long-term influence on many other abstract trees, from Linnaeus's taxonomy (1735) to Darwin's evolutionary tree of life (1837). But the Porphyrian tree was immediately also a theory of language. Umberto Eco, among other modern scholars, has shown that this tree, *qua* logic, is very rigid and it does not solve linguistic and conceptual aporias: it does not distinguish a dog from a horse, for instance. According to Eco, the only way to make this tree-based semiotics consistent would be by proliferating each node with another independent tree of genuses and species.[4] Eco was writing already in the age of hypertexts and networks, and his note is not surprising. According to him, the Porphyrian tree has to germinate and further proliferate in any direction to innervate all possible meanings of language and reach all the things of the universe, rather like a network.

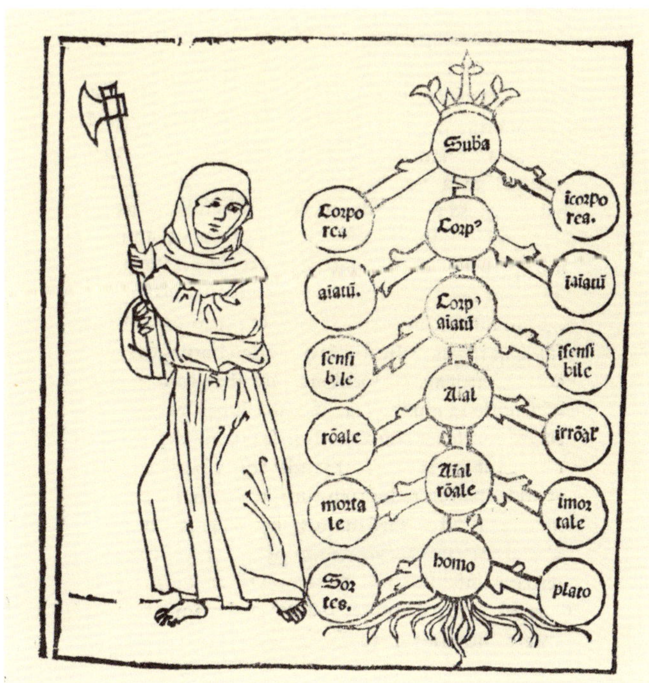

Fig. 3
Engraving in Augustinus Triumphus, *The Destruction of the Porphyrian Tree*, 1503

4. *Signatura rerum* (The Signature of All Things)

Plants and trees managed to escape their metaphorical destiny to become symbols of their own nature with the doctrine of signatures. The doctrine of signatures, also known to ancient physicians Dioscorides and Galen, states that herbs that resemble specific parts of the human body can be useful to treat the illness of those parts. For instance, St John's wort (*Hypericum perforatum*) was said to heal wounds and traumas, as the little transparent bubbles on its leaves look like lesions. The mandrake (*Mandragora officinarum*, in fact a hallucinogenic plant) was said to have deadly and magical properties, as its root resembles a homunculus (fig. 4). The doctrine of signatures was codified by the Swiss-German polymath Paracelsus in *De signatura rerum naturalium* (1537) and it can be considered a precursor of the methodology of modern science, as for the first time a logical correlation is established between the hidden nature of a being and its external appearance. For Paracelsus, 'nothing is without a sign [...] since nature does not release anything in which it has not marked what is to be found within that thing.'[5] And again: 'There is nothing exterior that is not an announcement of the interior.'[6] Then 'signatura is the science by which everything that is hidden is found, and without this art nothing of any profundity can be done.'[7] The innovation of the doctrine of signatures is that the morphology of the plant expresses the gestalt of its very nature, while it keeps resonating with the surrounding cosmos.

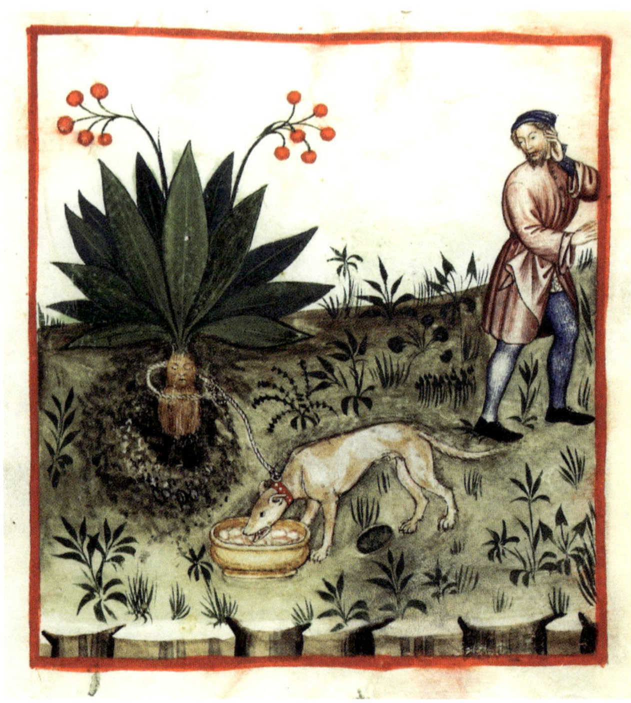

Fig. 4
Human-like mandrake root, in Ibn Butlan, *Tacuinum Sanitatis*, c.1390

5. The Metamorphosis of Plants

In September 1786 Johann Wolfgang von Goethe left Weimar to commence his Italian journey with the idea to search for the *Urpflanze*, or the archetypal plant that he thought would condense all the general forms of the vegetable kingdom (fig. 5). While in Sicily, he candidly wrote in his diary: 'There must be such a plant, after all. If all plants were not moulded on one pattern, how could I recognise that they are plants?'[8] In 1790 Goethe published *The Metamorphosis of Plants*, the first book of natural morphology that influenced the whole *Naturphilosophie* and the first evolutionary biology, from Alexander von Humboldt to Jakob von Uexküll (not to mention the artworks of Ernst Haeckel and Karl Blossfeldt). The first lines of *The Metamorphosis of Plants* read: 'Anyone who has paid even a little attention to plant growth will readily see that certain external parts of the plant undergo frequent change and take on the shape of the adjacent parts.' Goethe continues: 'In many plants we find that one node arises from another.'[9] Goethe defined his procedure 'genetic method', or a method for following the genesis of things. In Goethe the inner gestalt of beings emerges to acquire genetic power and to grow autonomously. The lineage of German vitalism (which recognised often and tragically the purity of nature's life over human life) sprouted from the *Urpflanze*, a plant that did not exist.[10]

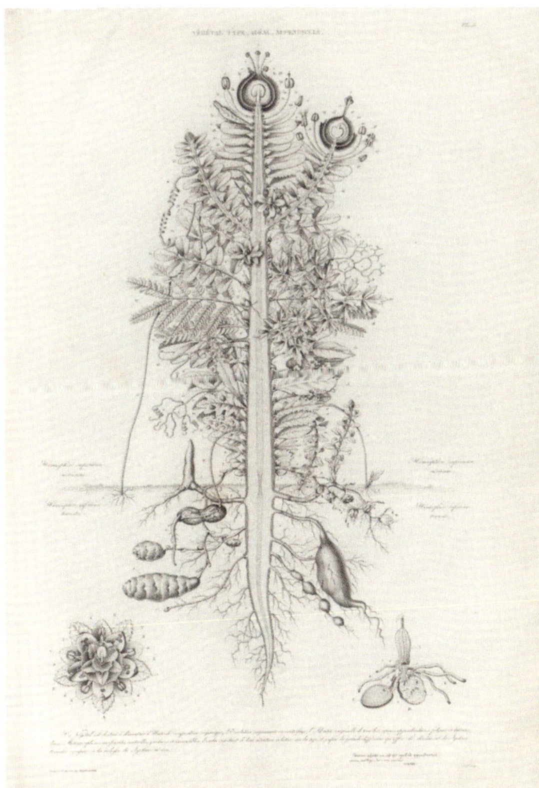

Fig. 5
The ideal plant, or the plant-idea, in J.W. Goethe, *Natural History Works*, 1873, plate 3, illustration by Pierre Jean François Turpin

In 1837 Charles Darwin sketched an abstract tree on his notebook to illustrate the evolution of species. Darwin's evolutionary tree is a very competitive one and branches fight and kill each other. In *On the Origin of Species* (1859) he writes: 'The affinities of all the beings of the same class have sometimes been represented by a great tree. I believe this simile largely speaks the truth. The green and budding twigs may represent existing species; and those produced during each former year may represent the long succession of extinct species. At each period of growth all the growing twigs have tried to branch out on all sides, and to overtop and kill the surrounding twigs and branches, in the same manner as species and groups of species have tried to overmaster other species in the great battle for life.'[11] It is often forgotten that Darwin's last book was *The Power of Movements in Plants* (1880), in which he stresses the similarities between animals and plants, such as sensitivity to touch (thigmotropism), light sensitivity (phototropism) and responsiveness to gravity (geotropism). The book concludes with the suggestive hypothesis that the plant's root functions like the brain in animals: 'The course pursued by the radicle in penetrating the ground must be determined by the tip; hence it has acquired such diverse kinds of sensitiveness. It is hardly an exaggeration to say that the tip of the radicle thus endowed, and having the power of directing the movements of the adjoining parts, acts like the brain of one of the lower animals; the brain being seated within the anterior end of the body, receiving impressions from the sense-organs, and directing the several movements.'[12]

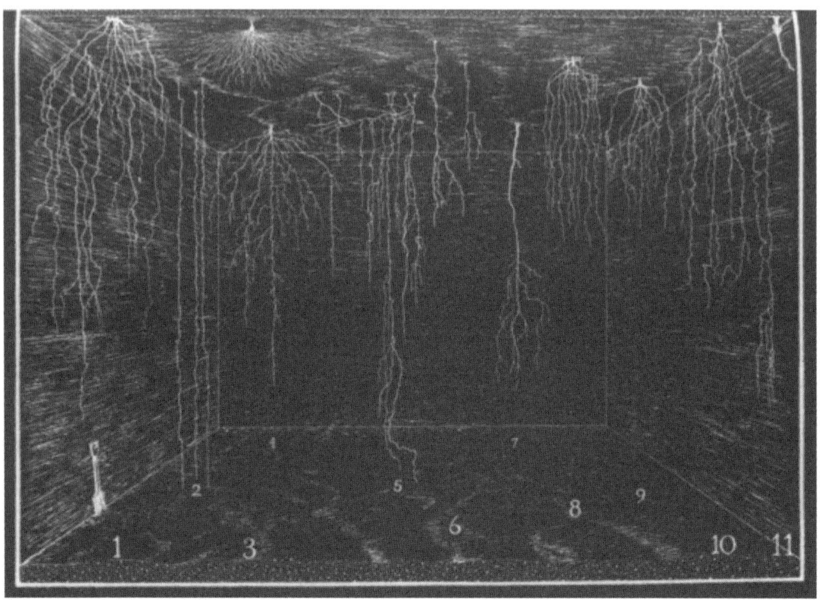

Fig. 6
Drawing of prairie plants' roots after excavation, in John Weaver, *Prairie Plants and Their Environment*, 1968

7. The Arborisation of Networks

In their introduction to *A Thousand Plateaus*, Gilles Deleuze and Félix Guattari write: 'The Tree or Root as an image endlessly develops the law of the One that becomes two, then of the two that become four [...] Binary logic is the spiritual reality of the root-tree.'[13] 'We should stop believing in trees, roots, and radicles. They've made us suffer too much. All of arborescent culture is founded on them, from biology to linguistics. Nothing is beautiful or loving or political aside from underground stems and aerial roots, adventitious growths and rhizomes.'[14] 'Thought is not arborescent, and the brain is not a rooted or ramified matter [...] Many people have a tree growing in their heads, but the brain itself is much more a grass than a tree.'[15] Against the vertical tree form, Deleuze and Guattari propose the horizontal rhizome form that would become popular across the 1990s as a metaphor of the network society.[16] Deleuze and Guattari's own dichotomy between tree and rhizome will be overcome by information technologies themselves and specifically by the neural networks of artificial intelligence (fig. 7). Neural networks elaborate horizontal layers of data into consistent patterns, that is by transforming a myriad of nodes into a gestalt (Warren McCulloch and Walter Pitts proposed the creation of artificial neural networks in 1943, after observing the disposition of neurons in a frog's eye).[17] Neural networks are able to turn rhizomic networks into the source of a centralising intelligence. The rise of global datacentres (and the new computational capitalism) indicates how the good old rhizome has been reversed into a new tree of power.[18]

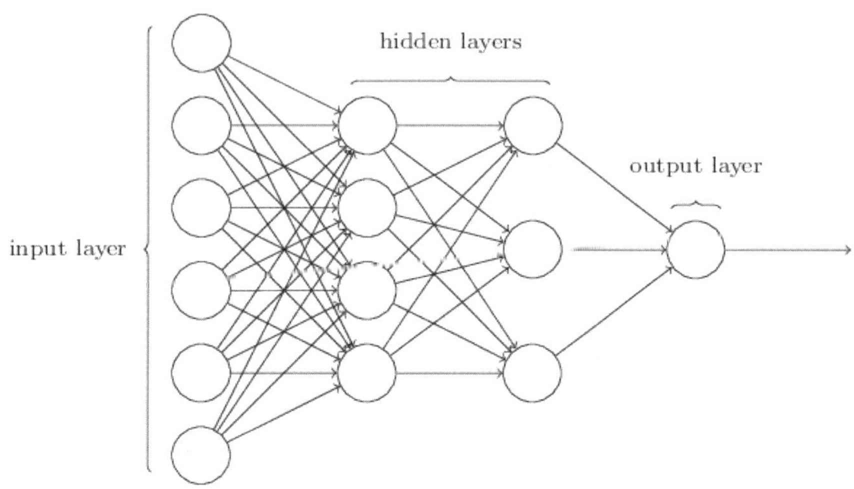

Fig. 7
Neural network architecture, in Michael A. Nielsen, *Neural Networks and Deep Learning*, 2015

1 Julien Pacotte, *Le Réseau Arborescent, Schème Primordial de la Pensée* (Paris: Hermann, 1936). Quoted and translated in Christy Wampole, *Rootedness: The Ramifications of a Metaphor* (Chicago: University of Chicago Press, 2016), p. 183

2 Mariana Giovino, *The Assyrian Sacred Tree: A History of Interpretations* (Freiburg: Academic Press, 2007)

3 Simo Parpola, 'The Assyrian Tree of Life: Tracing the Origins of Jewish Monotheism and Greek Philosophy', *Journal of Near Eastern Studies*, Vol. 52, No. 3 (July 1993), pp. 161–208

4 Umberto Eco, *Semiotics and the Philosophy of Language* (Bloomington: Indiana University Press, 1986)

5 Paracelsus, *Von den natürlichen Dingen* (1537), in Johannes Huser (ed.), *Die Bücher und Schriften* (Hildesheim/New York: Georg Olms, 1972 [1859]), Vol. 3, No. 7, p. 131. Translated in Giorgio Agamben, *The Signature of All Things: On Method* (New York: Zone Books, 2009), p. 33

6 Paracelsus, *Liber de podagricis,* in Huser, Vol. 2, No. 4, p. 259. Agamben, p. 33

7 Paracelsus (1537), in Huser, Vol. 3, No. 7, p. 133. Agamben, p. 33

8 J.W. Goethe, *Versuch die Metamorphose der Pflanzen zu erklären* (Gotha: Ettinger, 1790), in G.L. Miller (tr.), *The Metamorphosis of Plants* (Cambridge, MA: MIT Press, 2009)

9 Ibid.

10 The biologist and illustrator Ernst Haeckel expanded the idea of genetic gestalt in his famous phylogenetic trees, which were supposed to show family resemblance and difference among species in a more organic way compared to Charles Darwin's tree of life, in which the adaptation to and selection by the environment had a major role. See Benoît Dayrat, 'The Roots of Phylogeny: How Did Haeckel Build his Trees?', *Systematic Biology*, Vol. 52, No. 4 (August 2003), pp. 515–27. See also Nils Petter Hellström, 'Darwin and the Tree of Life: The Roots of the Evolutionary Tree', *Archives of Natural History*, Vol. 39, No. 2 (October 2012), pp. 234–52

11 Charles Darwin, *On the Origin of Species by Means of Natural Selection, or the Preservation of Favoured Races in the Struggle for Life*, in Gillian Beer (ed.), (Oxford: Oxford University Press, 2008 [1859]), p. 106

12 Charles Darwin (assisted by Francis Darwin), *The Power of Movements in Plants* (London: John Murray, 1880). See in particular František Baluška et al., 'The Root-brain Hypothesis of Charles and Francis Darwin', *Plant Signaling & Behavior*, Vol. 4, No. 12 (December 2009), pp. 1121–27

13 Gilles Deleuze and Félix Guattari, *A Thousand Plateaus: Capitalism and Schizophrenia*, Vol. 2 (Minneapolis: University of Minnesota Press, 1987), pp. 5–15

14 Ibid.

15 Ibid.

16 It must be noted that Deleuze and Guattari, writing in 1980, were already referring to the network form. See Deleuze and Guattari, p. 519, notes 13–15. Specifically they quoted Pierre Rosenstiehl and Jean Petitot, 'Automate Asocial et Systèmes Acentrés', *Communications*, Vol. 22 (1974), pp. 45–62

17 Warren McCulloch and Walter Pitts, 'A Logical Calculus of the Ideas Immanent in Nervous Activity', *Bulletin of Mathematical Biophysics*, Vol. 5 (1943), pp. 115–33

18 Deleuze and Guattari were aware that the concept of rhizome was introducing a new rhizome/tree dichotomy and tried to resolve it: 'There exist tree or root structures in rhizomes; conversely, a tree branch or root division may begin to burgeon into a rhizome. The coordinates are determined not by theoretical analyses implying universals but by a pragmatics composing multiplicities or aggregates of intensities. A new rhizome may form in the heart of a tree, the hollow of a root, the crook of a branch.' Deleuze and Guattari, p. 15

'The example of trees does suggest a harmony for which it seems right to dream.'

— Robert Adams

'I went for a walk in the woods [...] and as I was walking back I suddenly saw the building anew. I had no desire to paint it on its own, but seeing it through the trees, that is when I found it striking [...].'

— Peter Doig

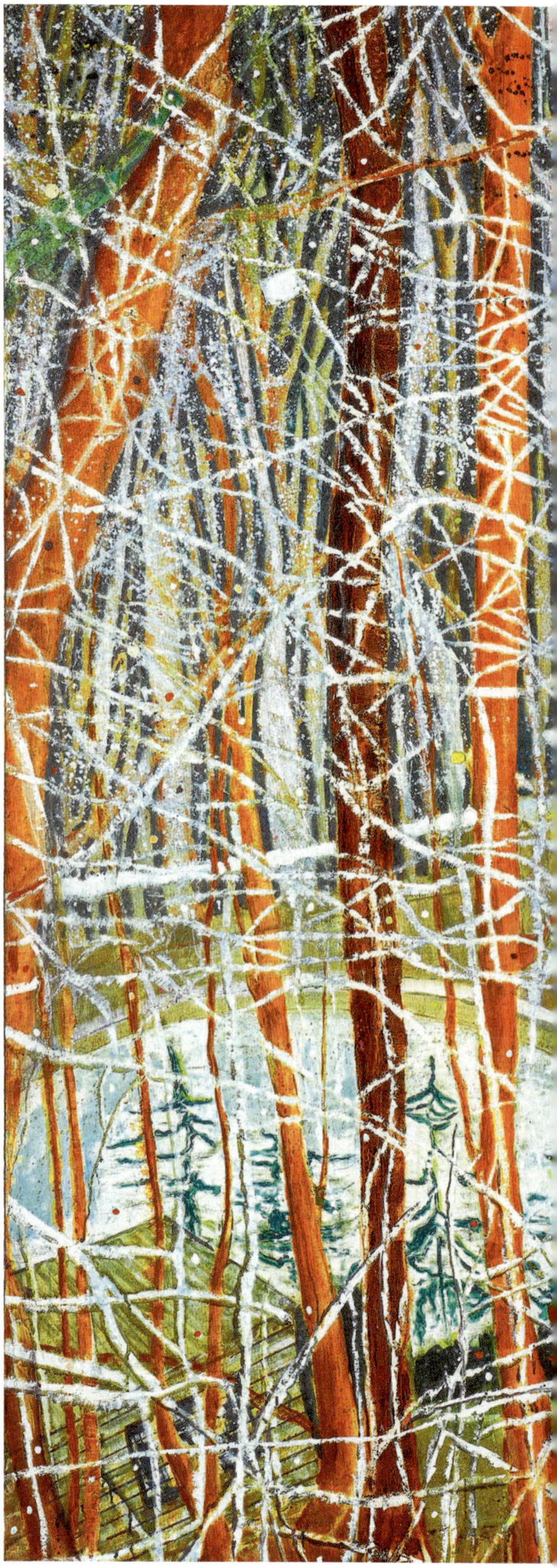

Peter Doig
The Architect's Home in the Ravine, 1991

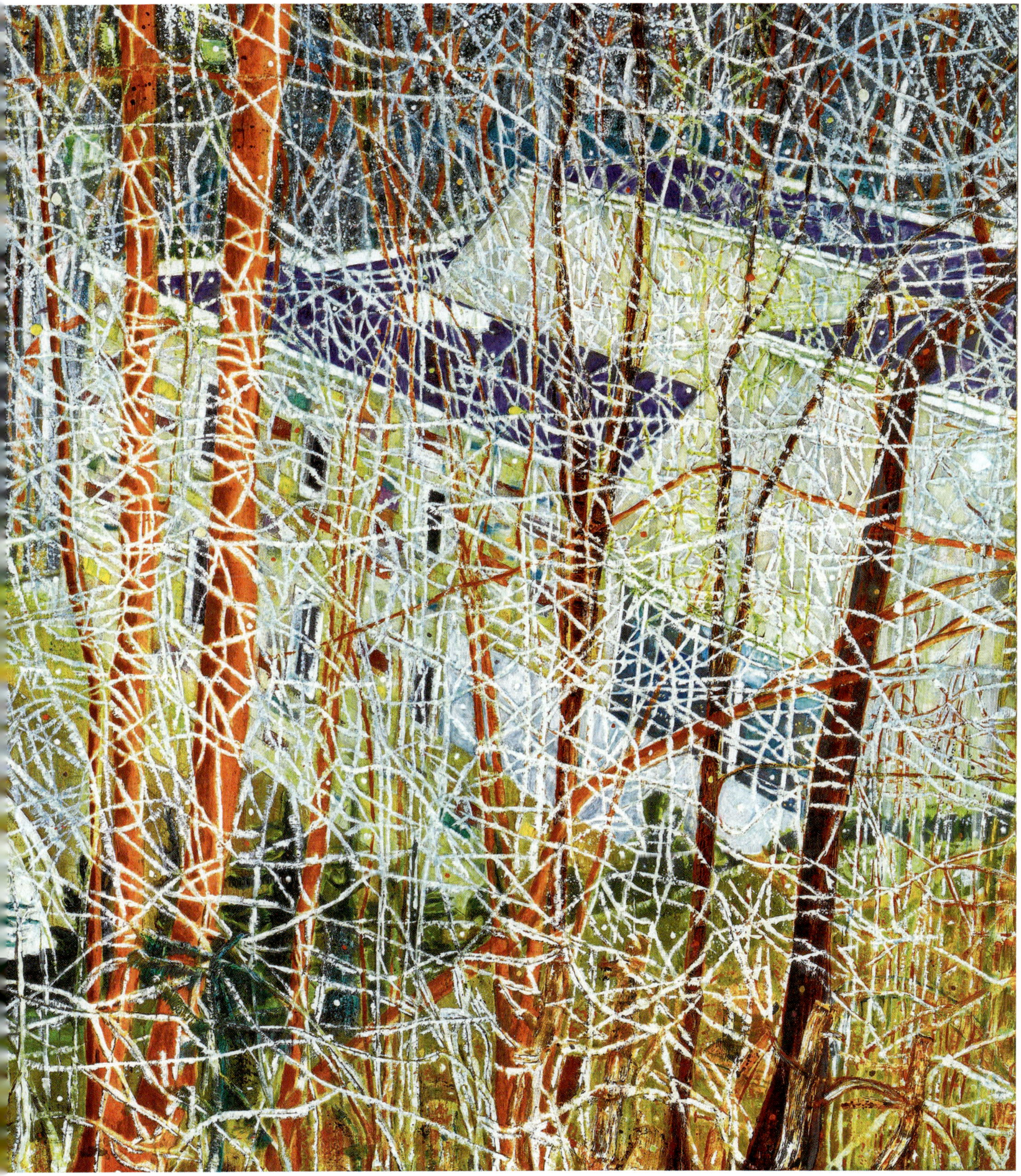

Luisa Lambri
Untitled (Palácio da Indústria #01), 2003

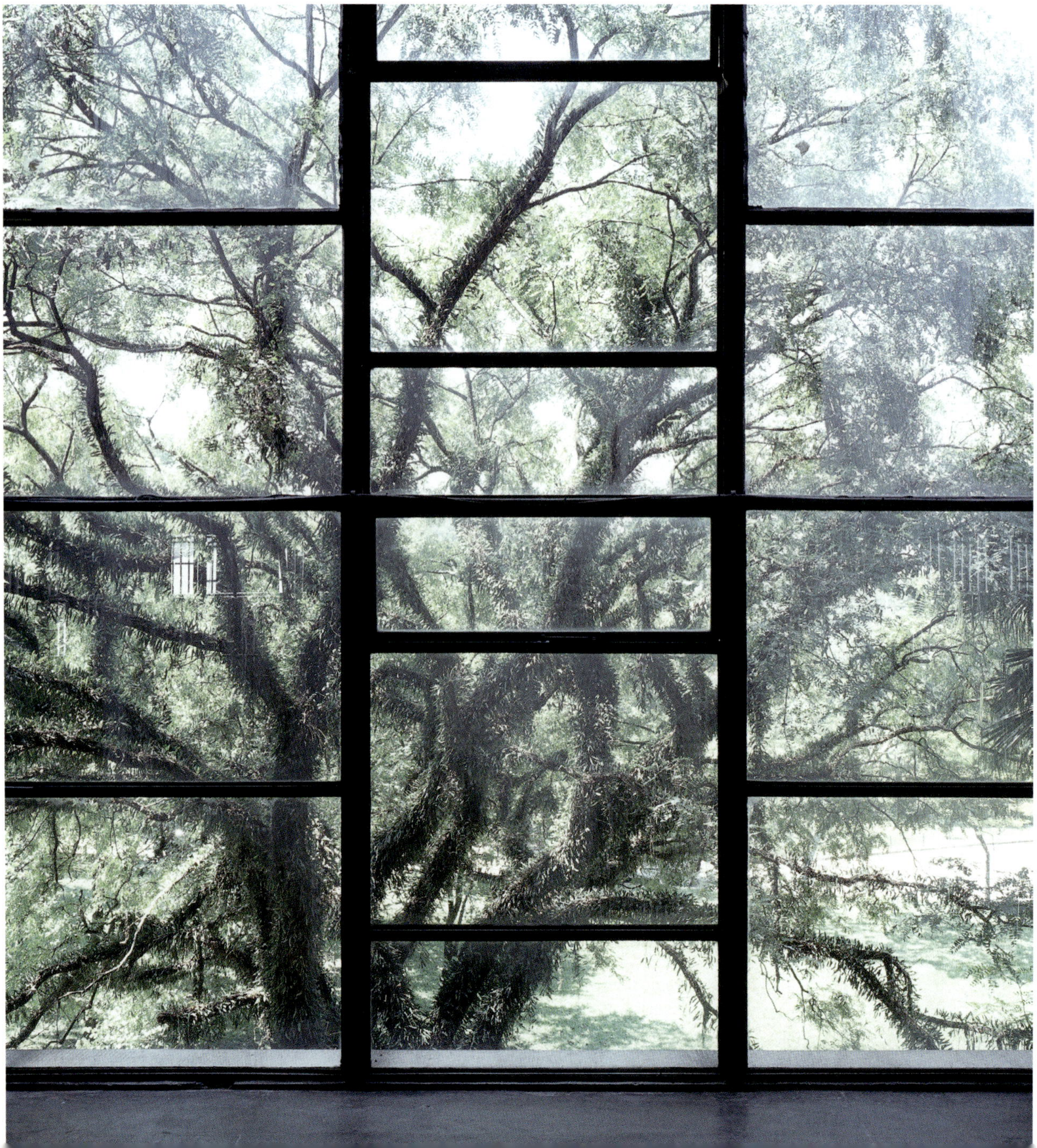

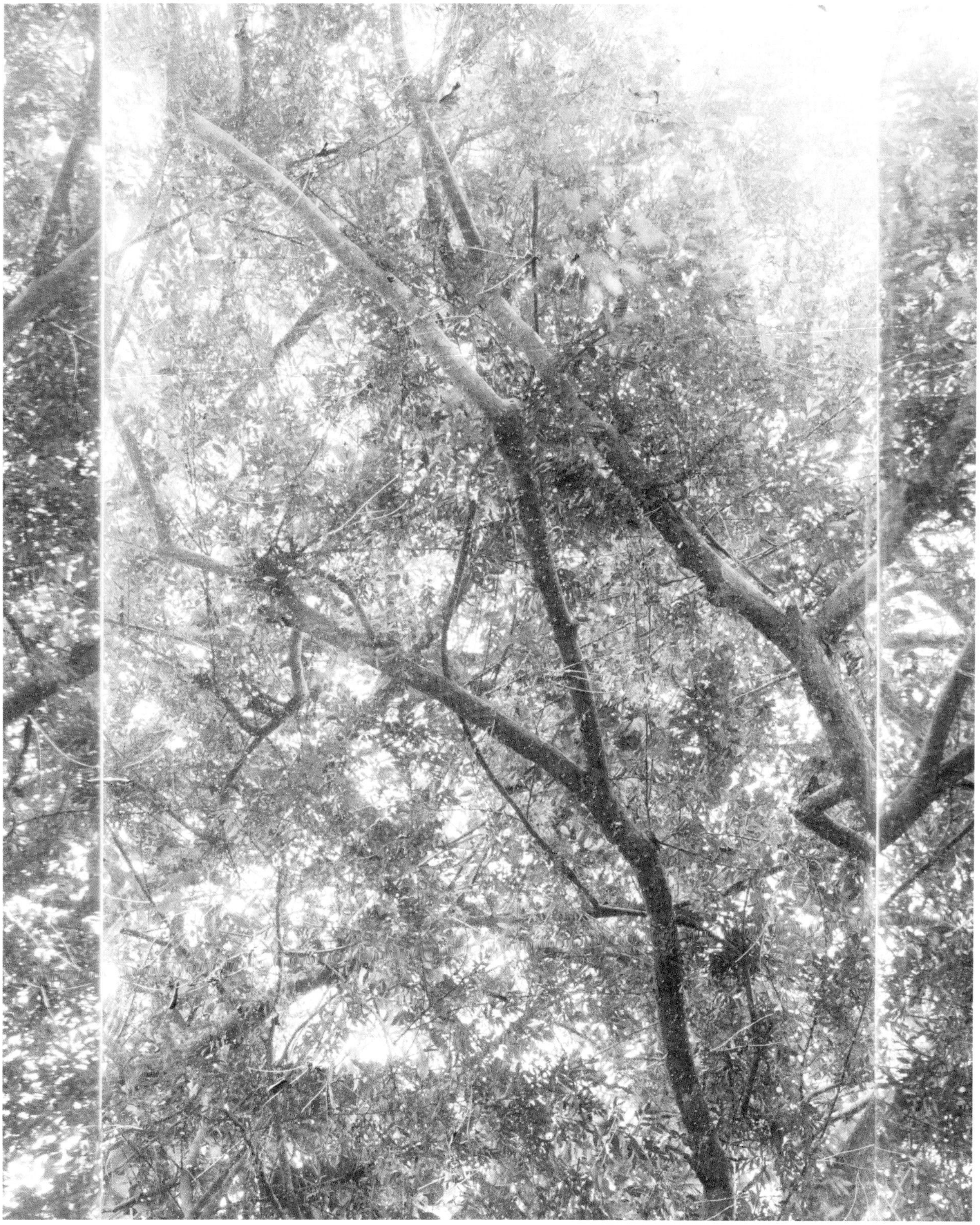

Luisa Lambri
Untitled (Sheats-Goldstein House #06), 2007

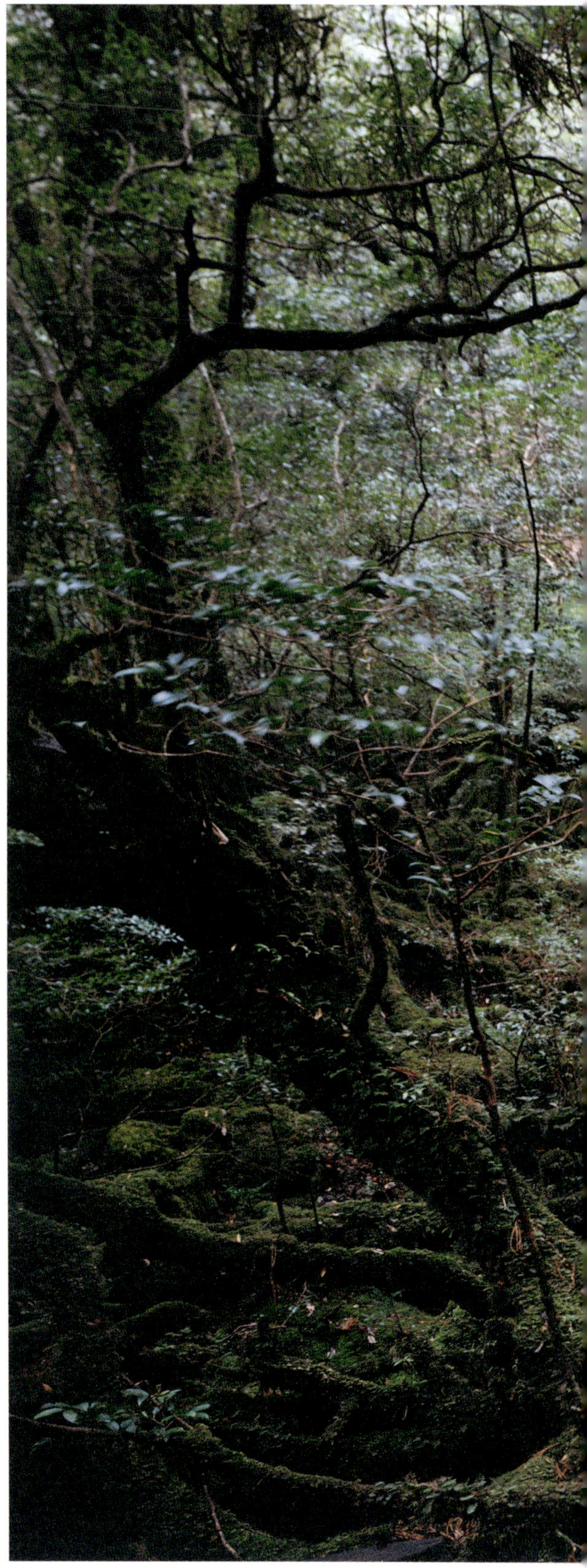

Thomas Struth
Paradise 13, Yakushima, Japan 1999, 1999

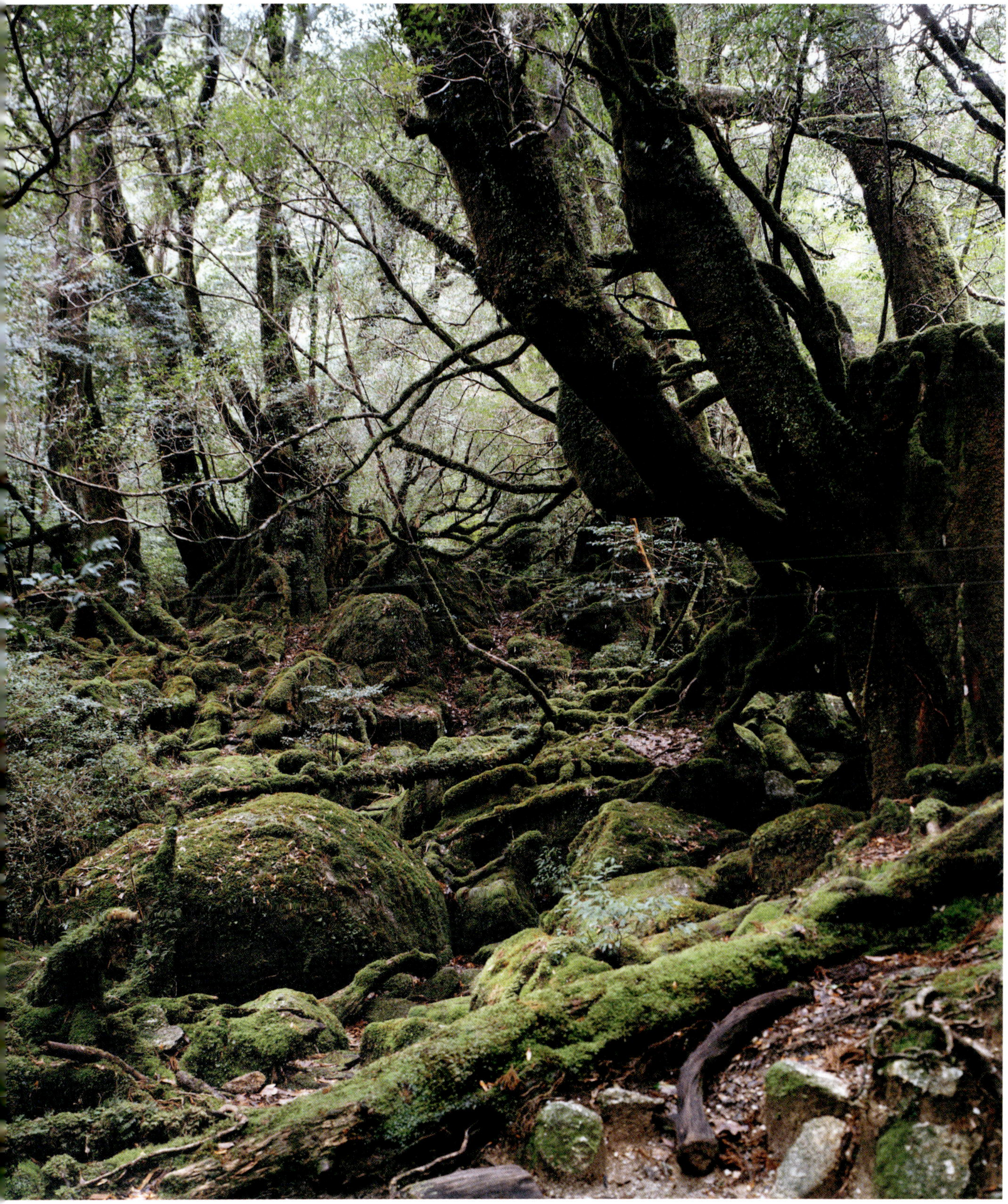

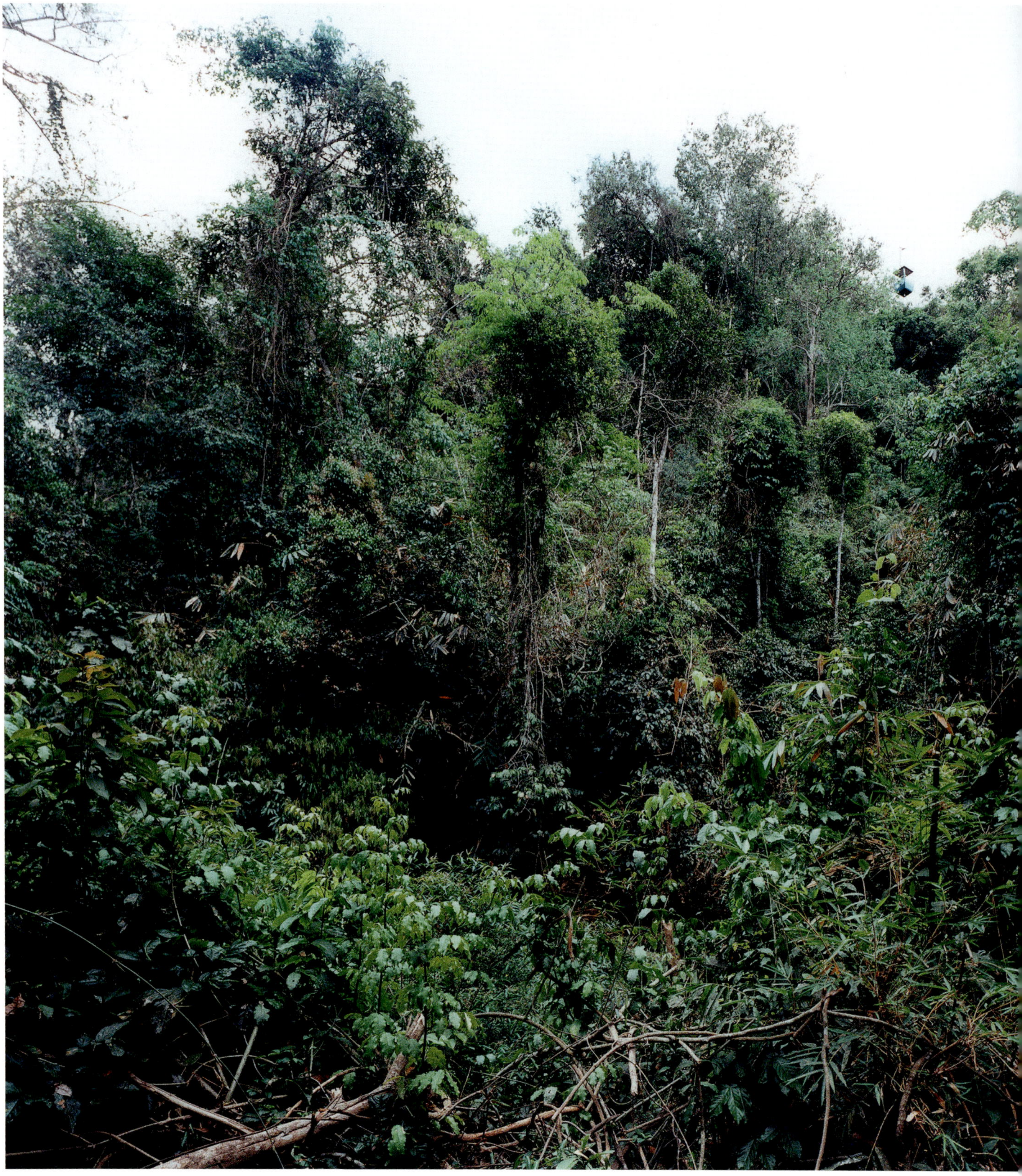

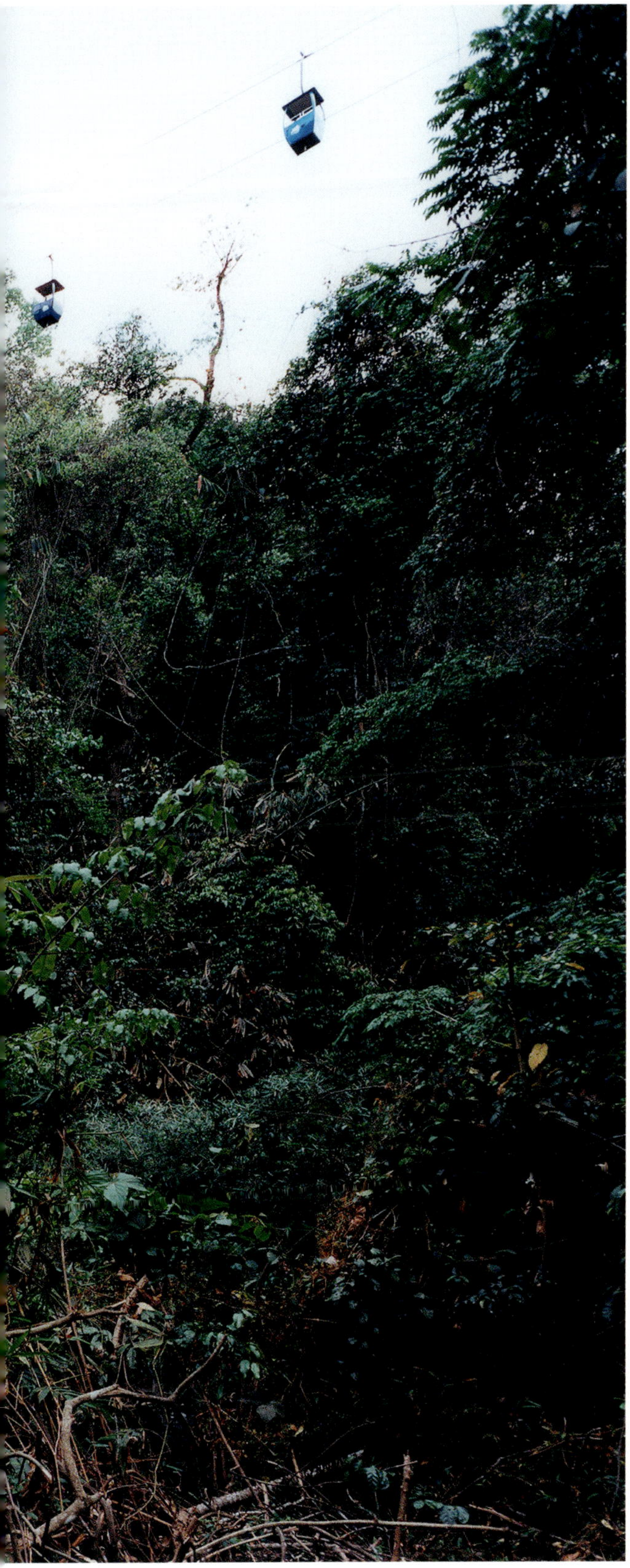

'I used to have an apartment in Düsseldorf for a long time with a terrace towards the back garden. I often used to have breakfast there, read the paper and observe the visual structure of the trees and branches, the information flow of these patterns. That stimulated the idea to make these kinds of pictures that would be very crowded with information which would make you surrender to the act of observation rather than interpretation. However, it could not be a German forest with pine trees and their dominating verticality. It needed to be something wilder, so I thought that jungle, primeval forests would be good [...]'

— Thomas Struth

Thomas Struth
Paradise 11, Xi Shuang Banna, Yunnan Province, China 1999,
1999

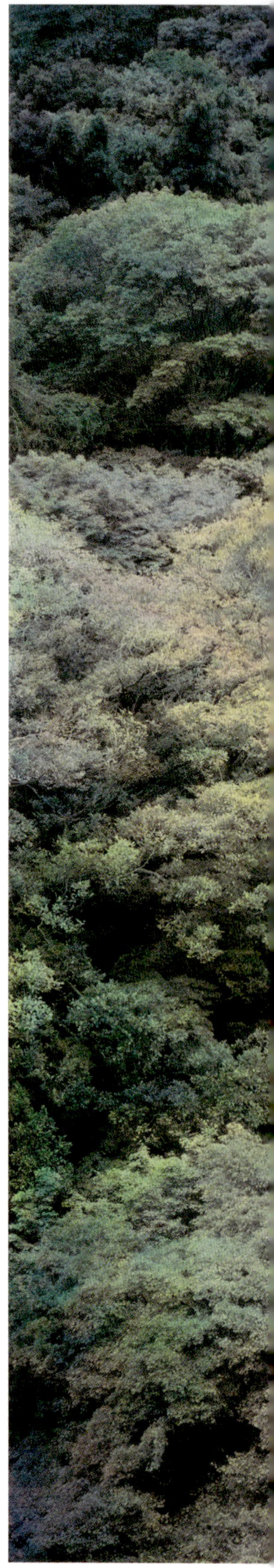

Shi Guowei
Kyoto, 2017

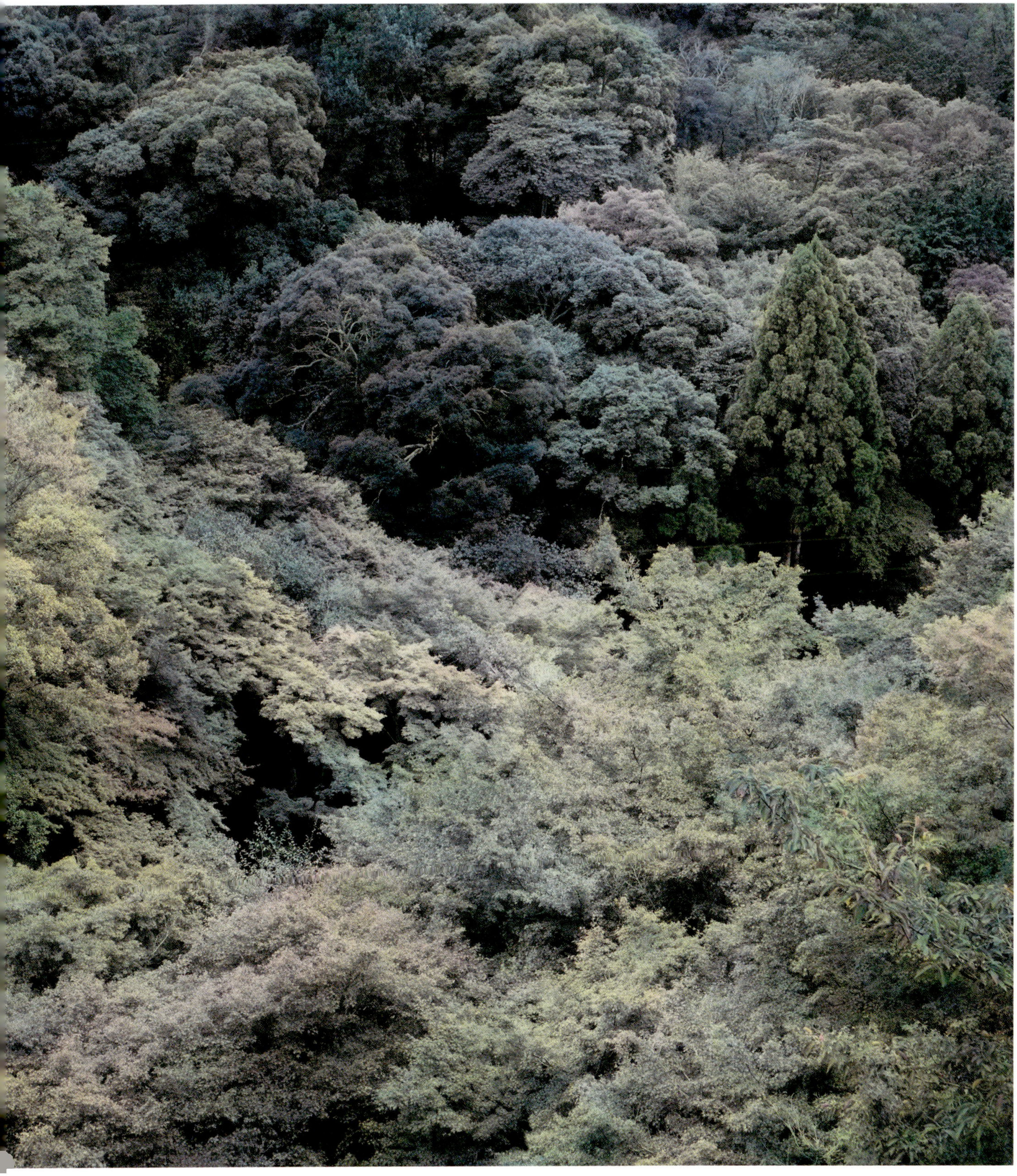

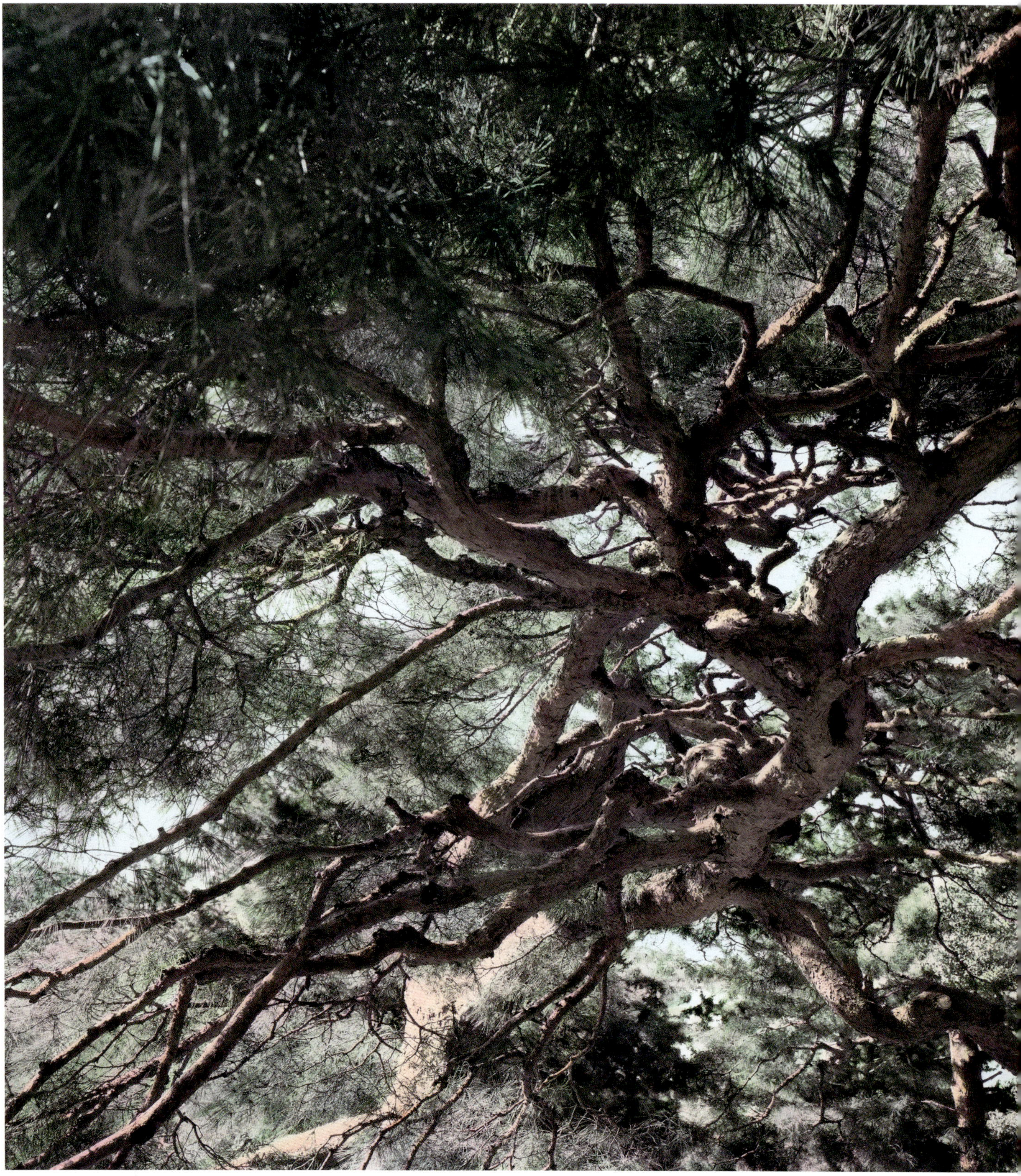

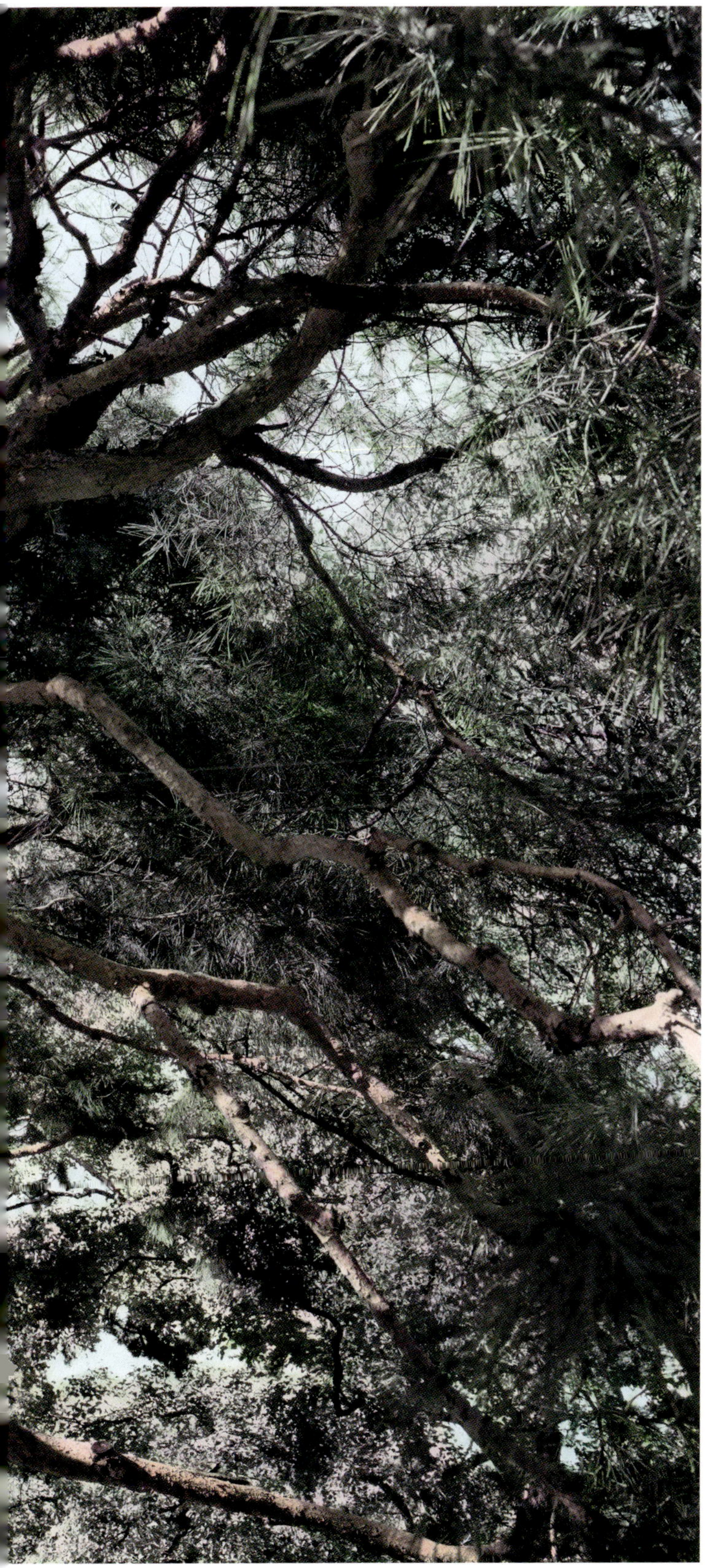

Shi Guowei
Pine, 2016

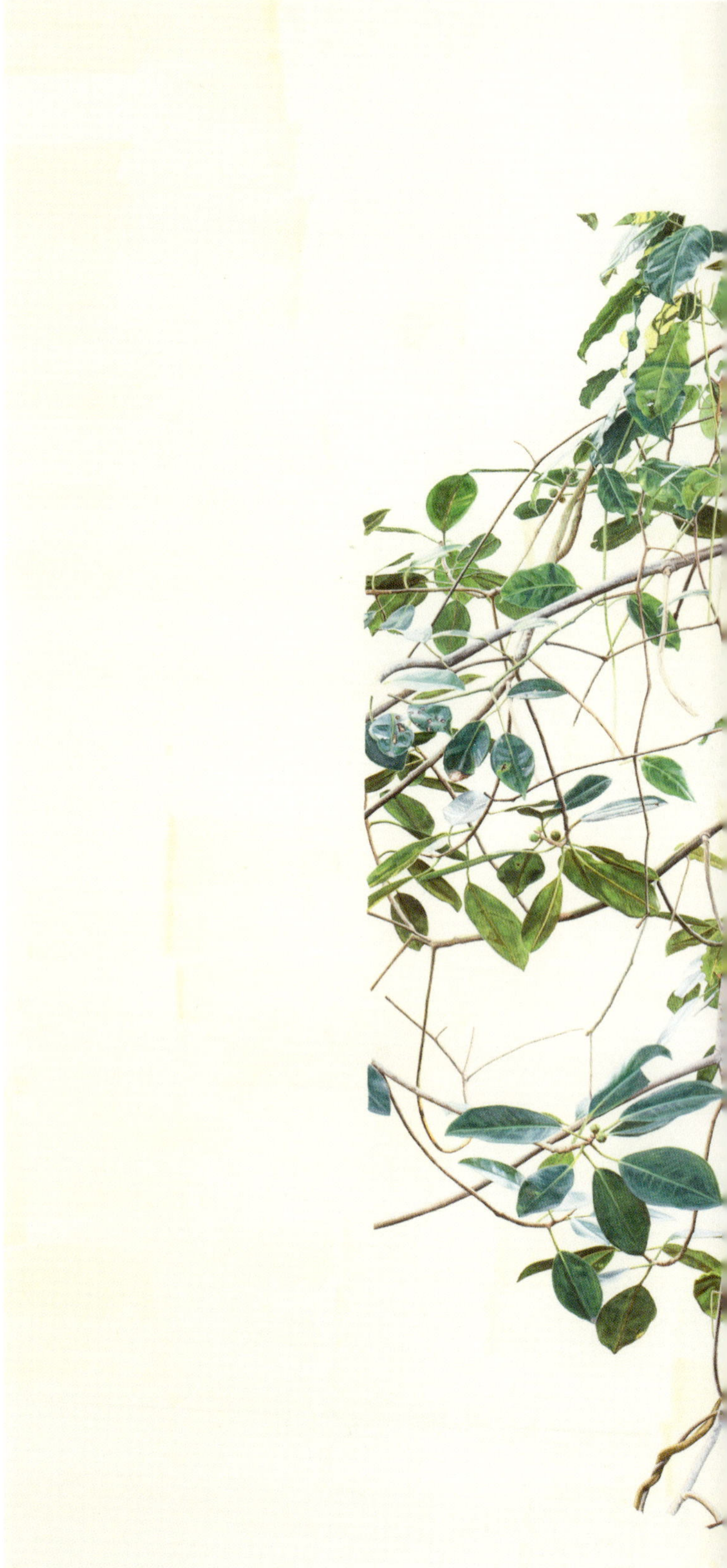

Toba Khedoori
Untitled, 2018

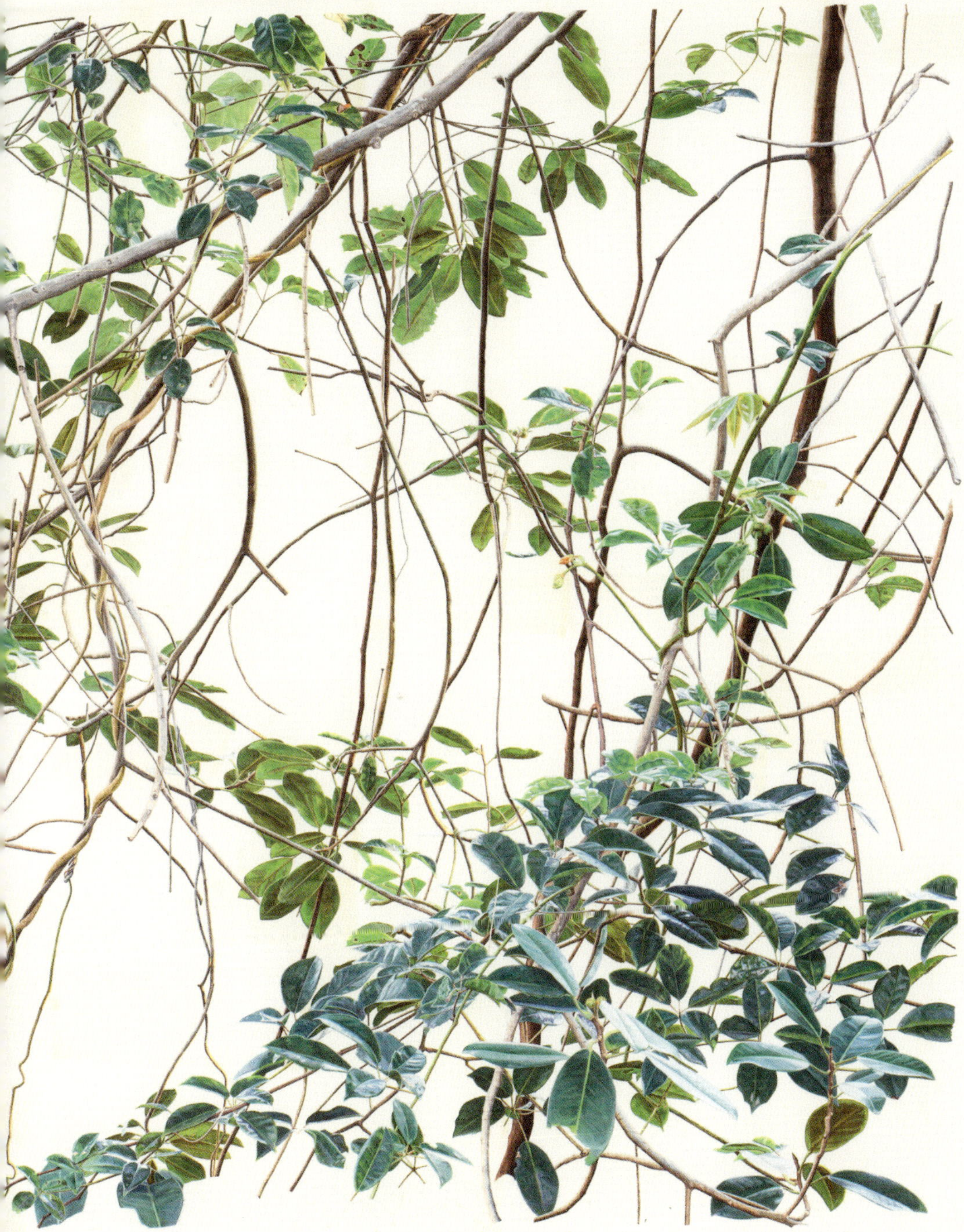

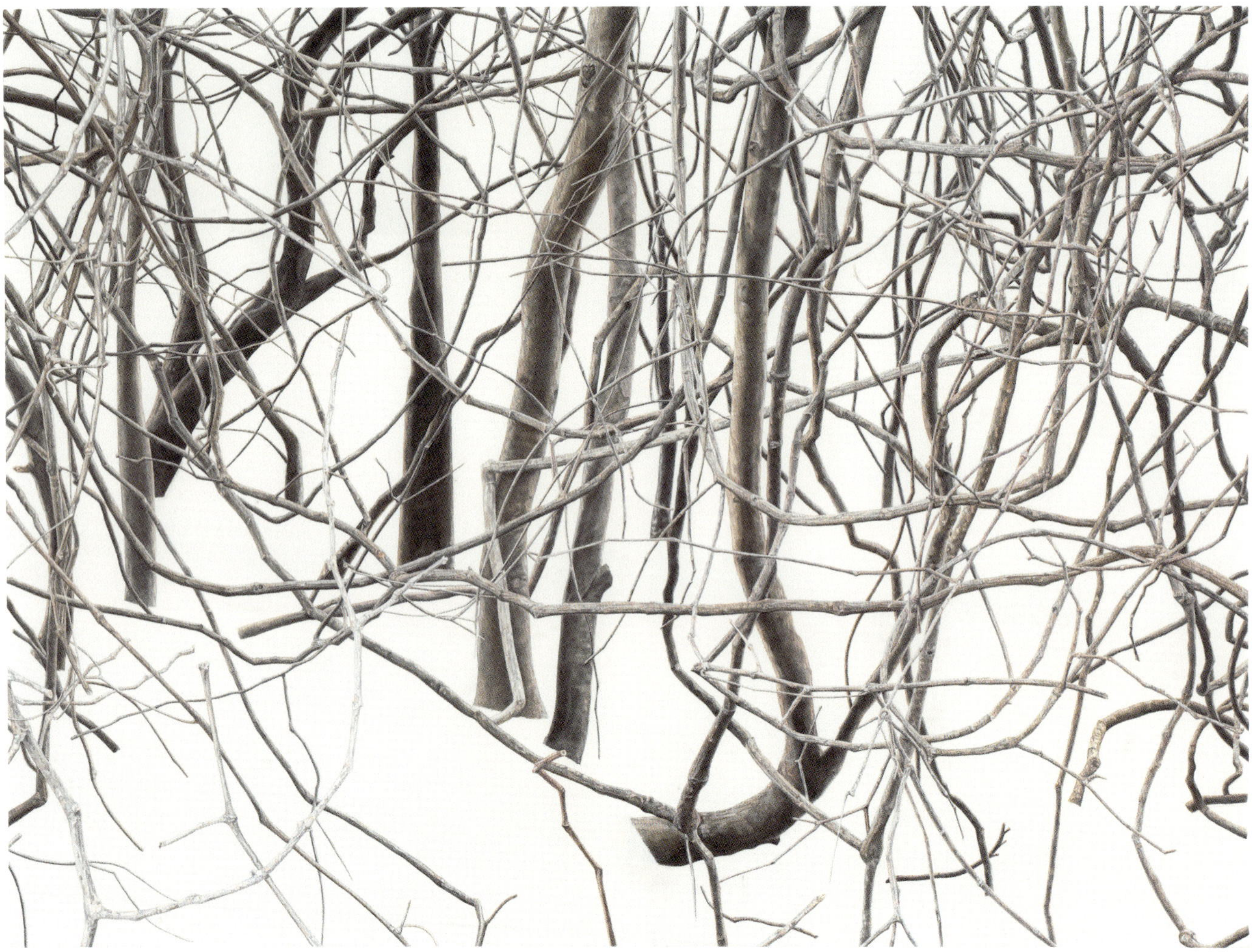

Toba Khedoori
Untitled (branches 1),
2011–12

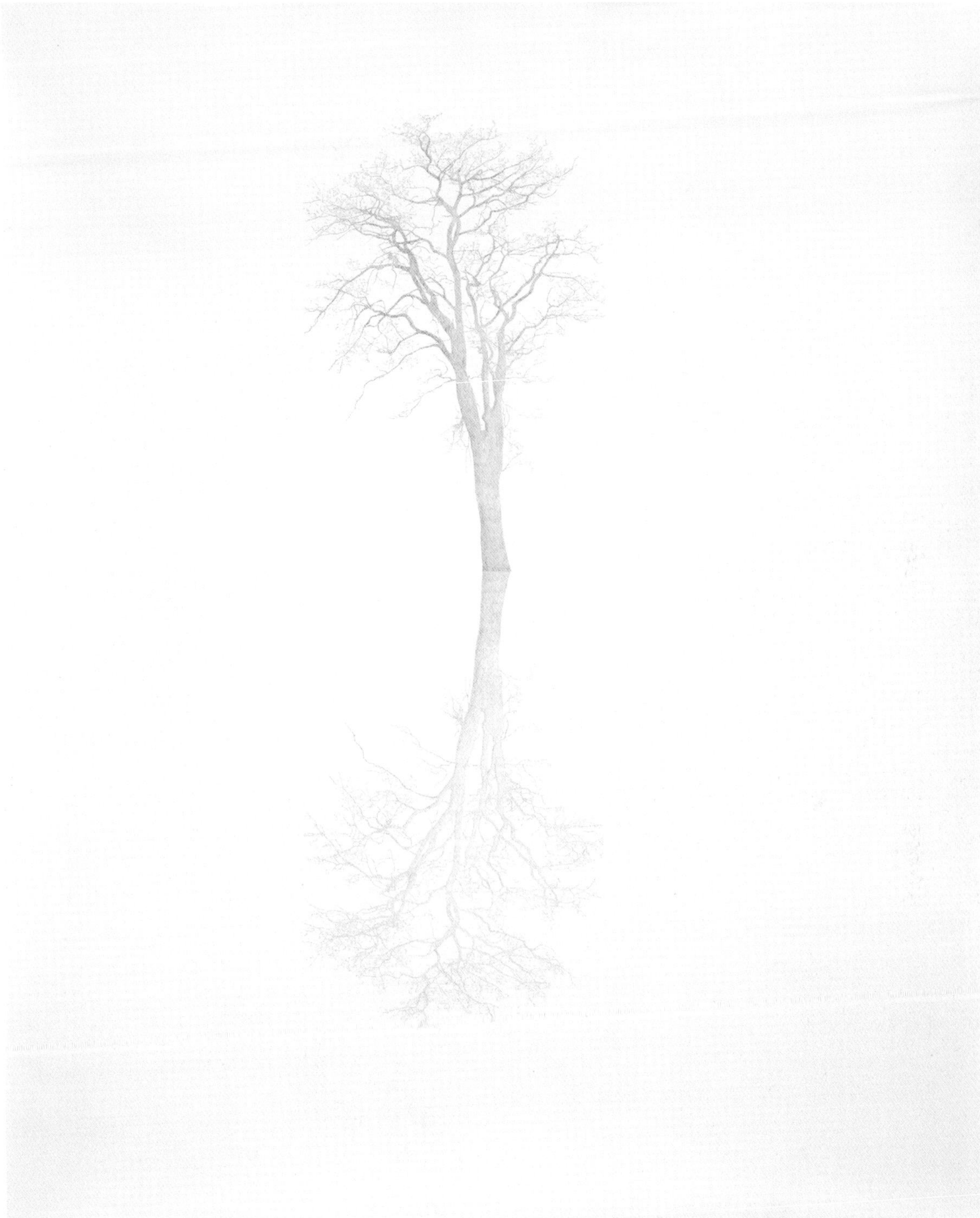

Toba Khedoori
Untitled, 2008

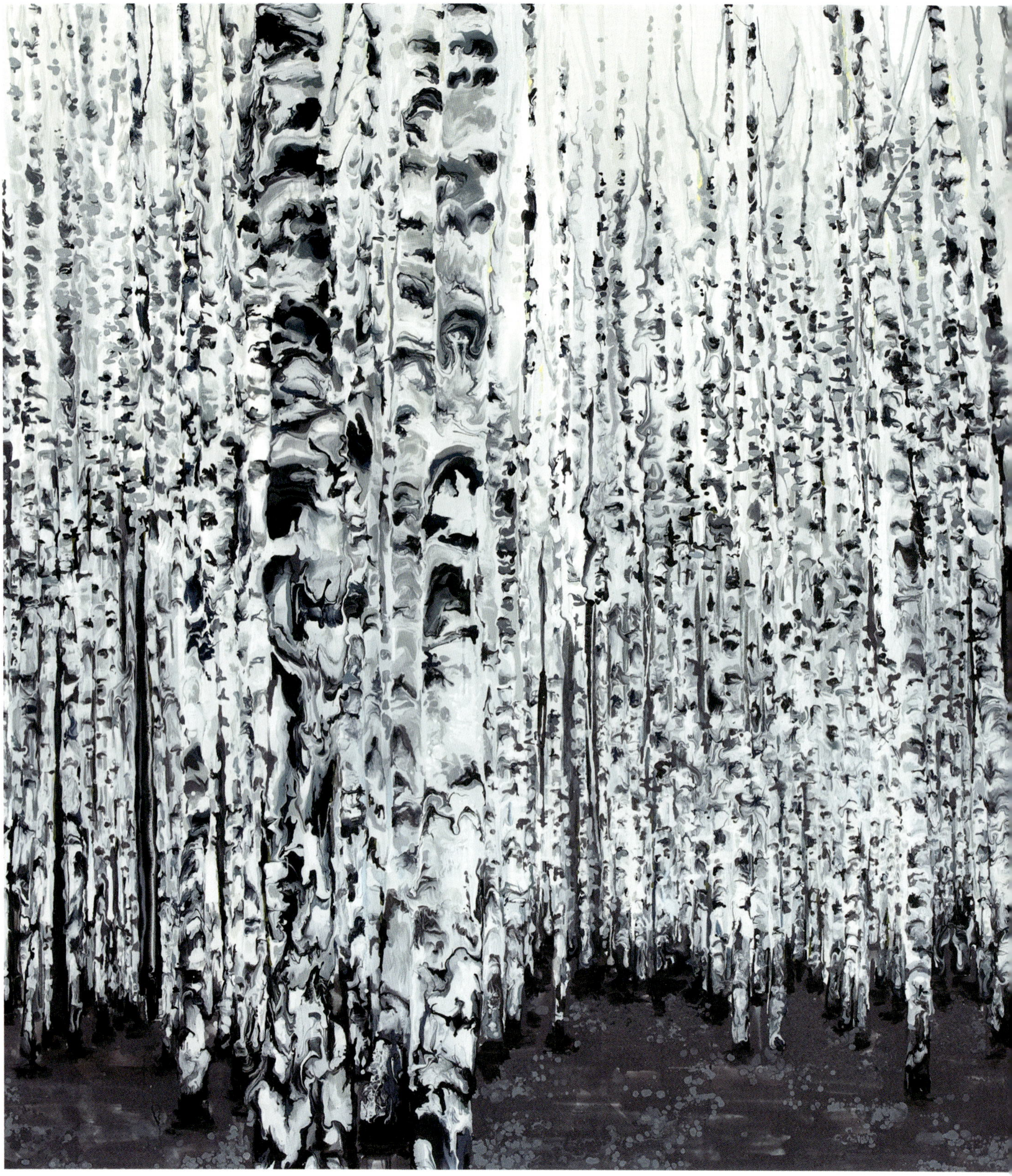

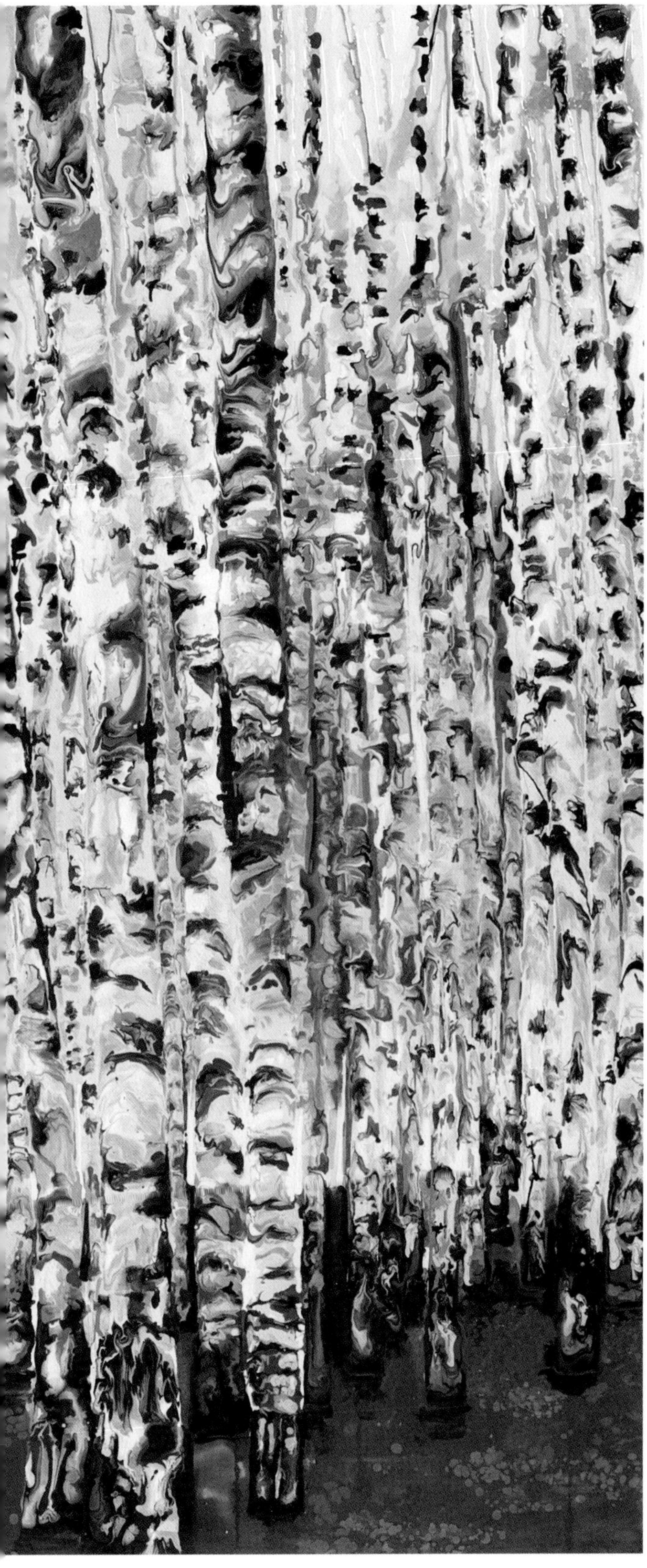

Kirsten Everberg
White Birch Grove, South
(After Tarkovsky), 2008

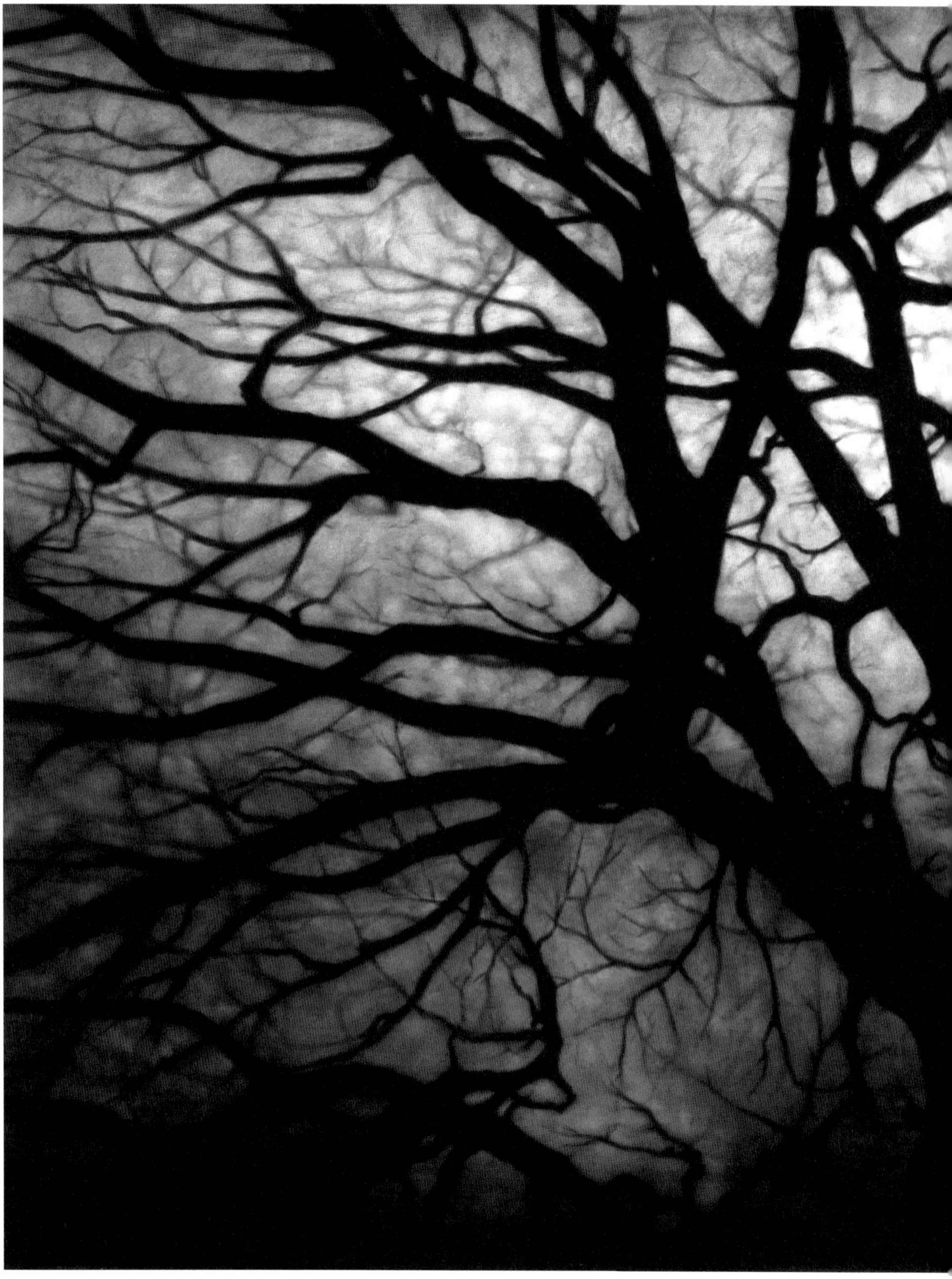

Robert Longo
Untitled (Sleepy Hollow), 2014

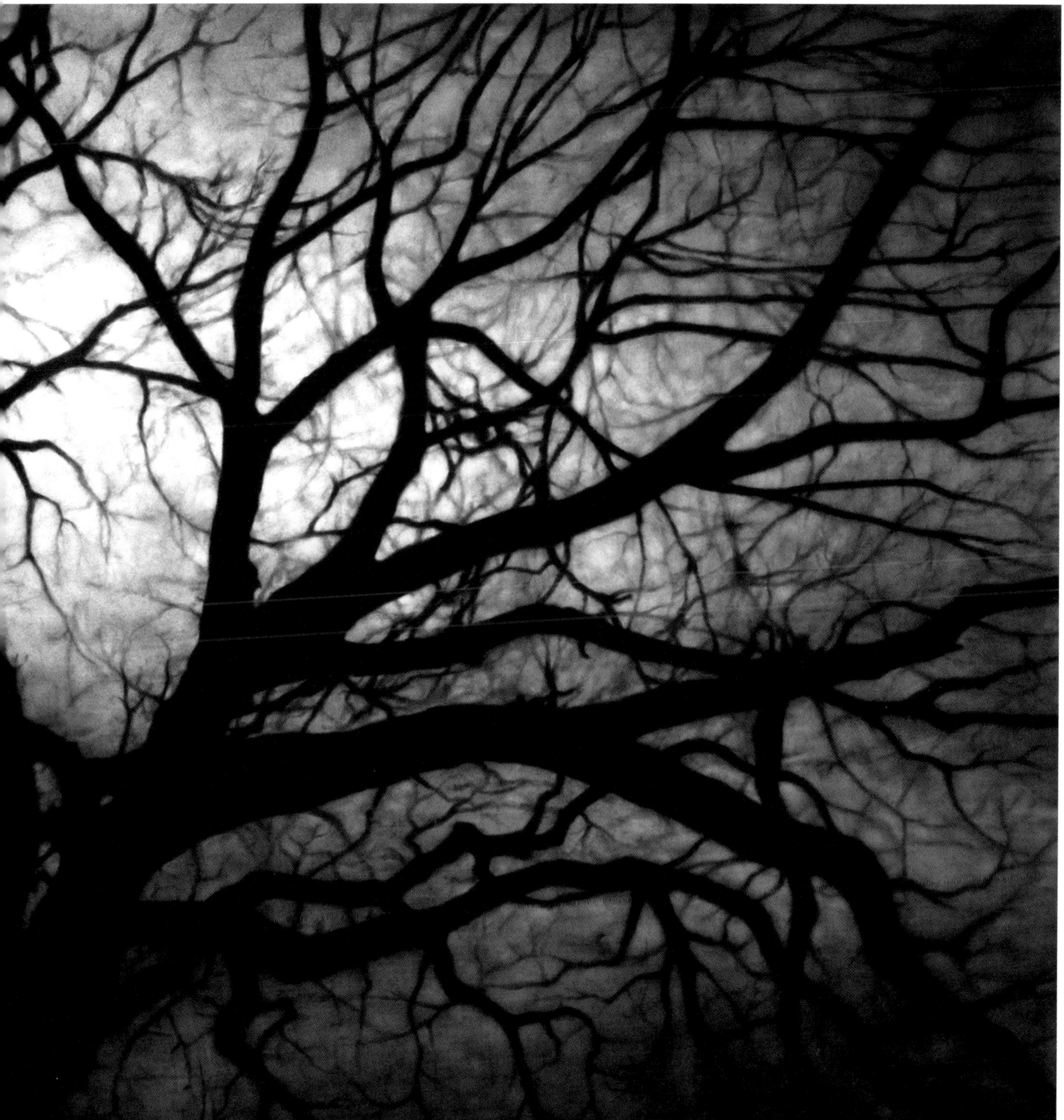

'The first [upside-down tree was planted] in Alfred, New York State, the second is in Captiva Island, Florida; lines drawn on a map will connect them. Are they totems of rootlessness that relate to one another? [...] Flies would come and go from all over to look at the upside-down trees, and peer at them with their compound eyes [...] The "trees" are dedicated to the flies. Dragonflies, fruit flies, horseflies. They are all welcome to walk on the roots with their sticky, padded feet, in order to get a closer look.'

— Robert Smithson

Robert Smithson
Upside Down Tree I, 1969

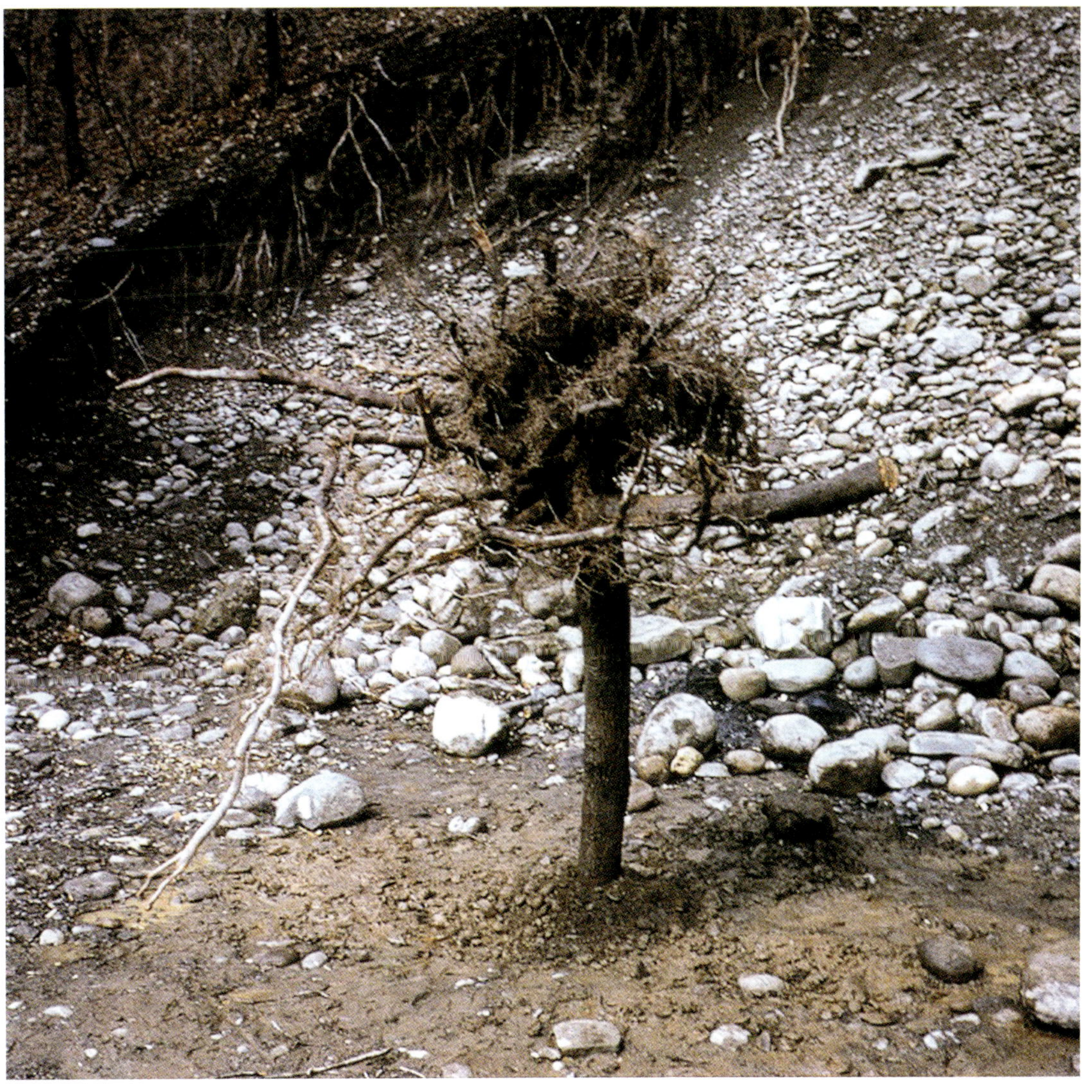

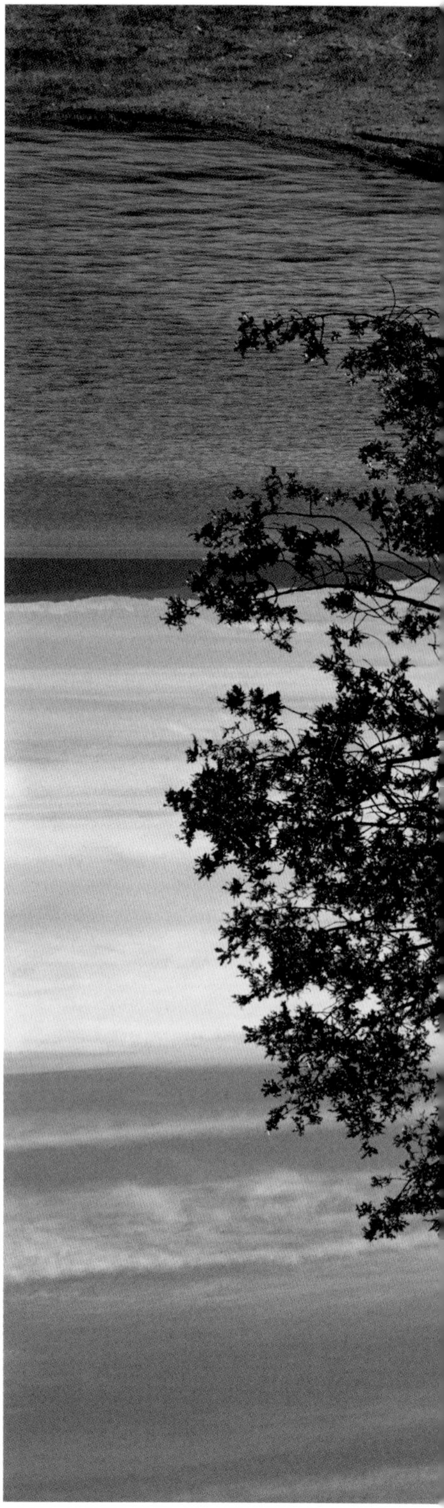

Rodney Graham
Gary Oak, Galiano Island, 2012

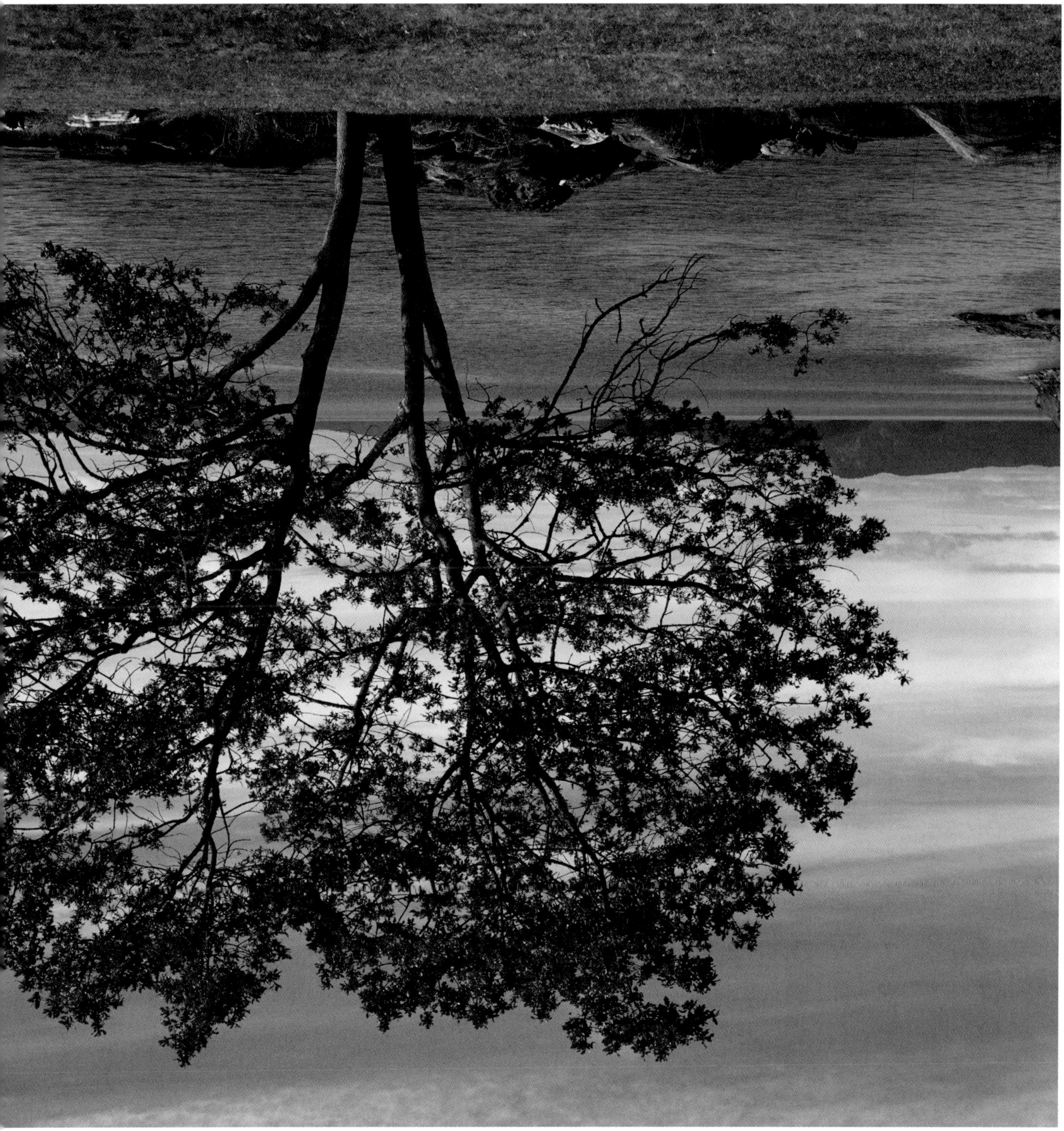

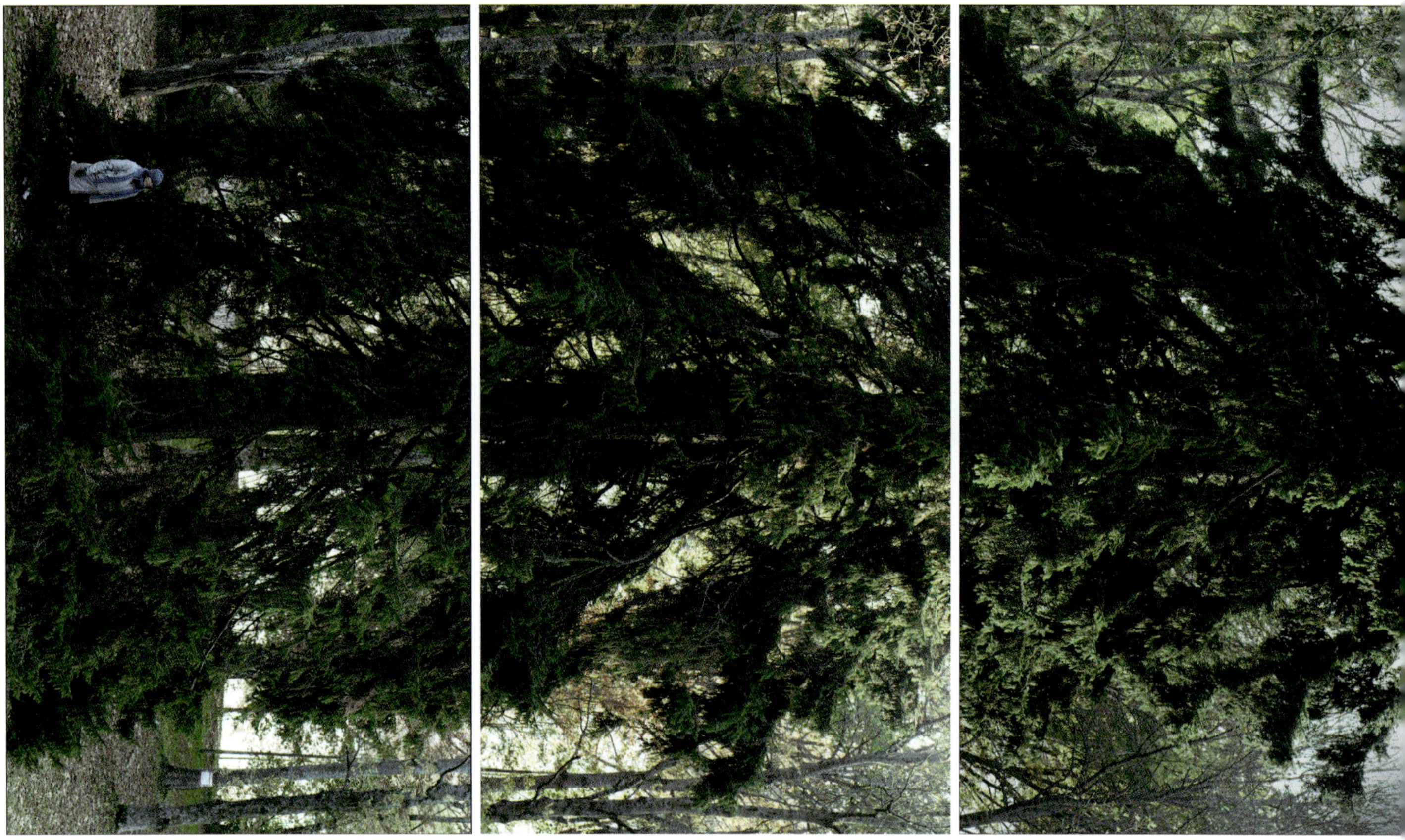

Eija-Liisa Ahtila
Horizontal –
Vaakasuora, 2011

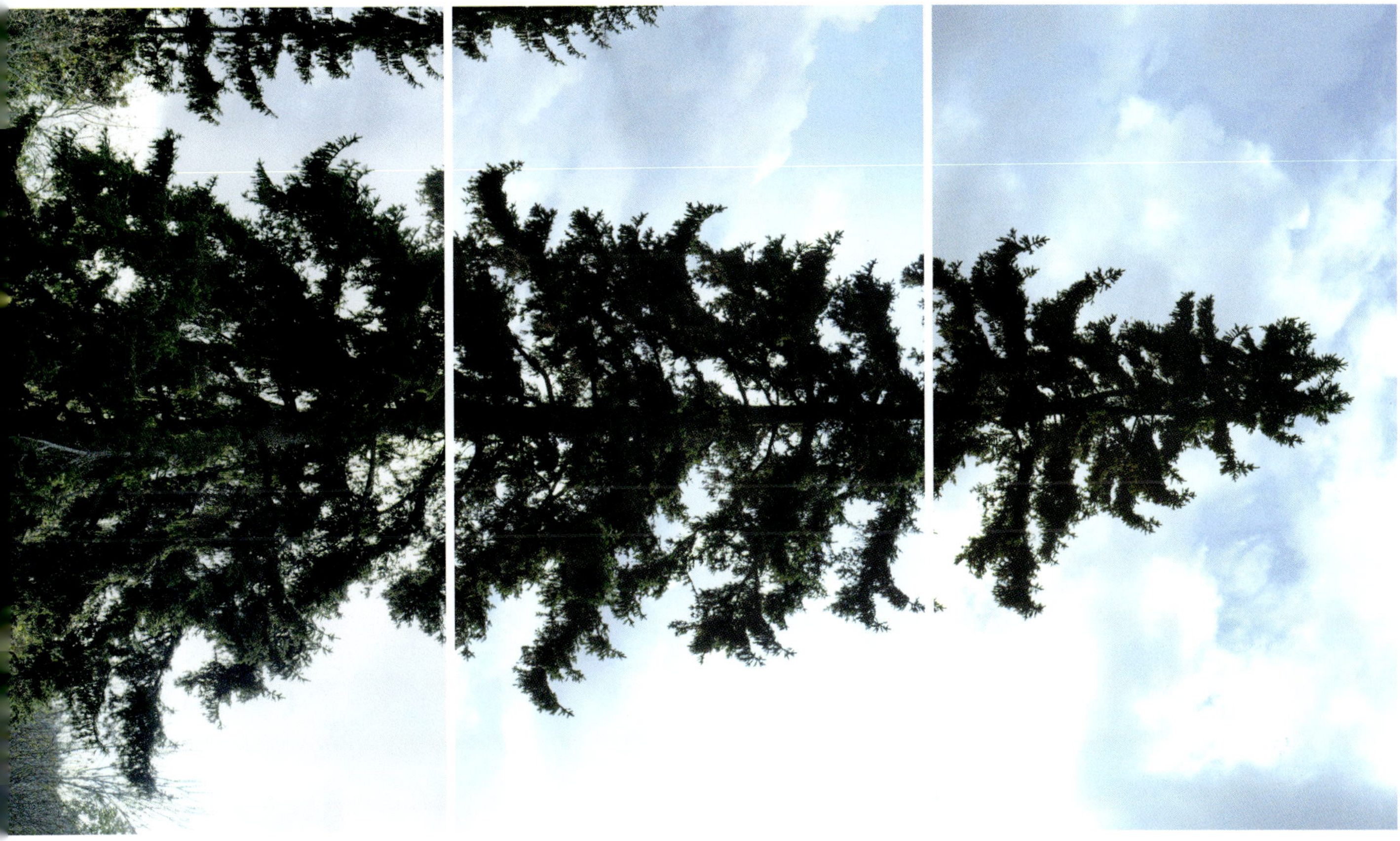

'Soon, it became clear how difficult it is to really portray a tall tree because of the size of the film image – its aspect ratio... I want[ed] to somehow make visible the limits, or edges, of human perception and to try to show the idea introduced by Jakob von Uexküll – of the simultaneous existence of different worlds, different times and spaces.'

— Eija-Liisa Ahtila

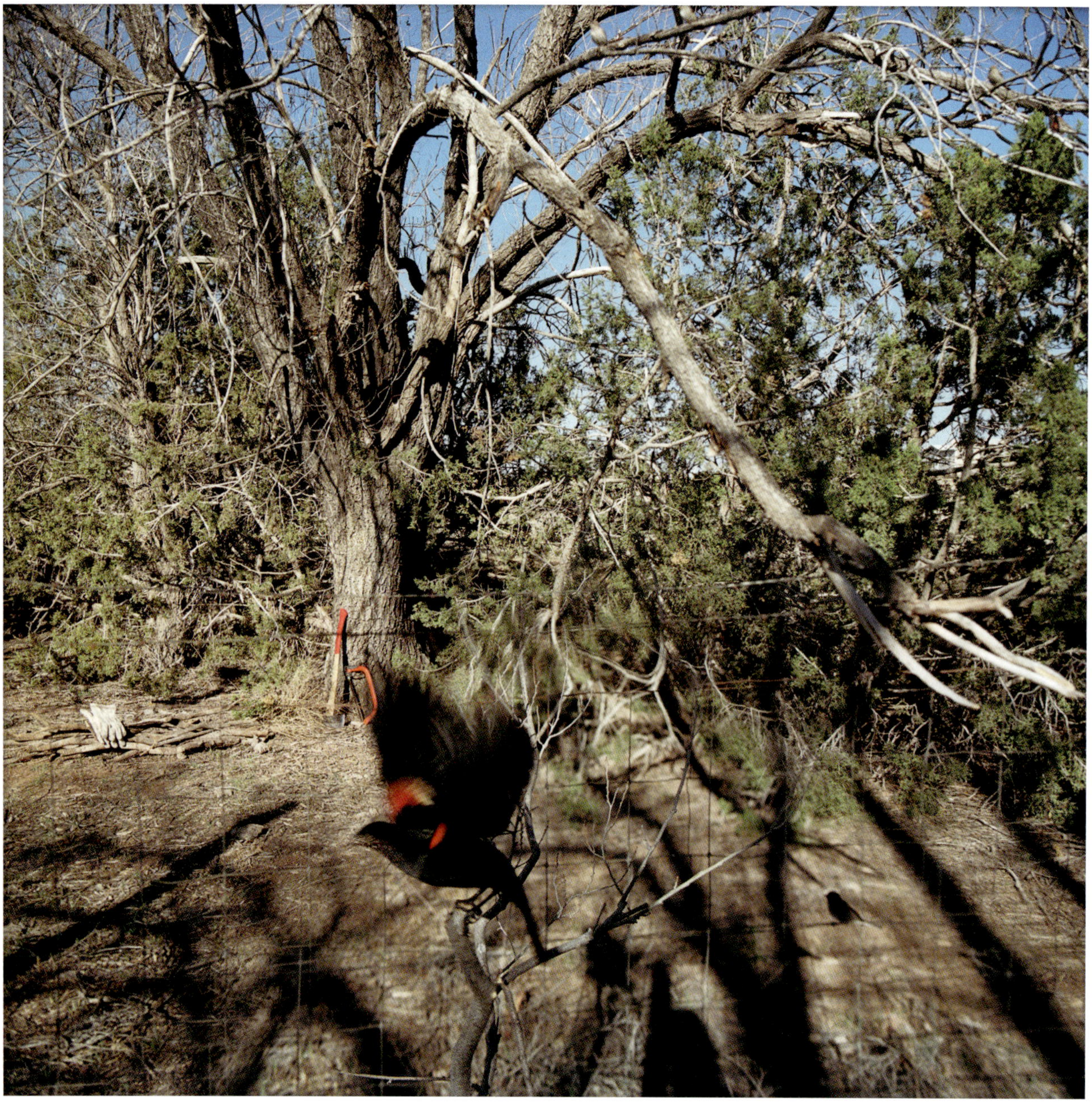

Jean-Luc Mylayne
No. 284, Février Mars 2004, 2004

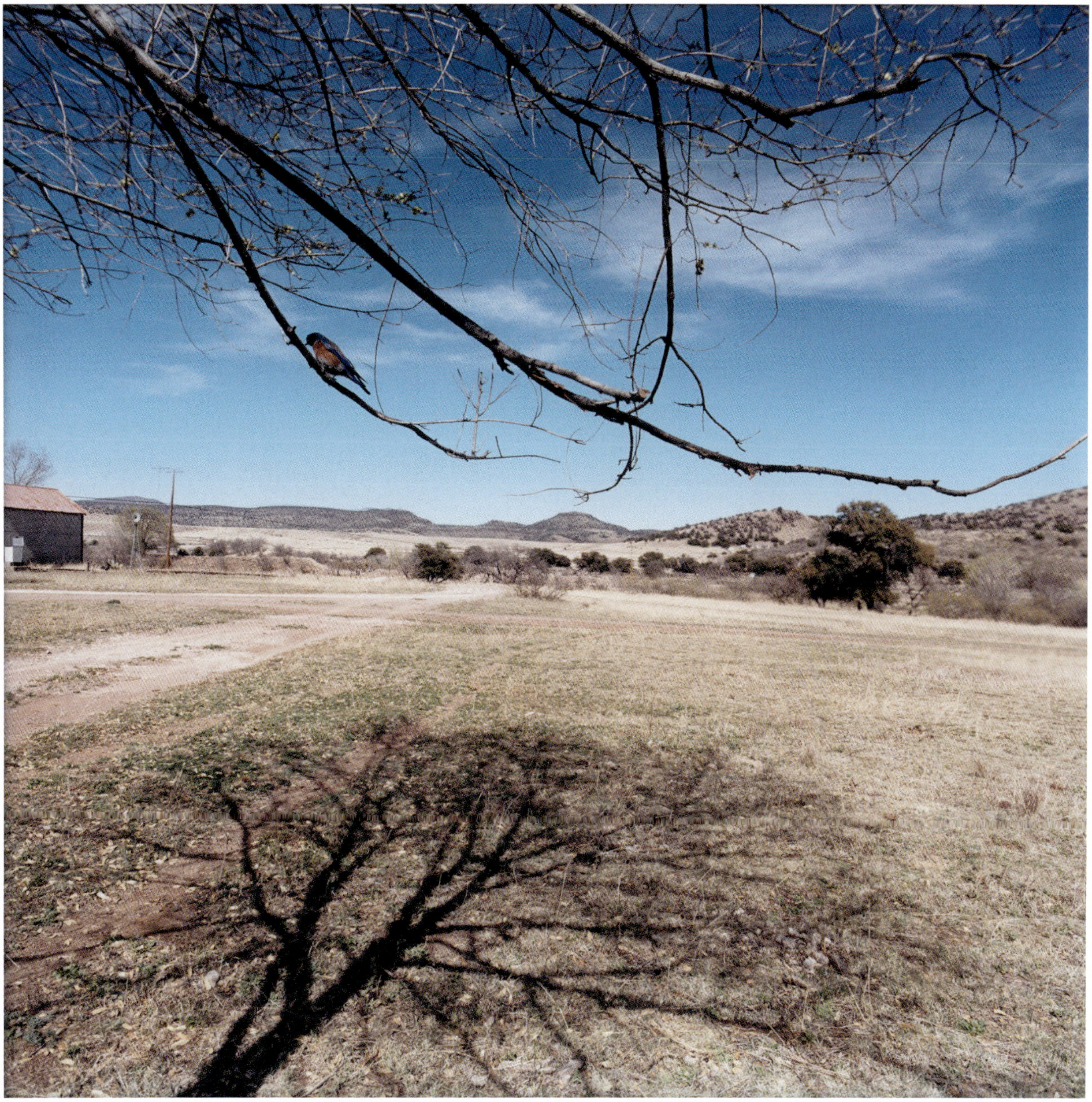

Jean-Luc Mylayne
No. 304, Mars Avril 2005, 2005

'The tree is a spectacular creation because each part of the tree is necessary to its life. It is the perfect sculpture.'

— Giuseppe Penone

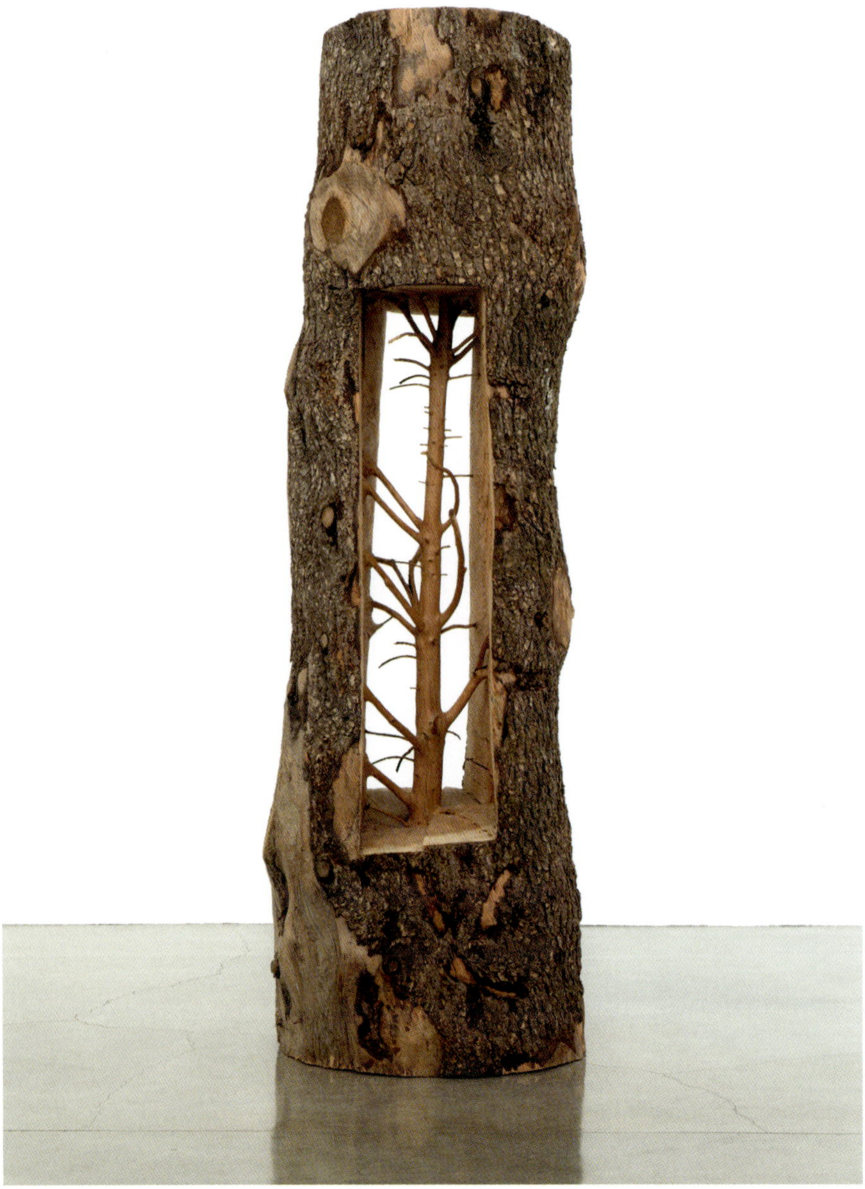

Giuseppe Penone
Albero Porta – Cedro
(Door Tree – Cedar), 2012

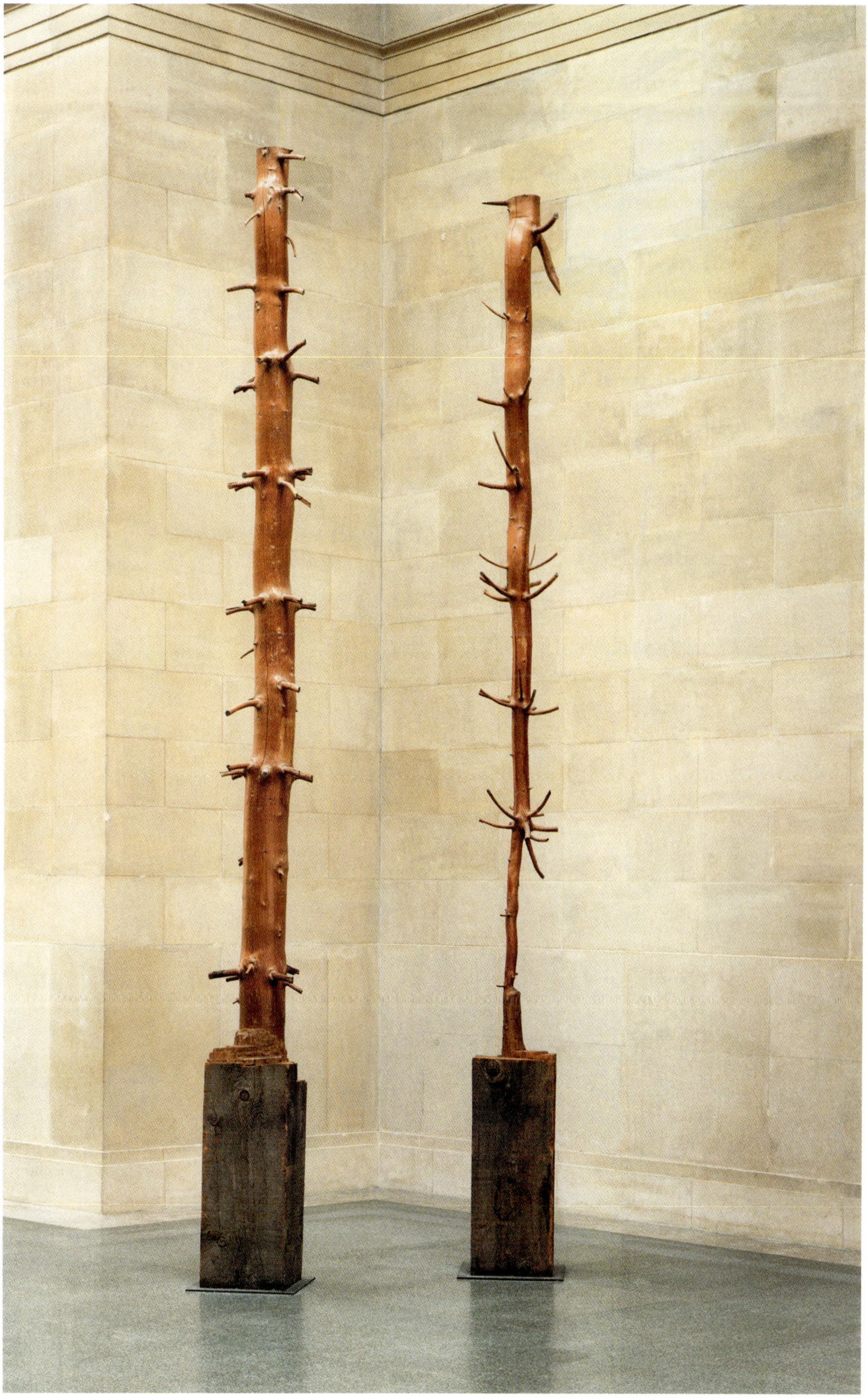

Giuseppe Penone
Tree of 12 Metres,
1980–82

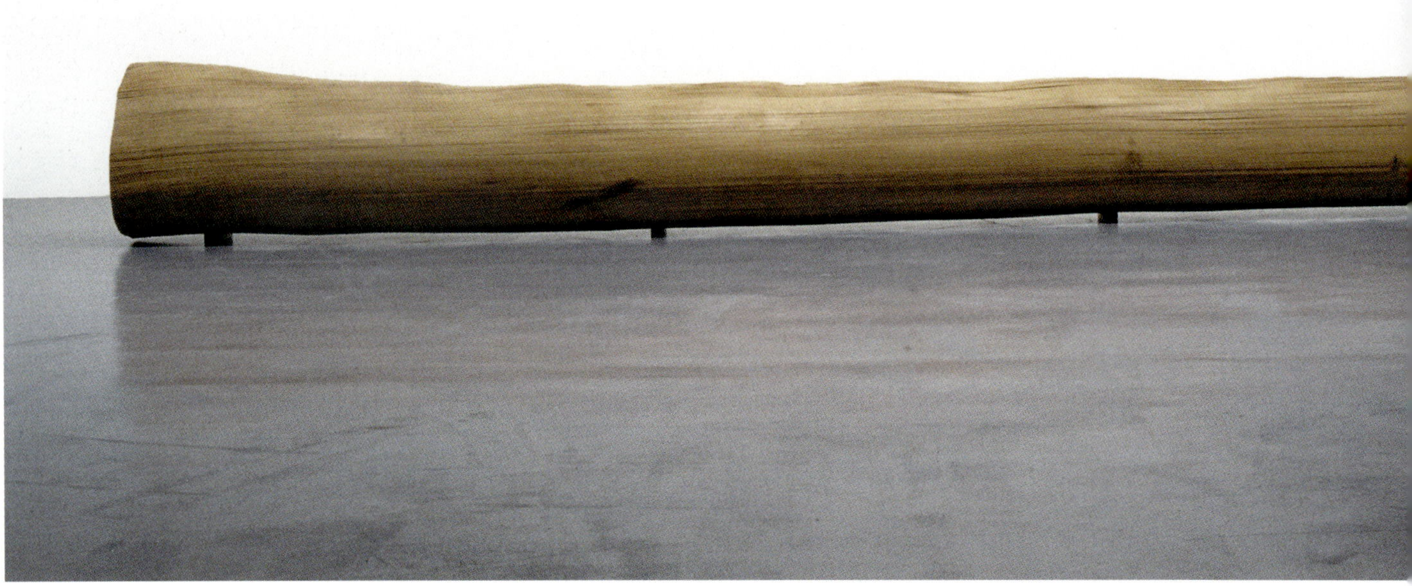

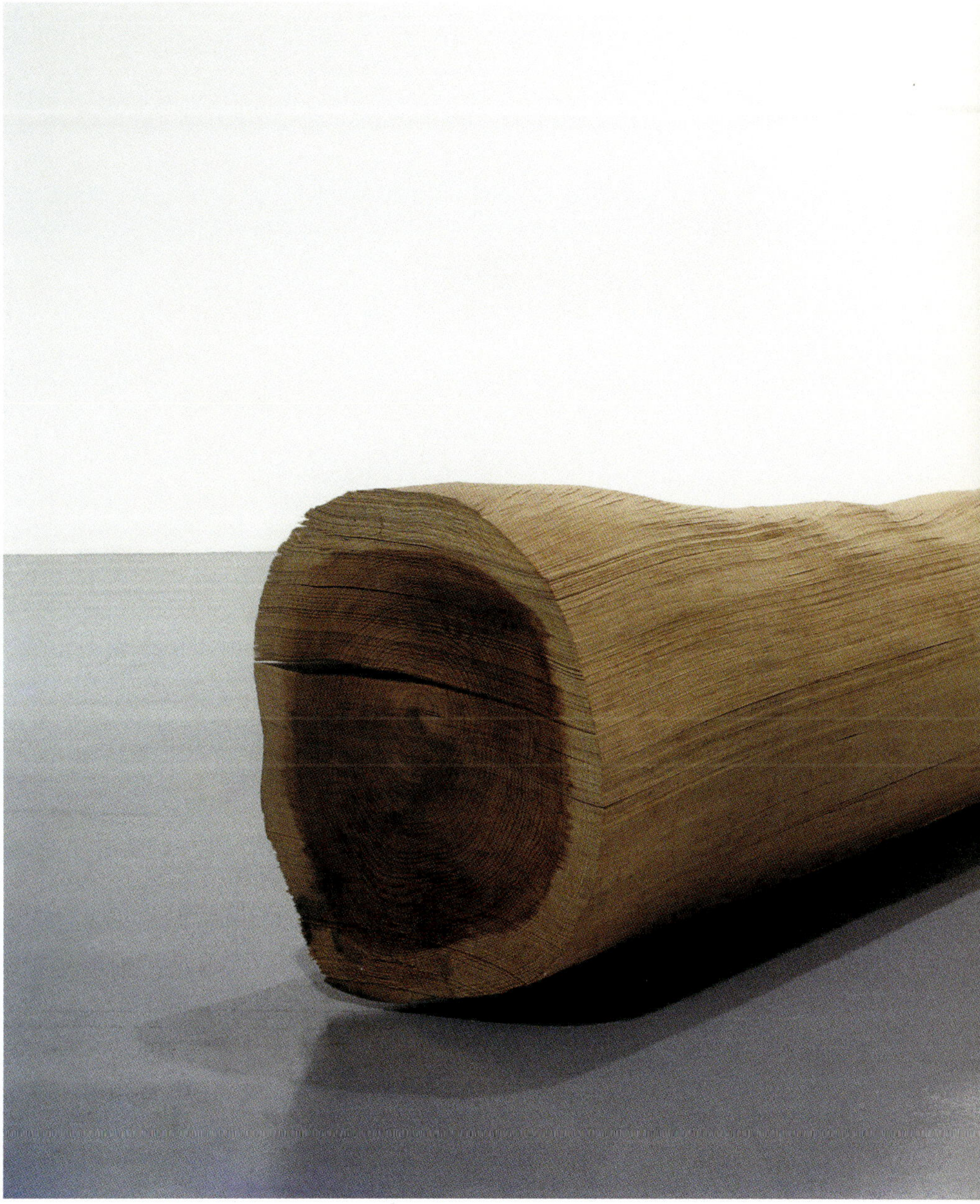

Kazuo Kadonaga
Wood No. 5 CH, 1984

'The number and variety of existing trees are astounding. This era should clearly be the Age of Trees. It would certainly be that, were it not so obviously the Age of Humans. Of course we can see that the general physicalities of the earth have made us continually more human – every other animal knows that we can throw rocks, and strictly human ability has given us math, computing and, indirectly, music. But it is the trees that have most directly and complexly contributed to our development. We say we learned to use fire. We learned to burn wood – for heat, light, cooking and destroying each other's homes, which were usually made of wood. We used these wood fires to extract and heat metals, with which we could stab each other and cut down trees.'

— Jimmie Durham

Jimmie Durham
It should work, 2012

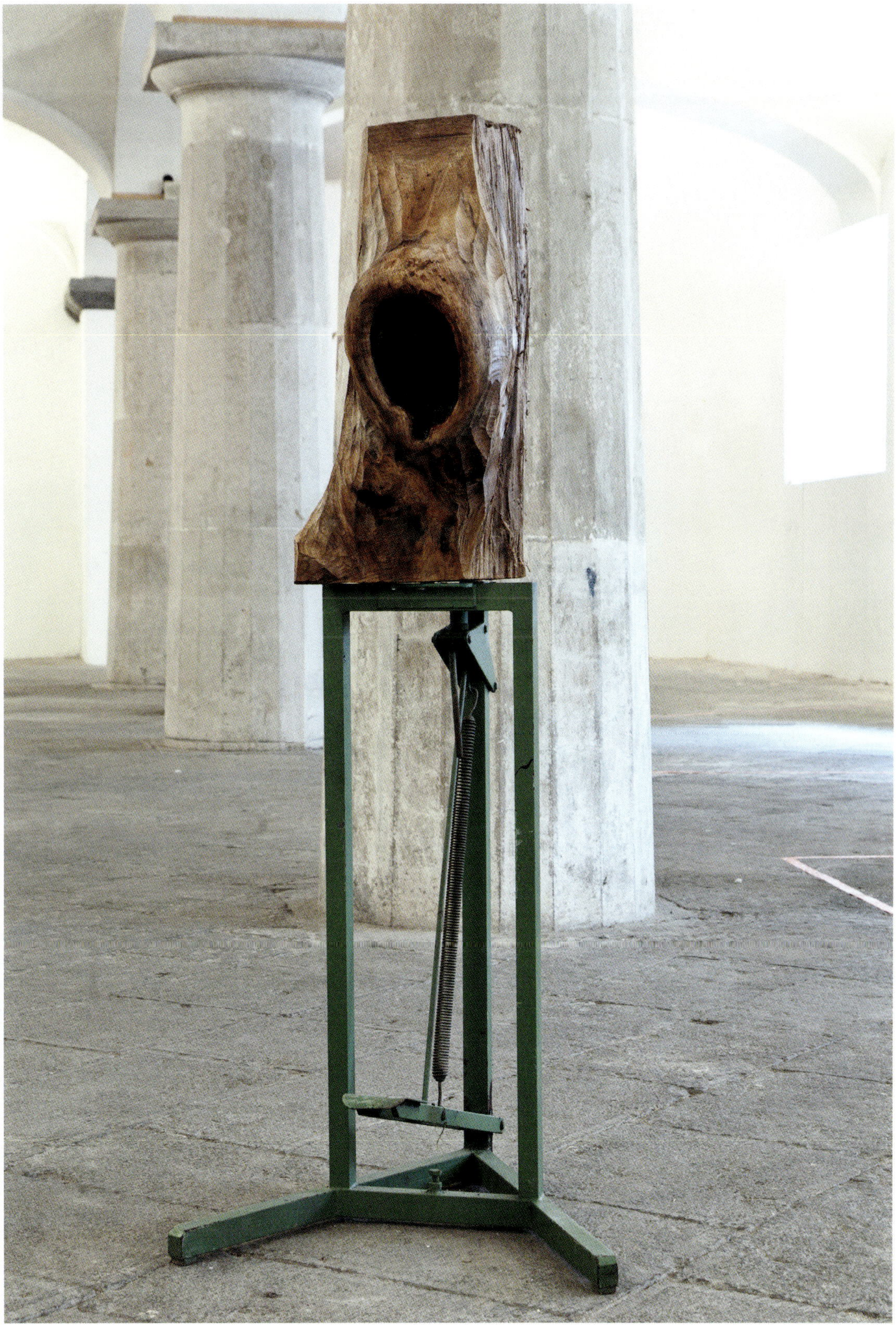

Hugh Hayden
Zelig 3 / Untitled (trunk), 2014

'Historically [cedars are] one of the most abundant materials at least in the United States. Although they're indigenous to Texas they're considered as "trash trees" [...] they tend to excel when other vegetation struggles [...] Politically I'm interested in the idea of a tree having a rightful sense of belonging and also being despised.'

— Hugh Hayden

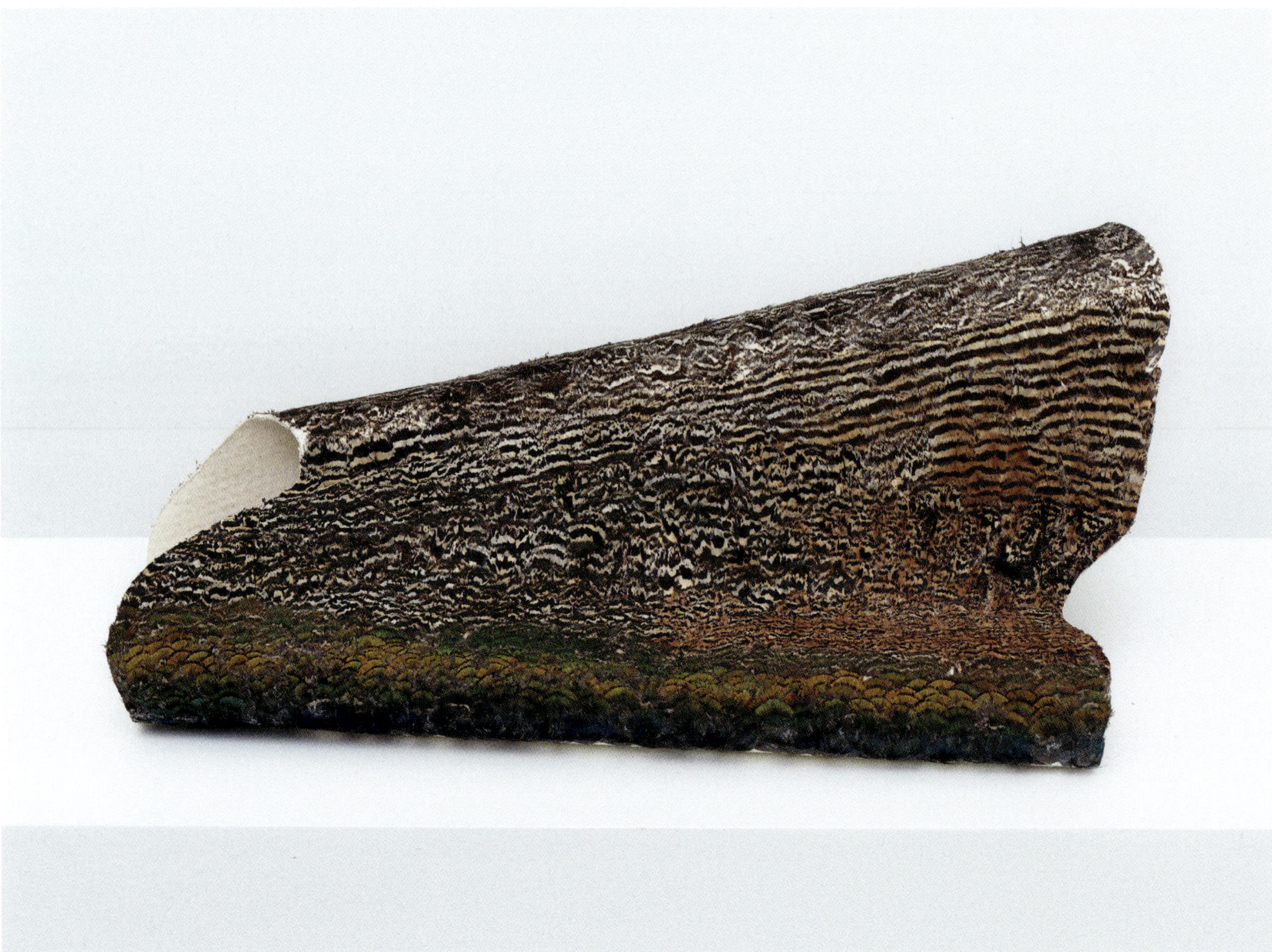

Overleaf:
Virginia Overton
Untitled (Juniperus virginiana), 2016

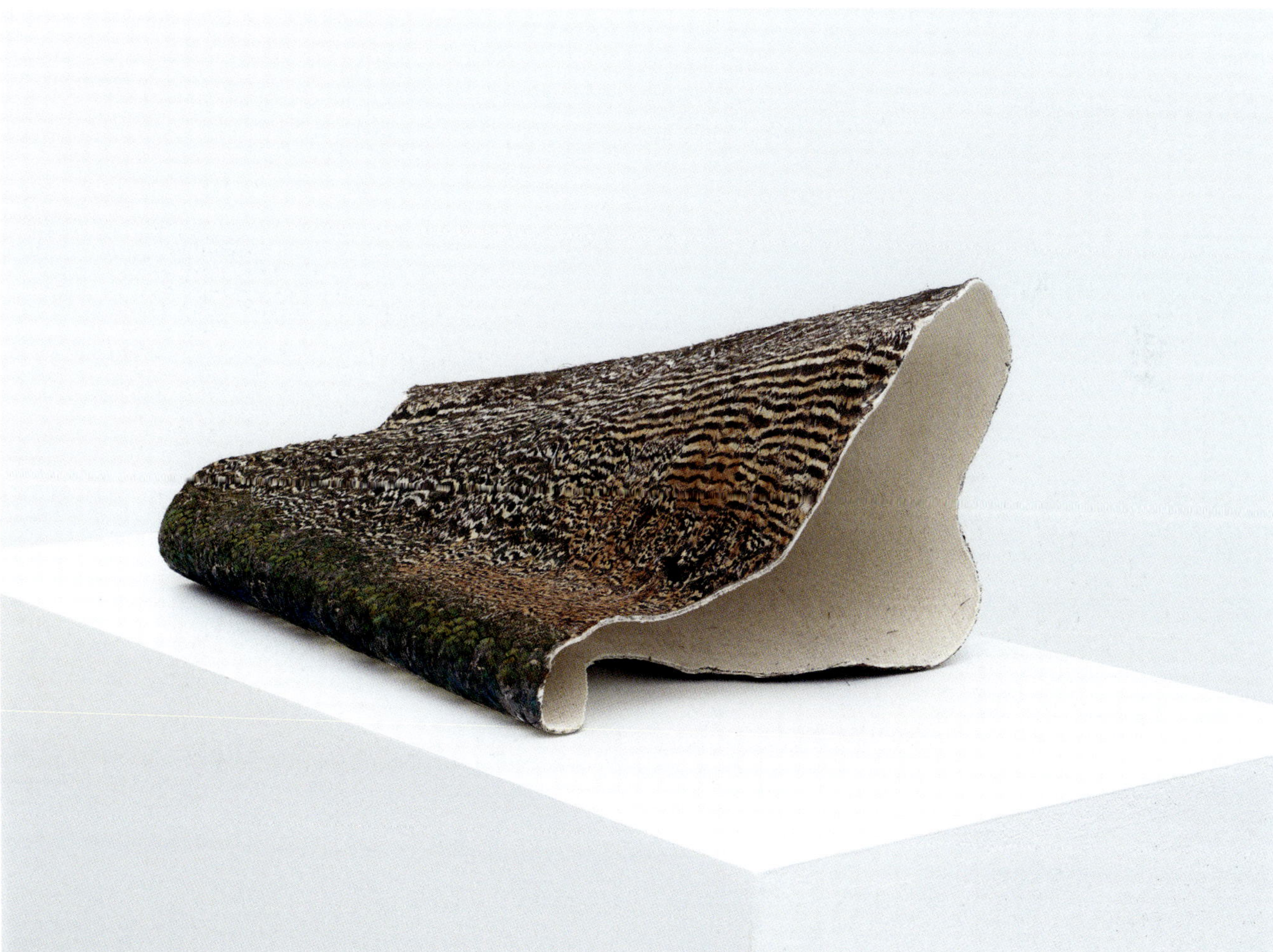

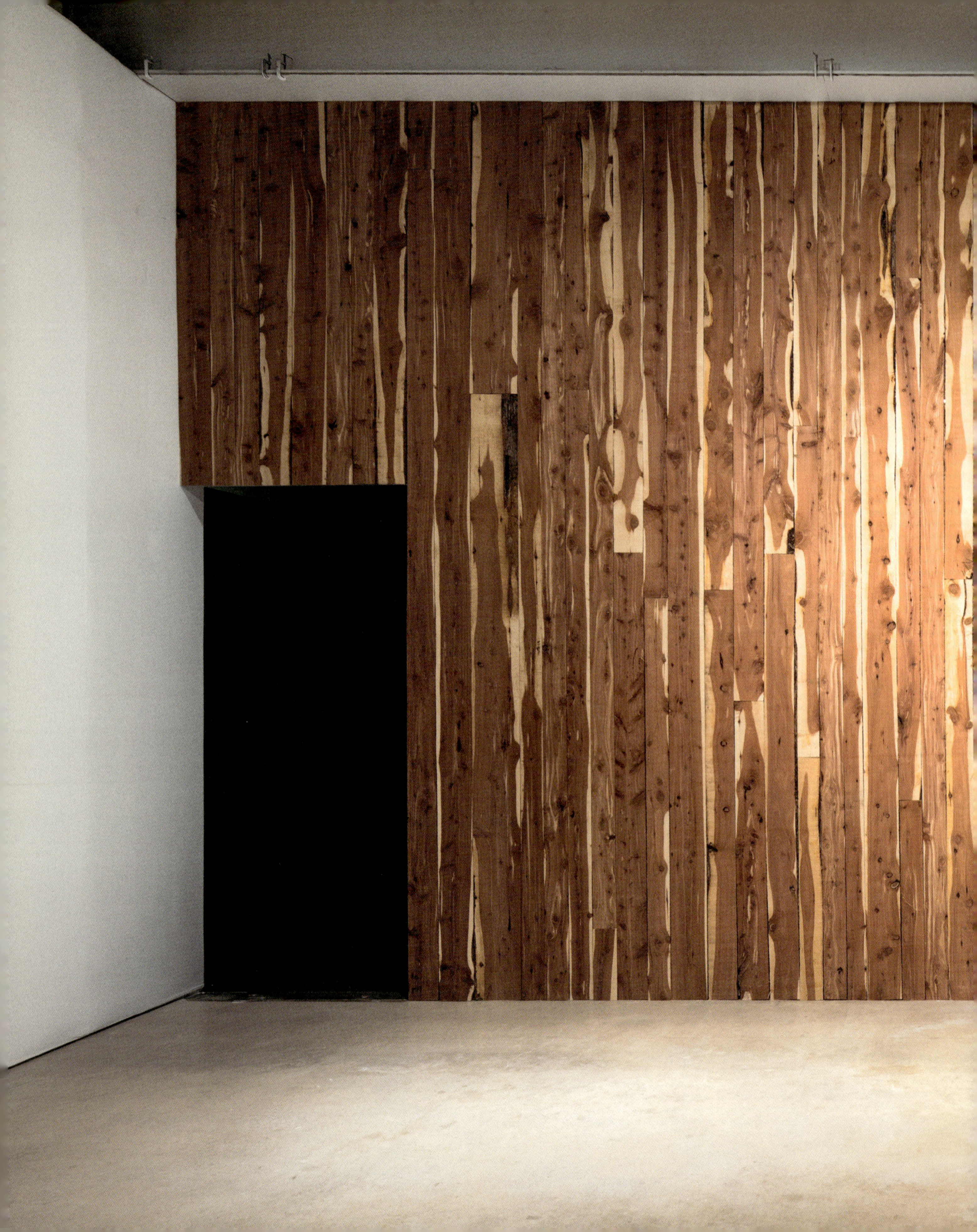

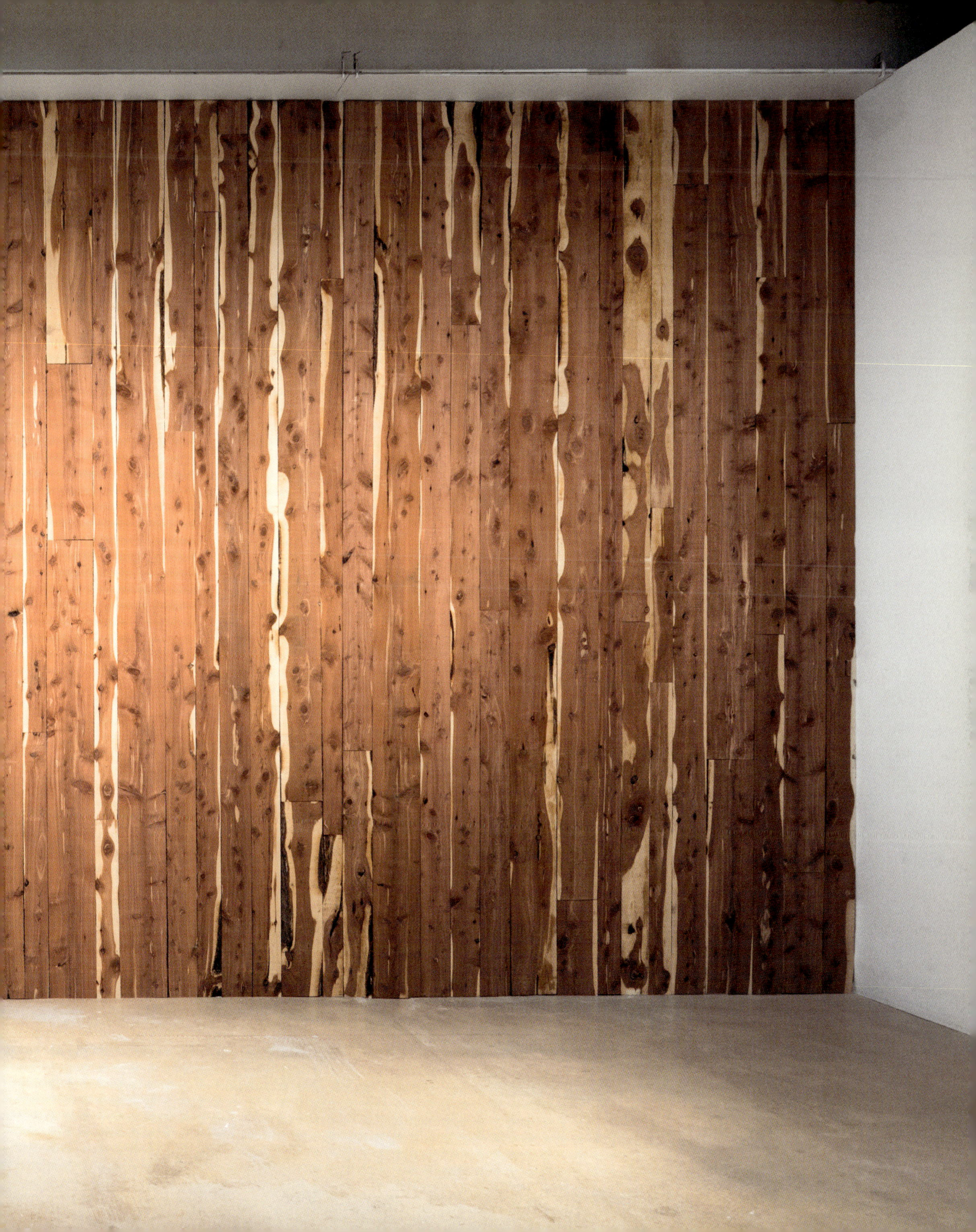

'Historically people planted trees in the belief they would be used for something. It was an investment in the future, a legacy, proof of faith in a continuing existence. It's like the story about the hall at New College, Oxford, and how the people who built it planted a grove of oaks at the same time in case, hundreds of years hence, the beams would need replacing. I'm interested in that kind of economy, in the social aspect of plants.'

— Anya Gallaccio

Anya Gallaccio
because I could not stop, 2002

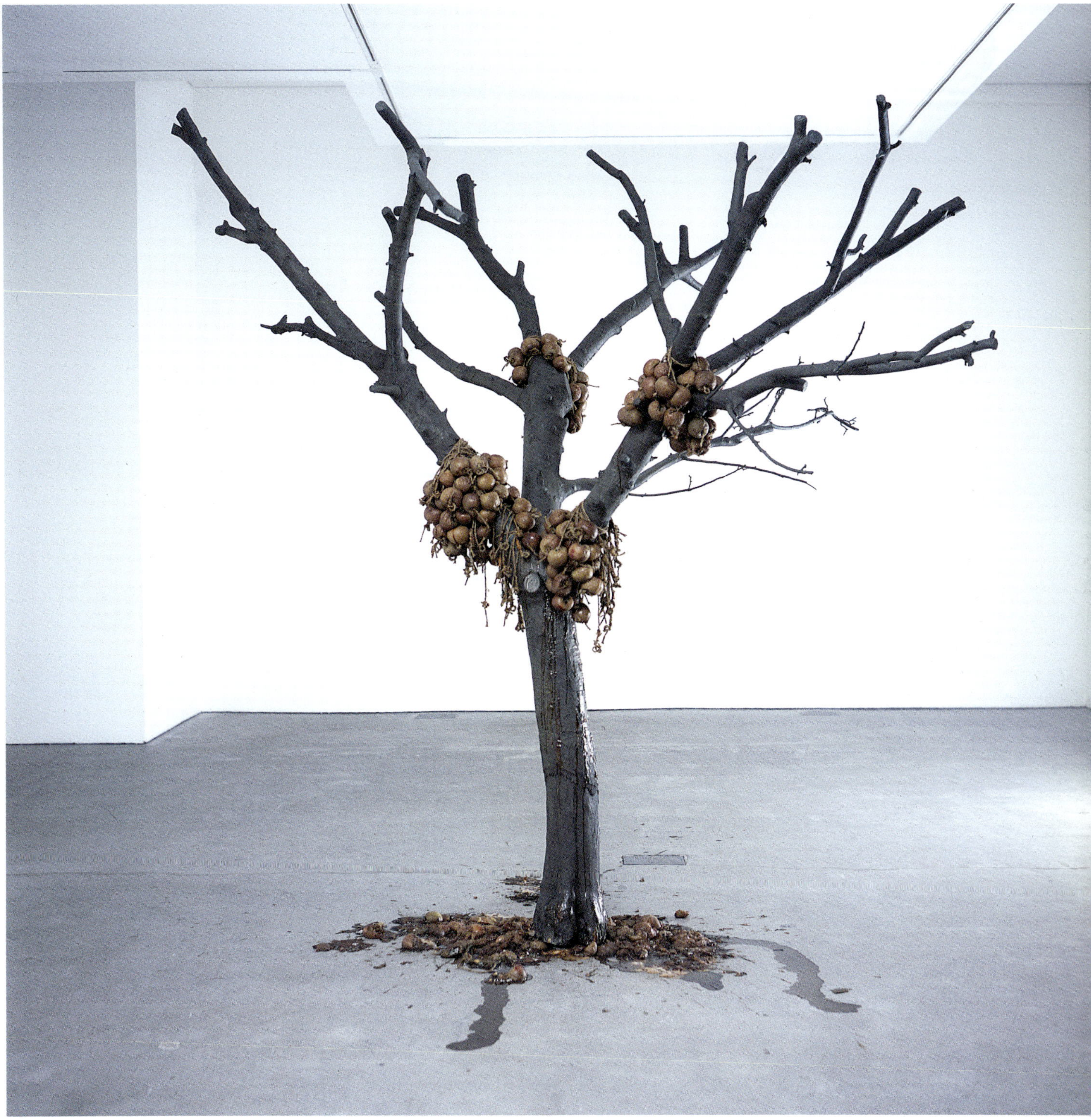

Roxy Paine
Rotoplasm, 2012

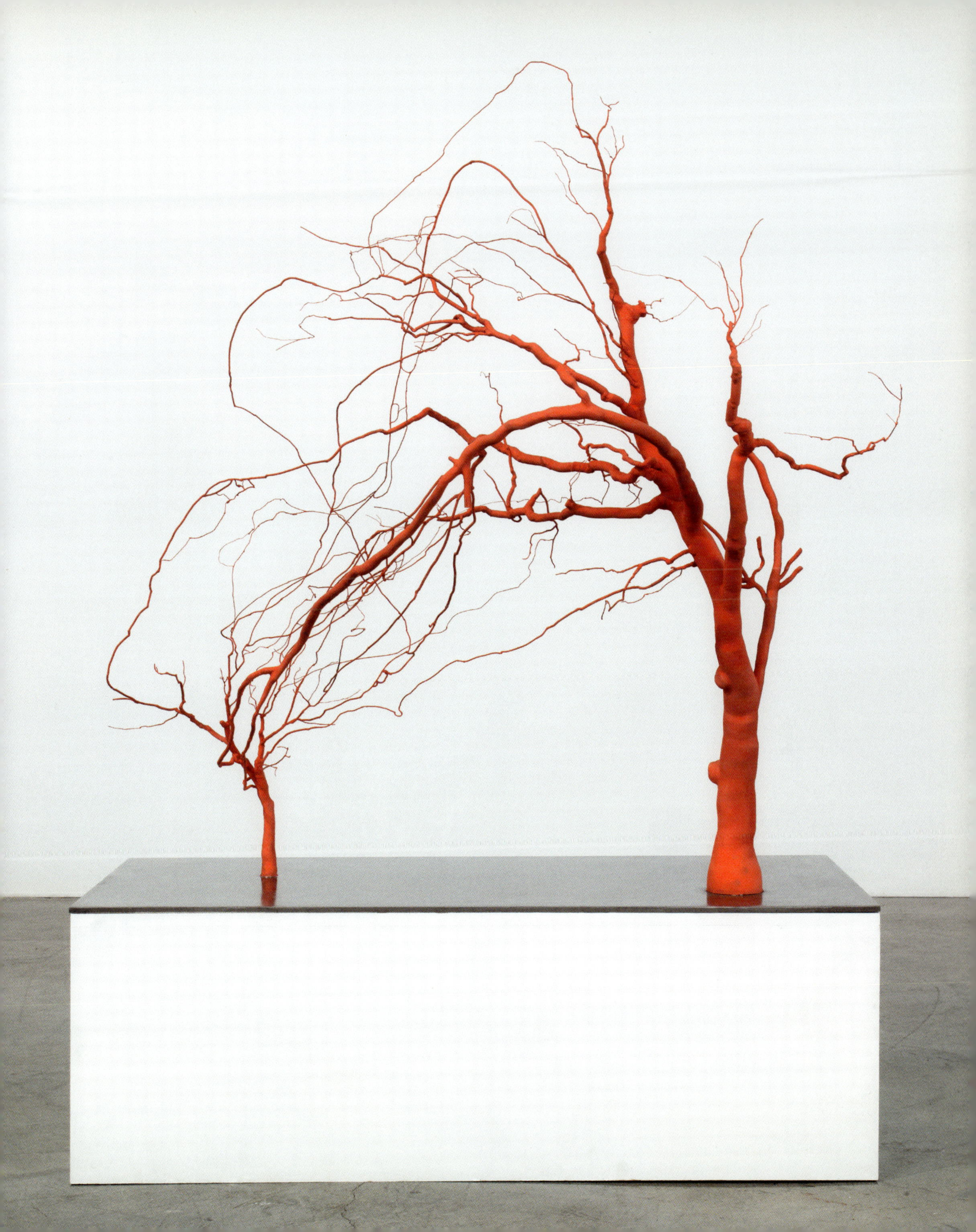

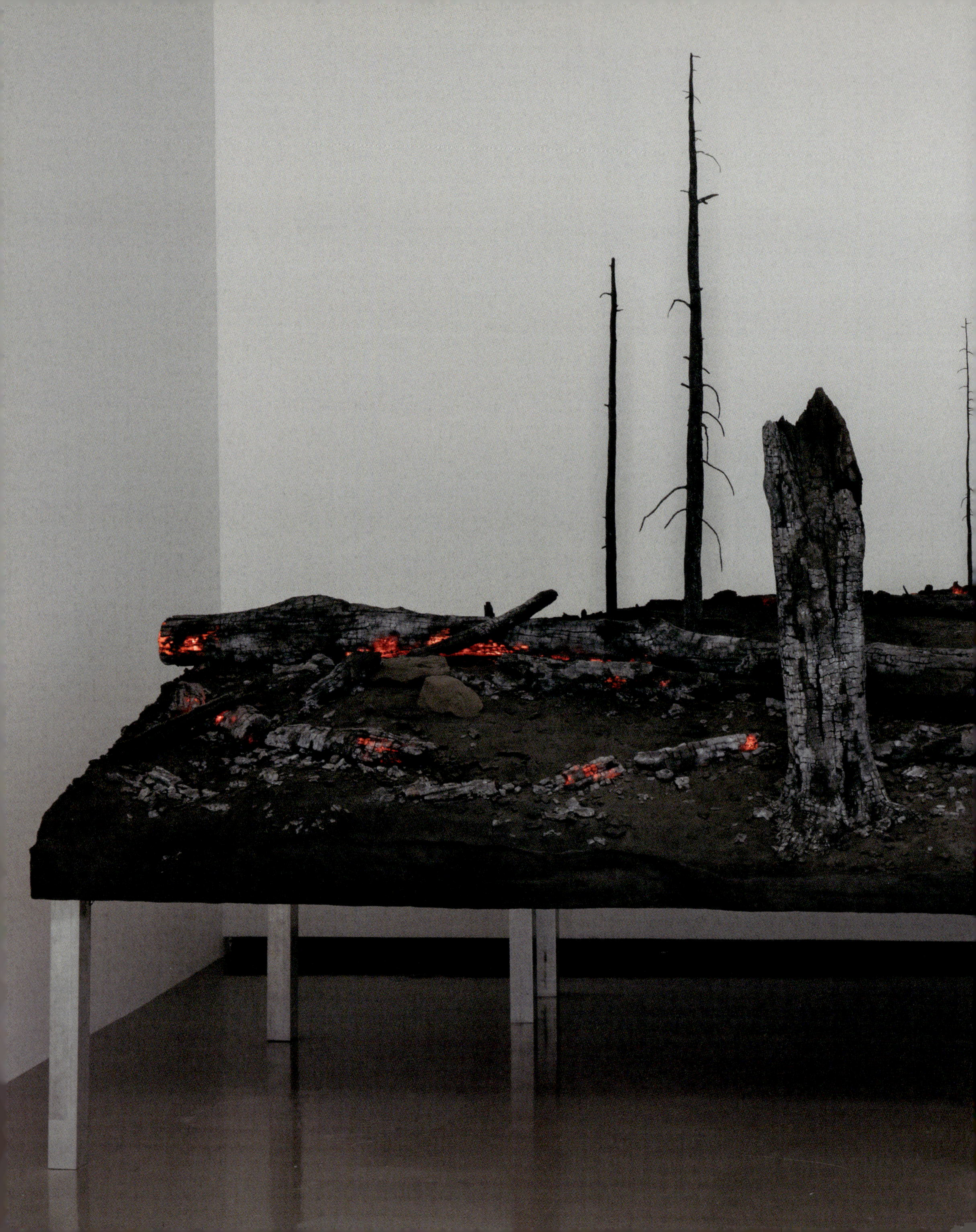

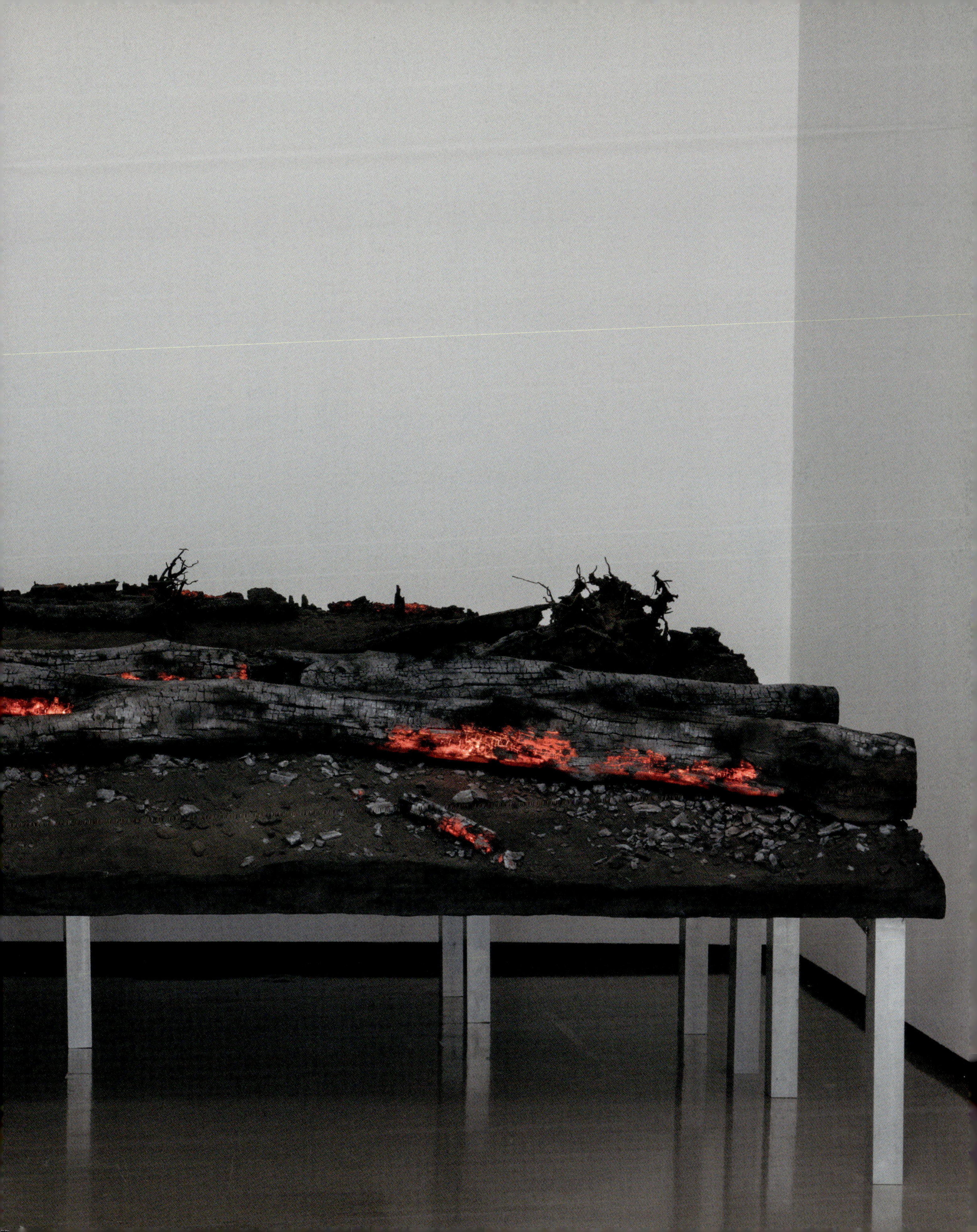

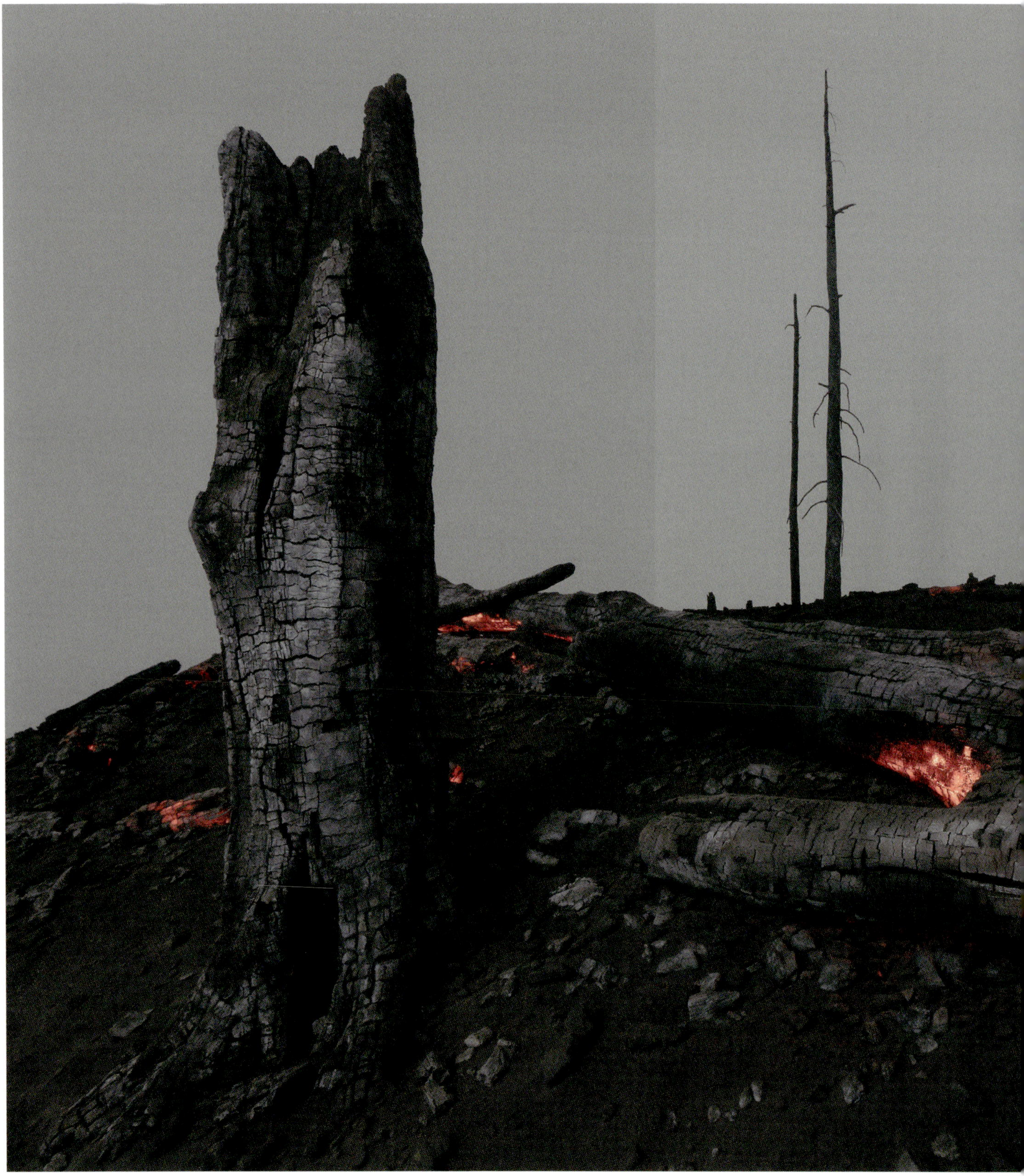

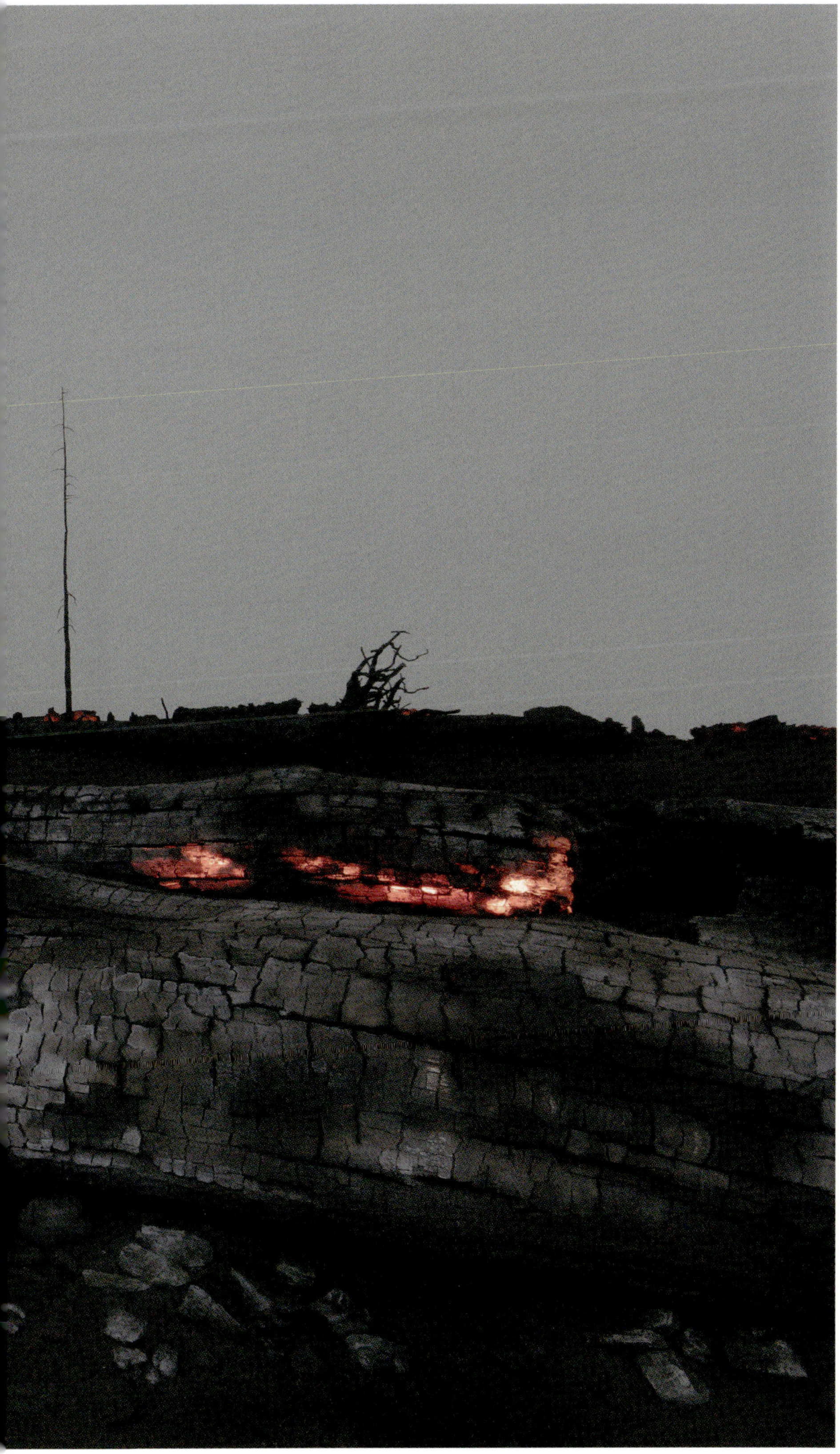

This page and previous pages:
Roxy Paine
Desolation Row, 2016

'Landscapes are charged with personal and universal histories, with politics and ideas that cut deep into our conscious- and subconsciousness. In the work And Then the World Changed Colour: Breathing Yellow, *I wish to evoke an immersive experience, as well as a detached one. You are both inside the forest, and clearly outside of it; you inhabit the space in your mind – simultaneously drawn in close and physically distanced by glass, refraction and reflection. The forest itself is impenetrable, a primal and dark place, yet pierced by the streaky, yellow light. The real and imaginary collide, as you are looking and breathing in the saturated air in the space – and inside the tank.*

Is it all in your head? The trees witness in silence: our past, present and future. There is nothing to guide your gaze here: just trees – and more trees, and a lot of enchanting, dappled yellow light on both sides of the glass.'

— Mariele Neudecker

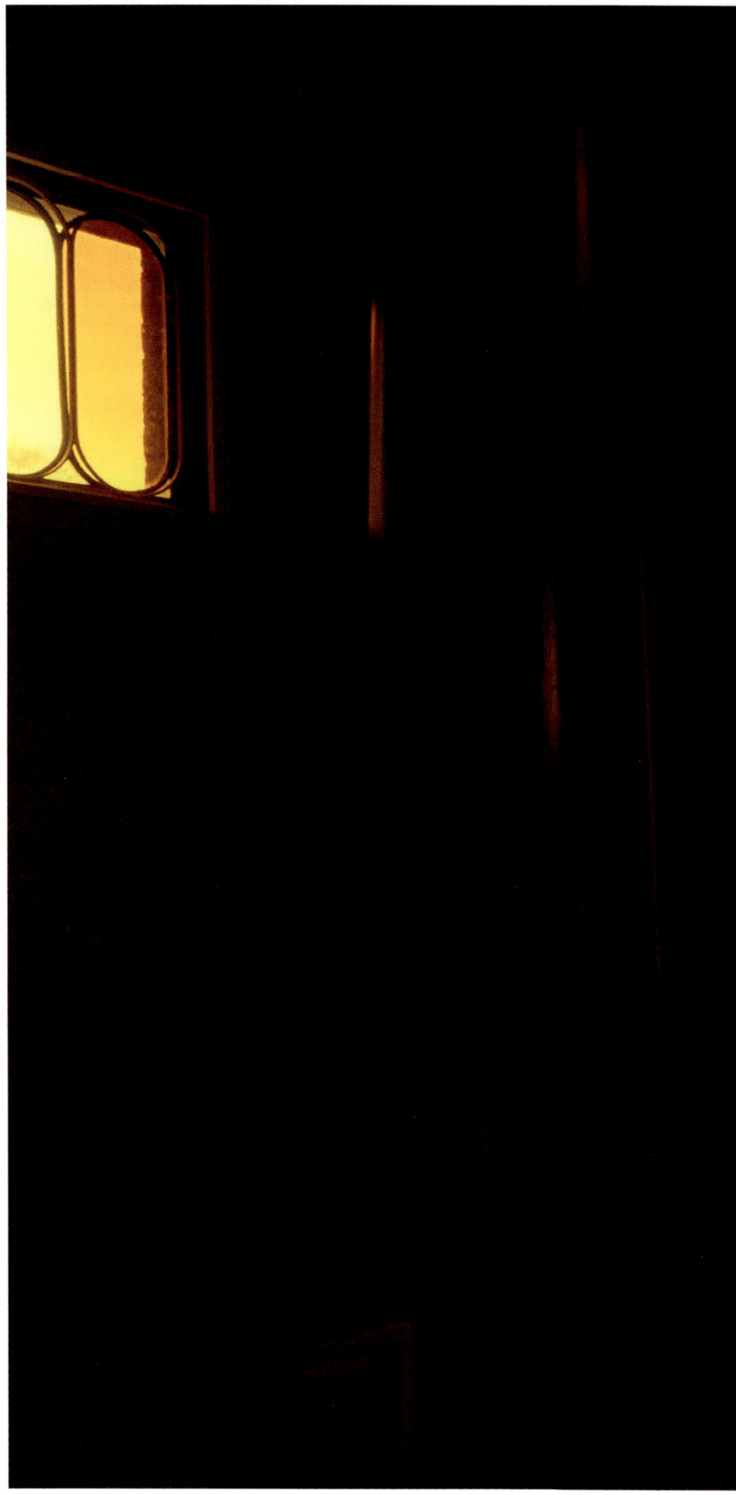

Mariele Neudecker
And Then the World Changed Colour: Breathing Yellow, 2019

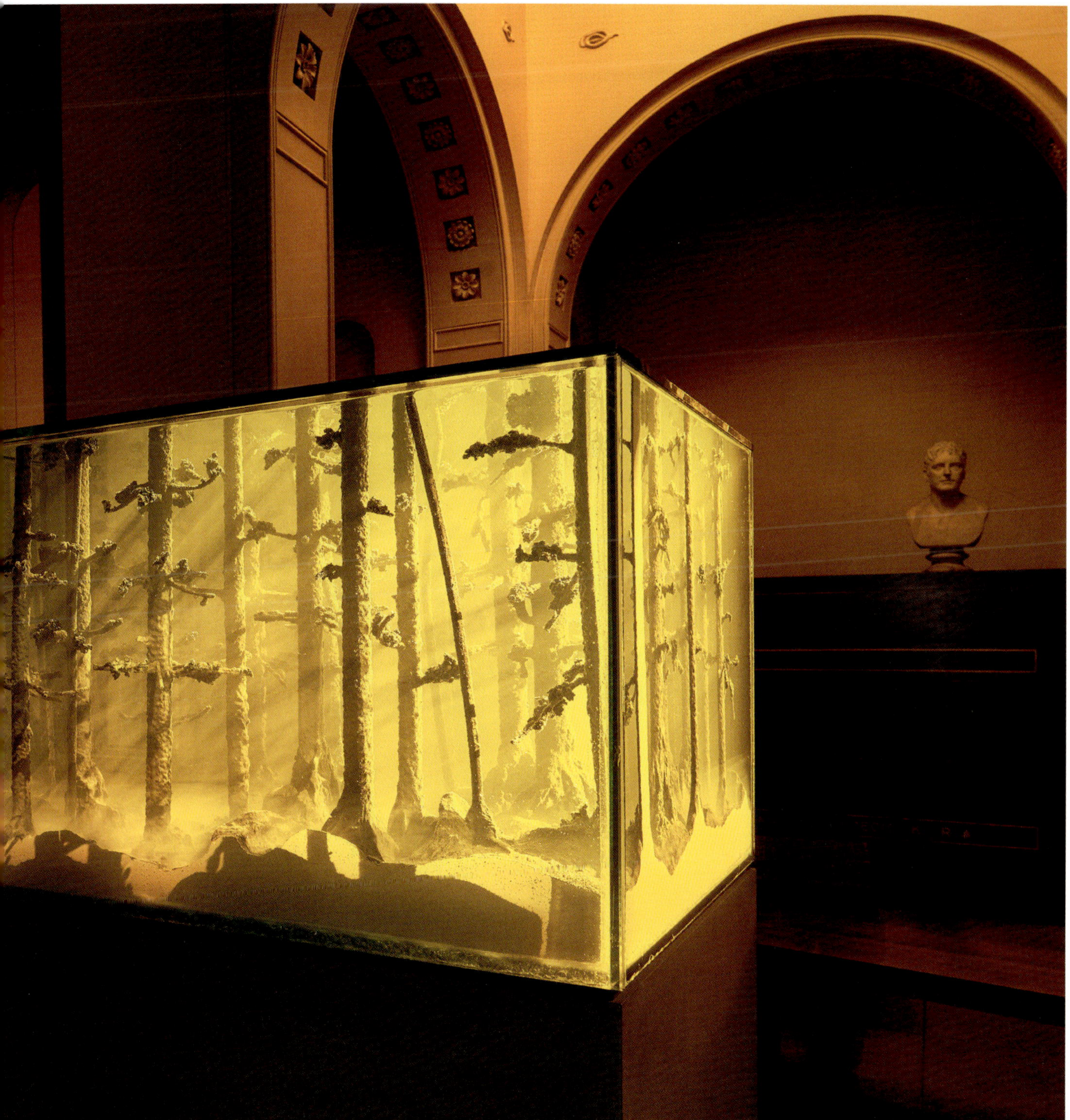

Gillian Carnegie
Black Square, 2003

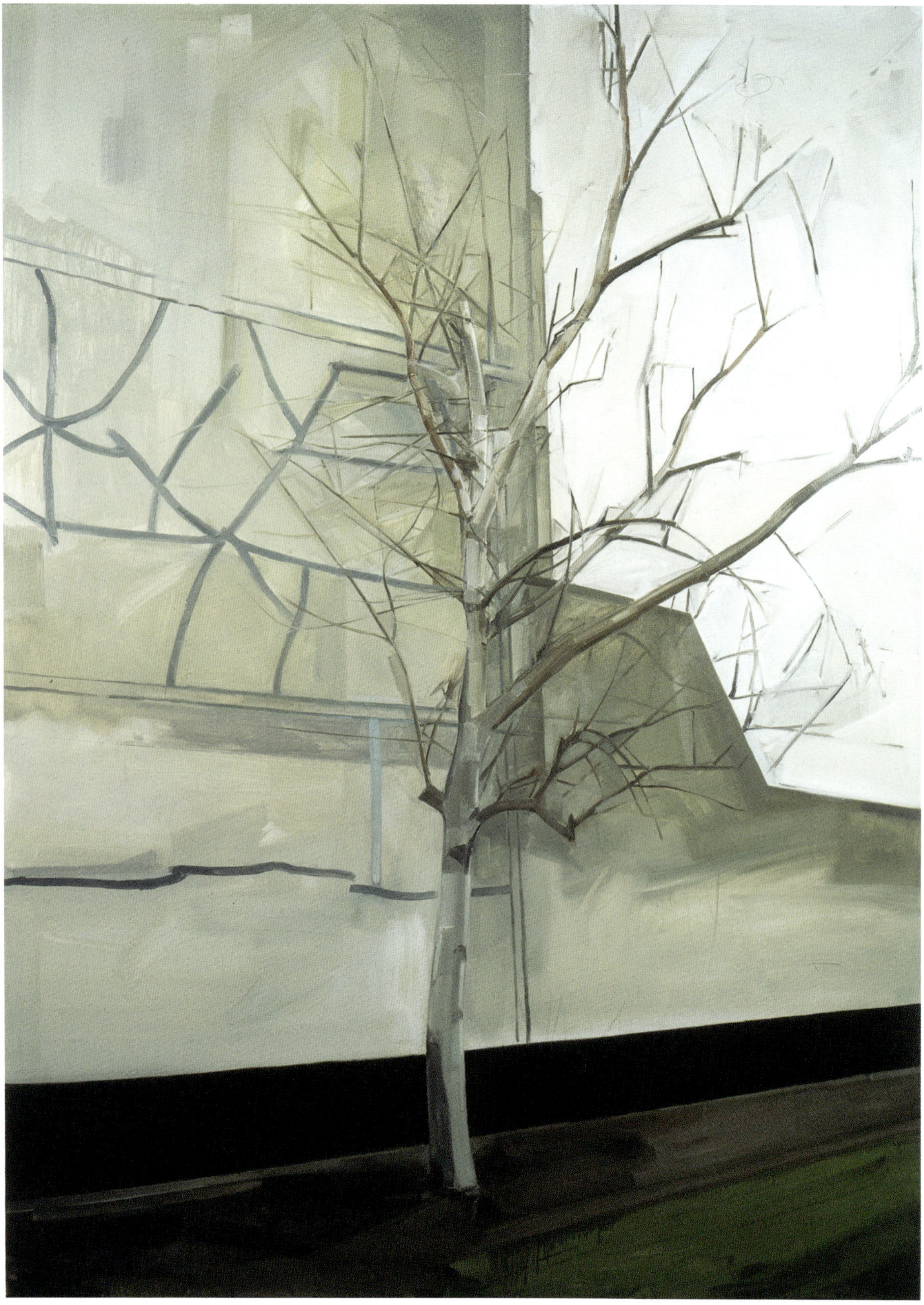

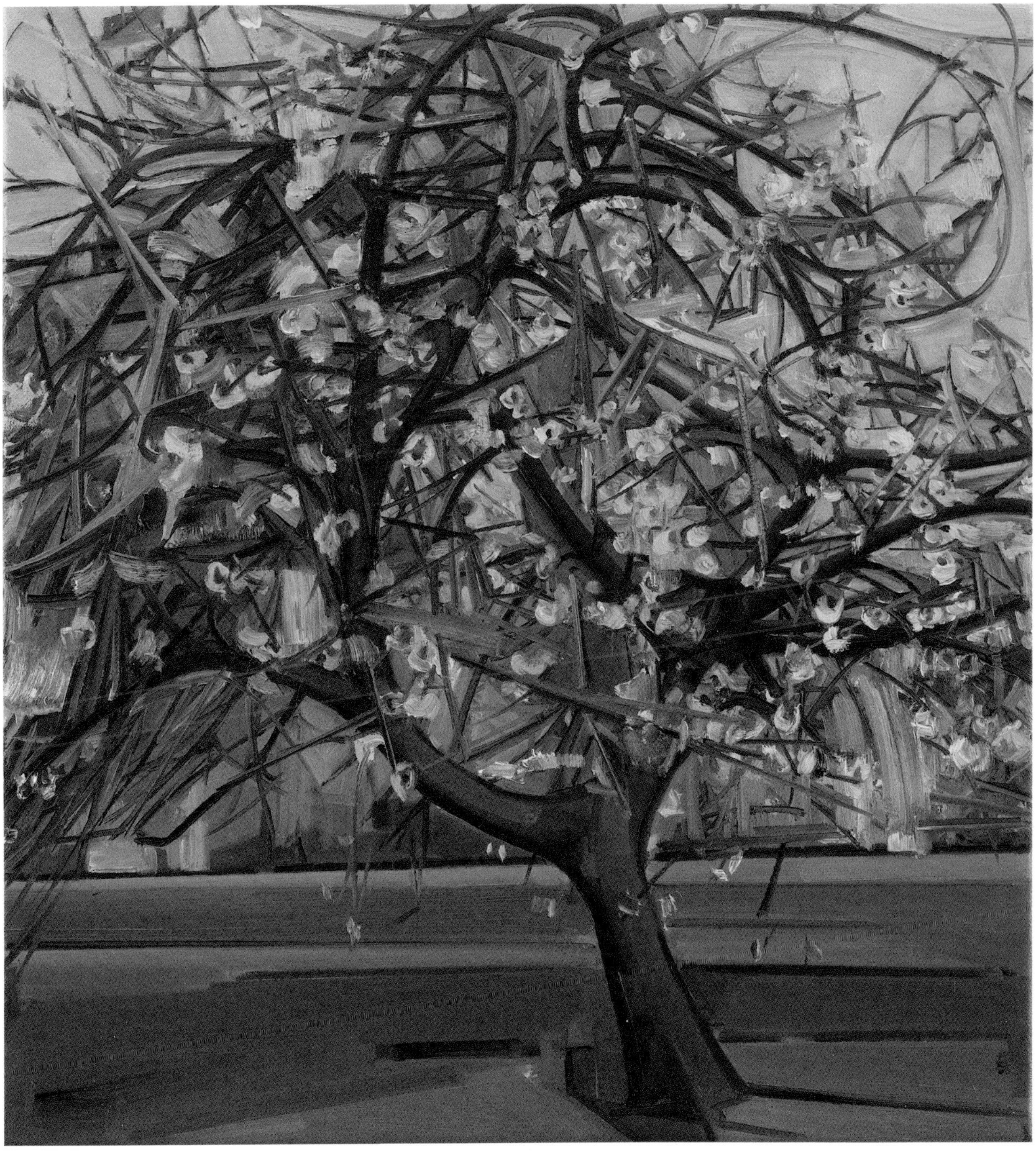

Gillian Carnegie
Green and Silver, 2005

Gillian Carnegie
Section, 2015

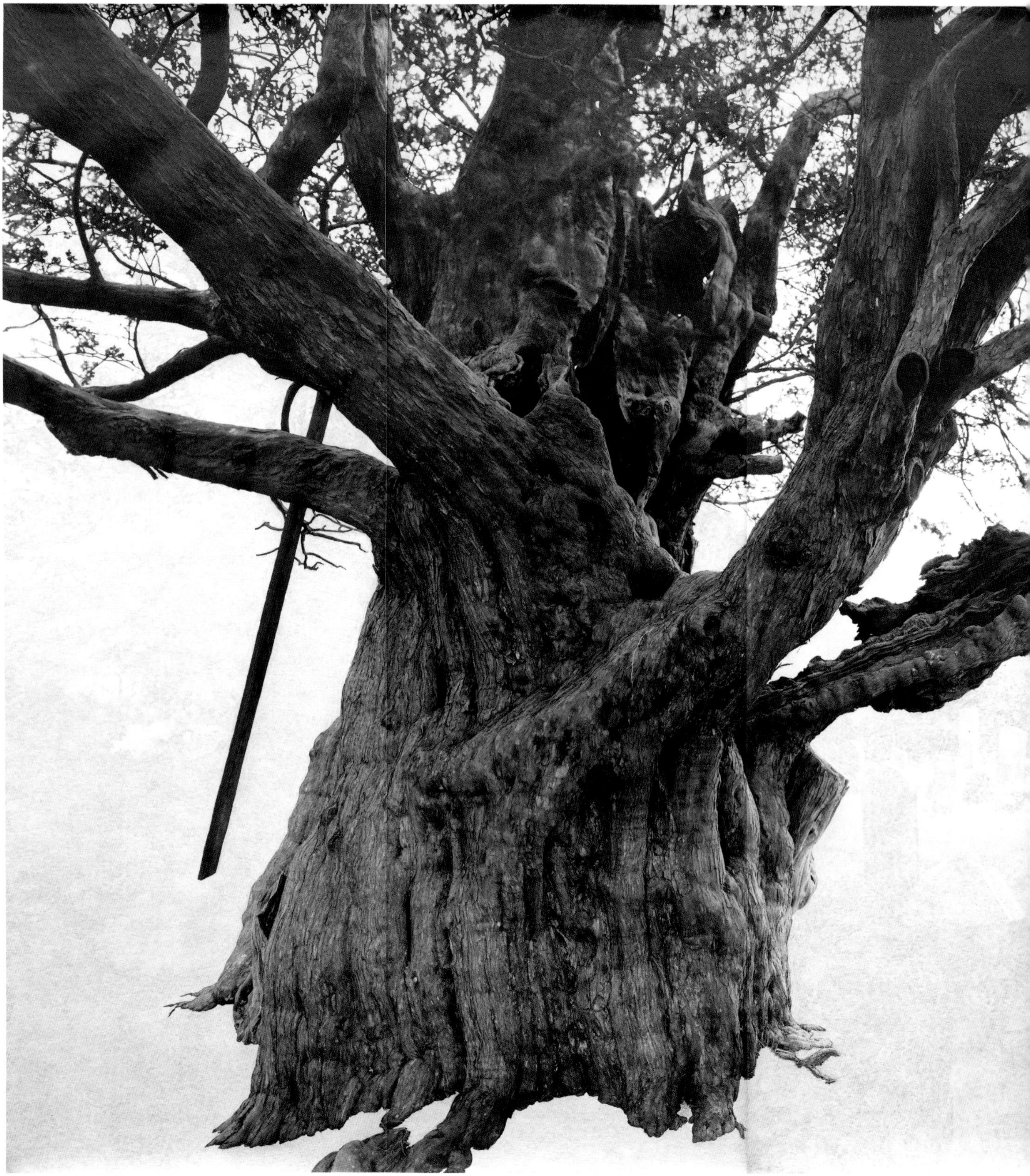

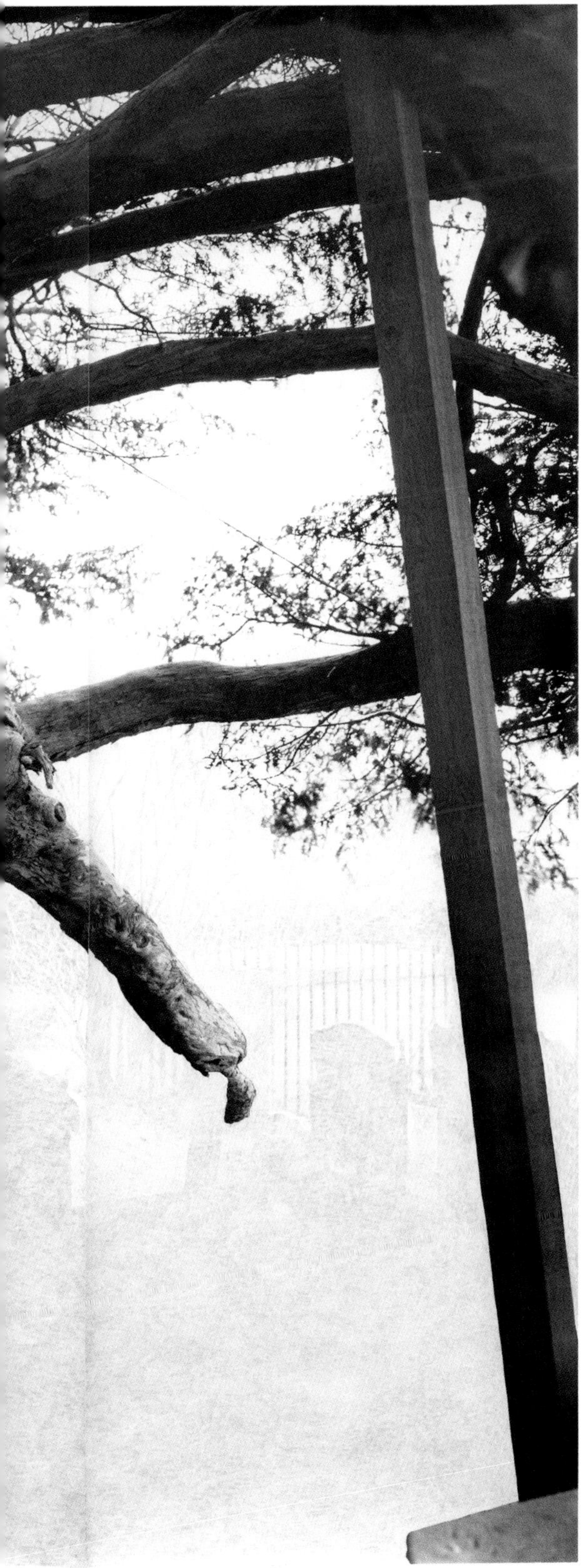

'I had found all these old postcards of the Forest of Fontainebleau [France] when I was in Kitakyushu in Japan, and I remember thinking that's so strange, why would they have so many postcards of Fontainebleau? And then I went onto the internet and I looked up the Forest of Fontainebleau, which led me to the famous oak of Fontainebleau, which in turn led me to look up old oak trees and then the oldest of trees in England, the yew tree. Before I knew it, the tiny village where I grew up came up as the place where there once was a 1,400-year-old yew tree.'

— Tacita Dean

Tacita Dean
Crowhurst II, 2007

'A cast of a 2,000-year-old olive tree is a memorial of condensed time. Through a cast olive tree one can experience the lapse of real time, frozen in its given form. It's an experience of a different calibrated temporality. Time becomes a lived abstraction, where the shape of the ancient olive tree is formed by an accumulation of time, and the force of air, water, wind, and fire.'

— Ugo Rondinone

Ugo Rondinone
Wind Moon, 2011

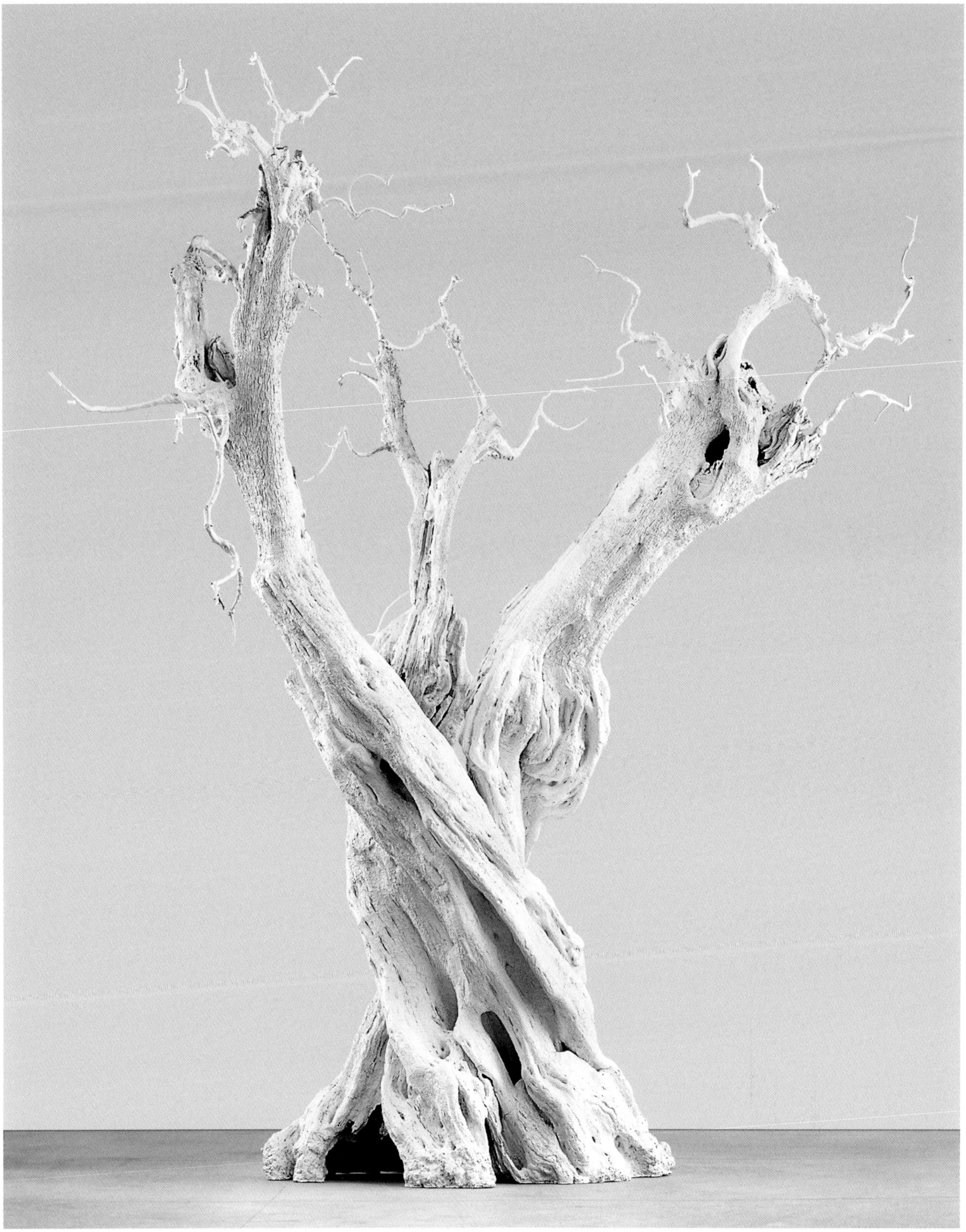

'It's as if the tree unites all: the ground, the sky and man in between. In East Asian philosophy the universe breaks down into three parts: Chun-Ji-In. Chun means the sky, Ji means the ground, and In means human. Since a tree connects all three, I feel very much that a tree is like a universe.'

— Myoung Ho Lee

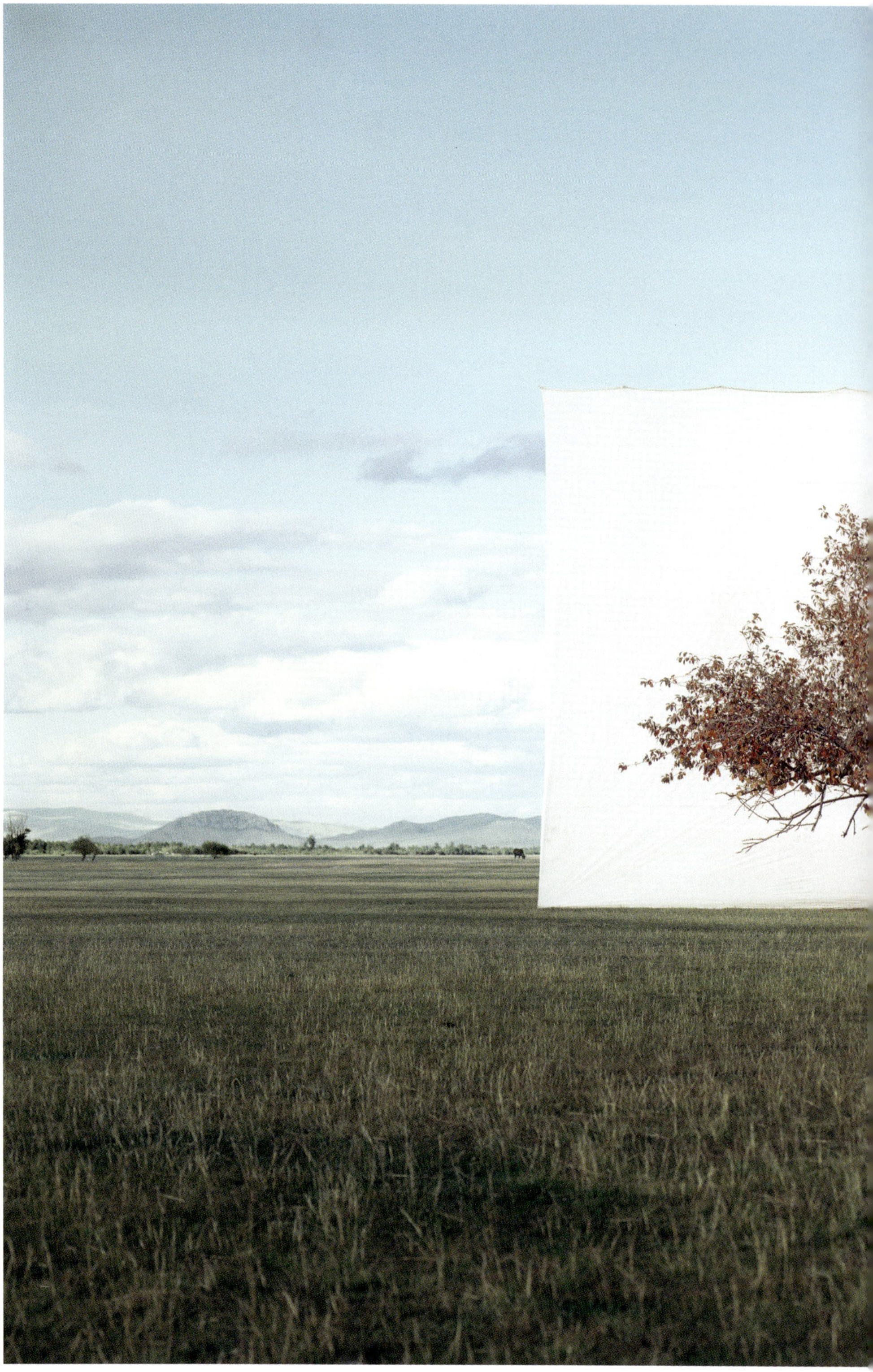

Myoung Ho Lee
Tree... #2, 2012

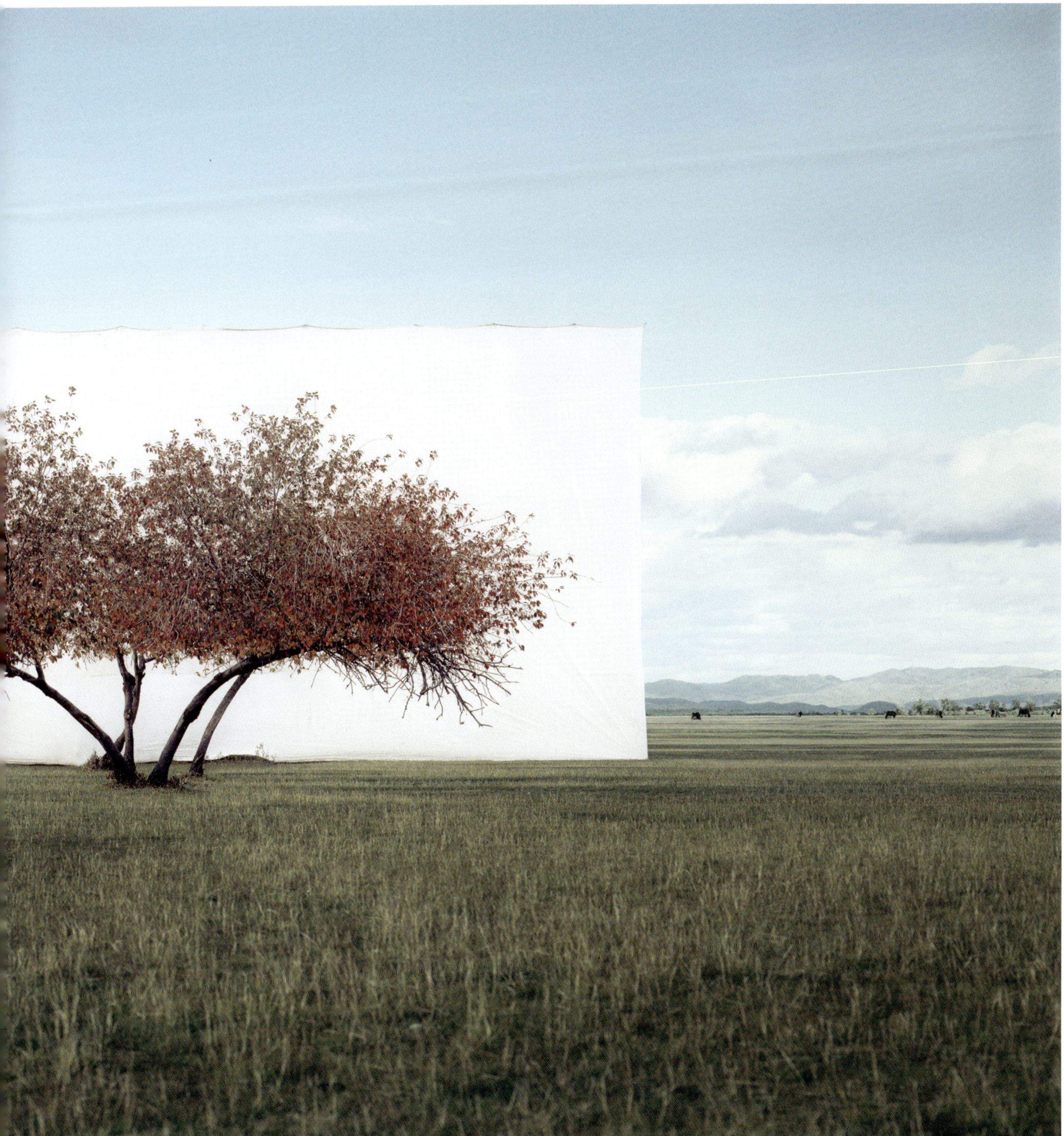

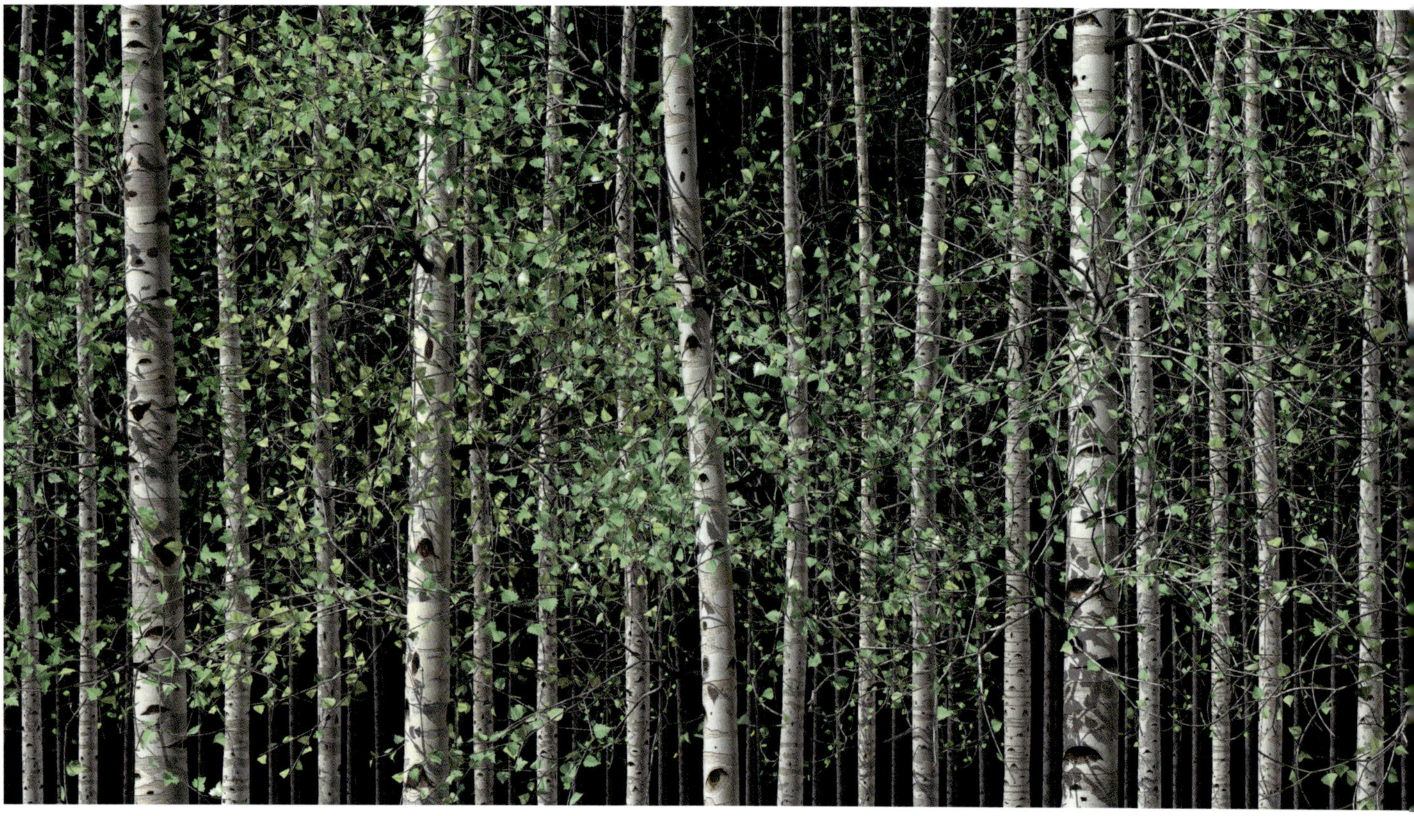

Jennifer Steinkamp
Blind Eye, 1, 2018

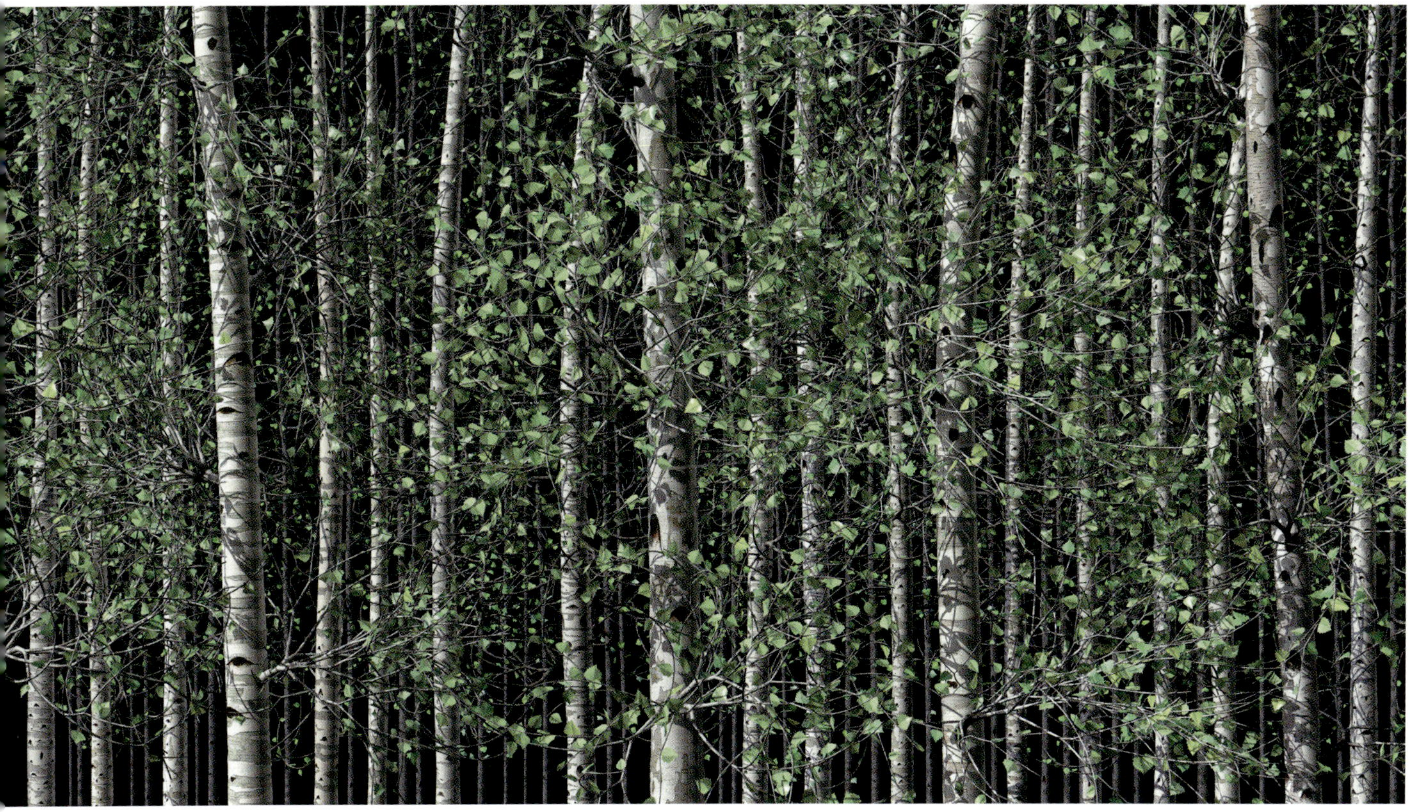

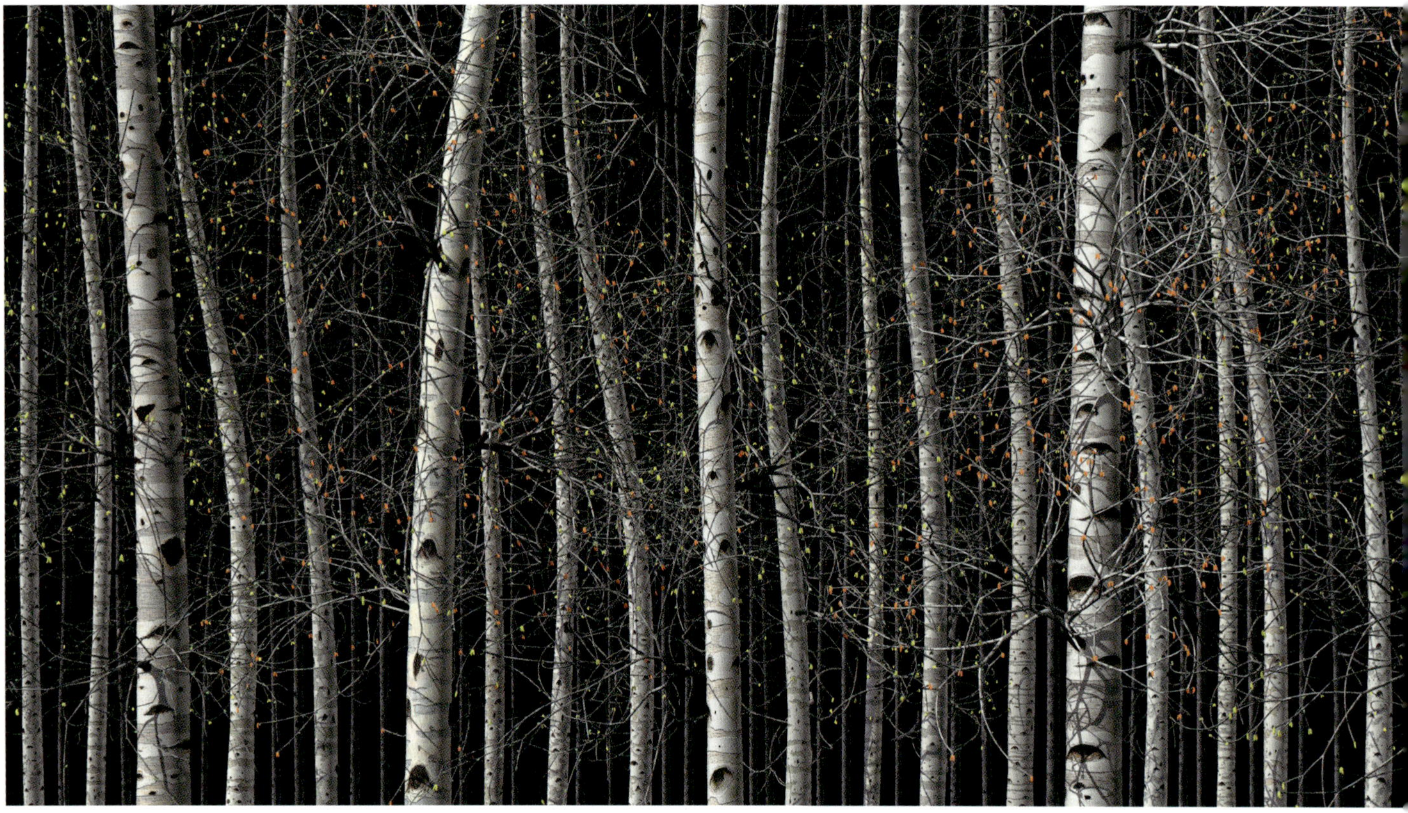

Jennifer Steinkamp
Blind Eye, 1, 2018

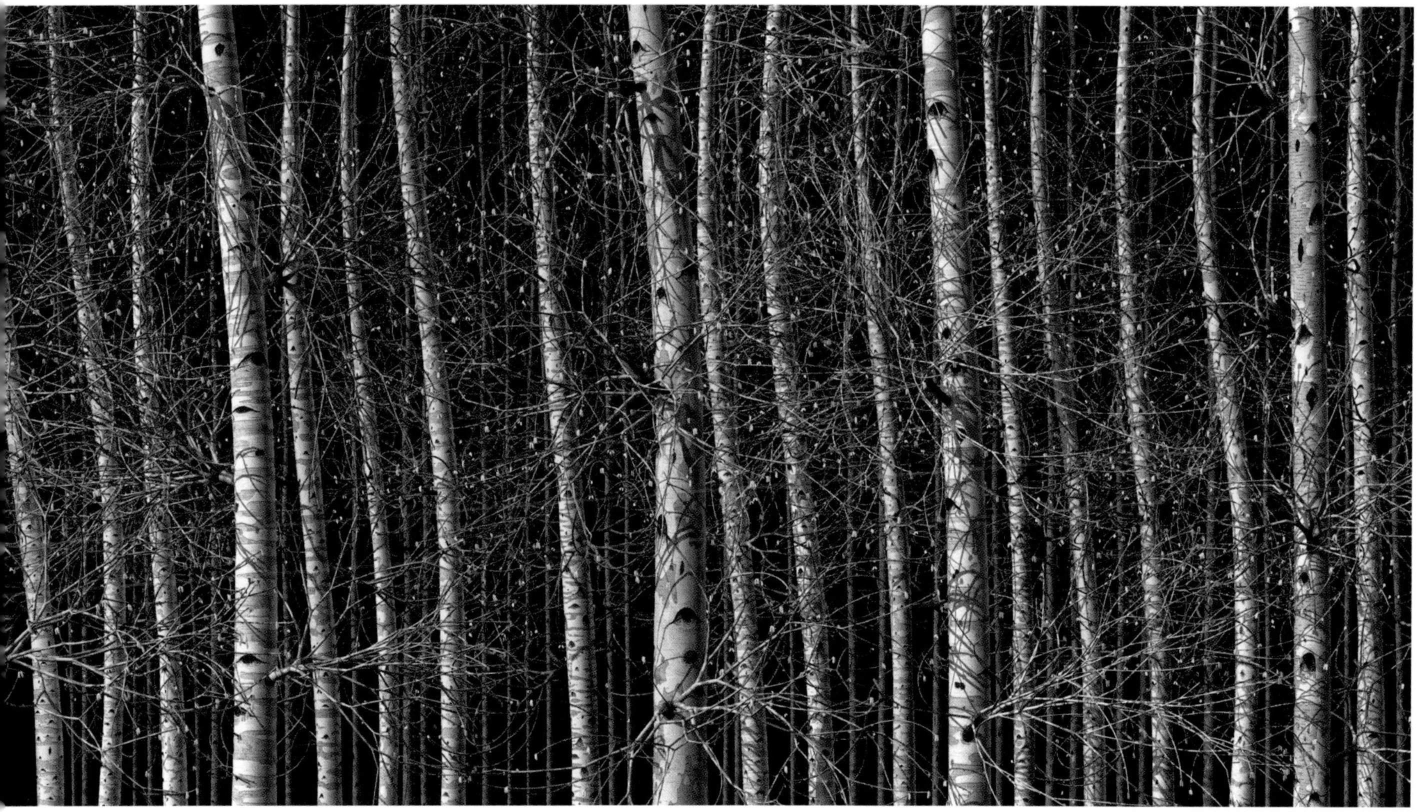

'I am fascinated by the recent discoveries that trees communicate through an underground chemical exchange [...] You can certainly sense the incorporeal in nature. If anything, this is a consistent current in my work. There is so much we can just barely sense and feel; yes, I believe we are surrounded by sentience.'

— Jennifer Steinkamp

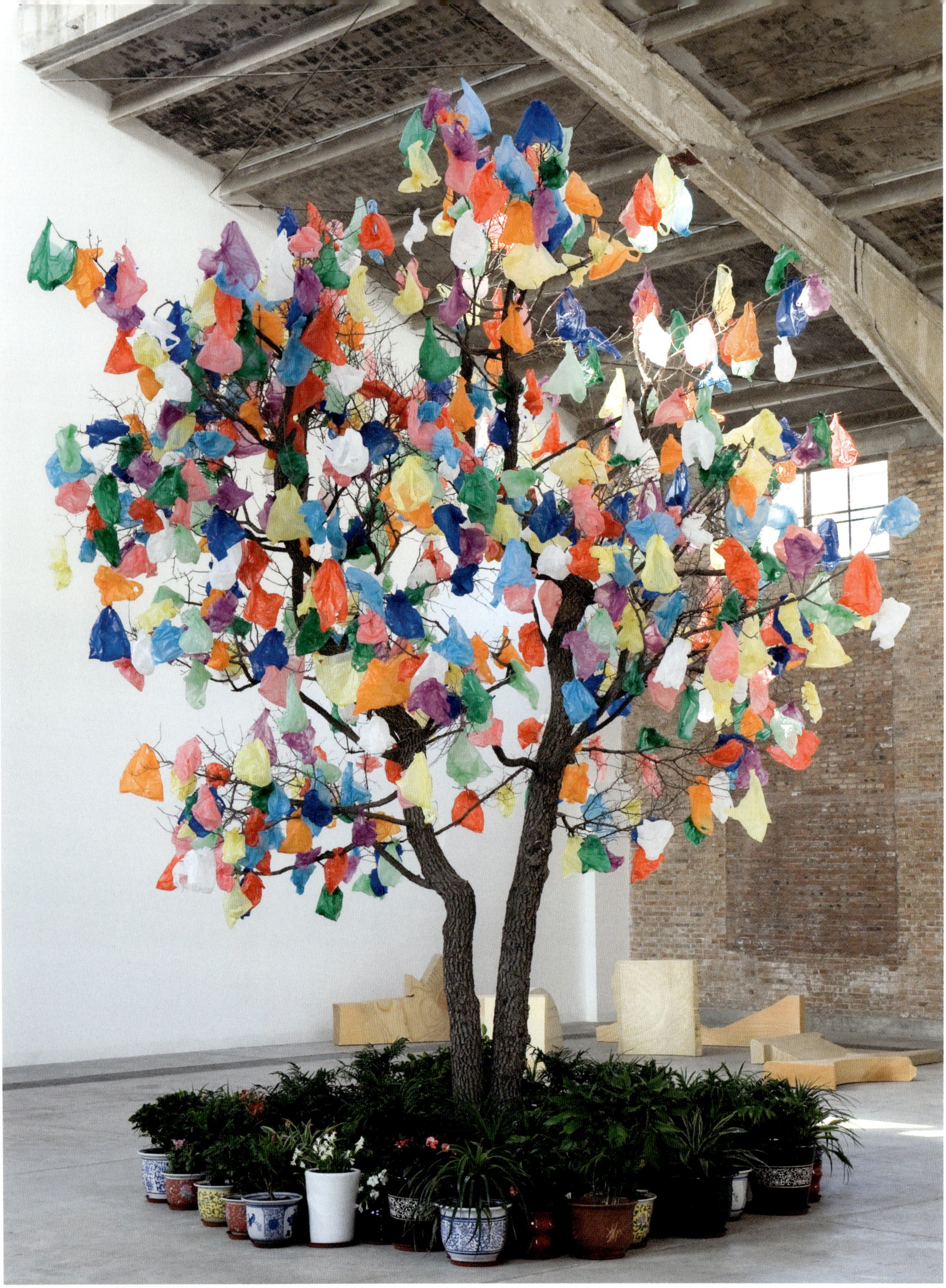

Pascale Marthine Tayou
Plastic Tree B, 2010

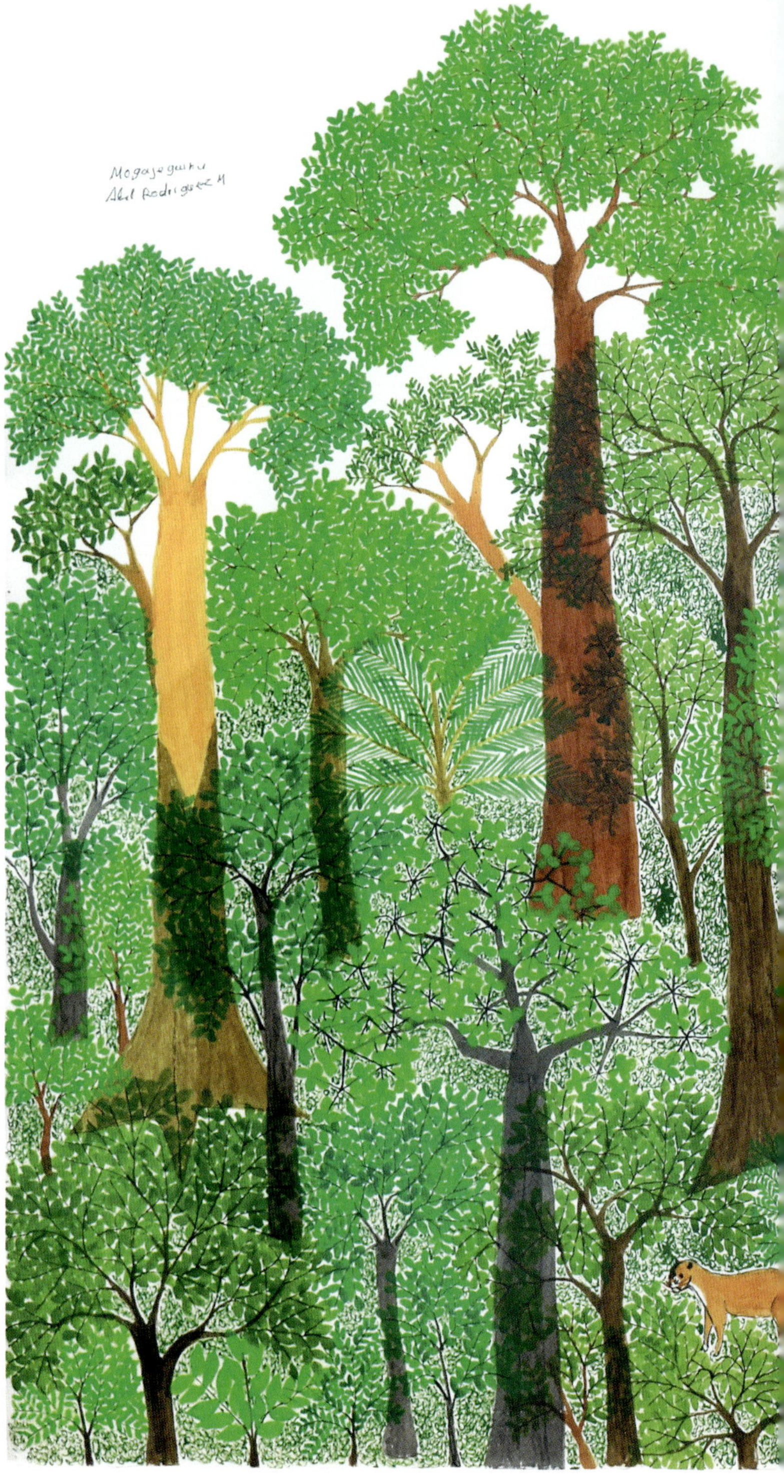

Abel Rodríguez
Terraza Alta II, 2018

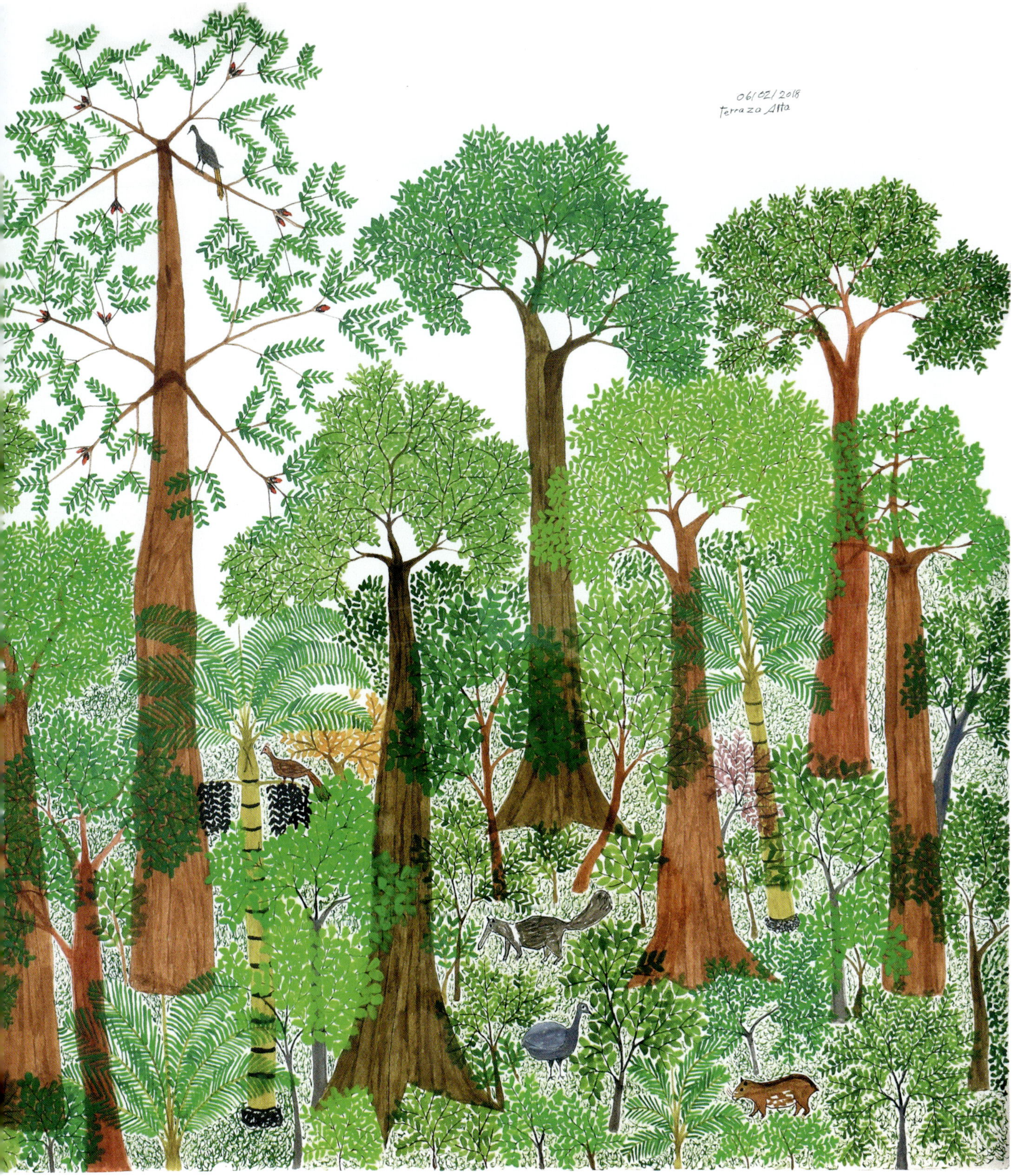
06/02/2018
terrazo Alta

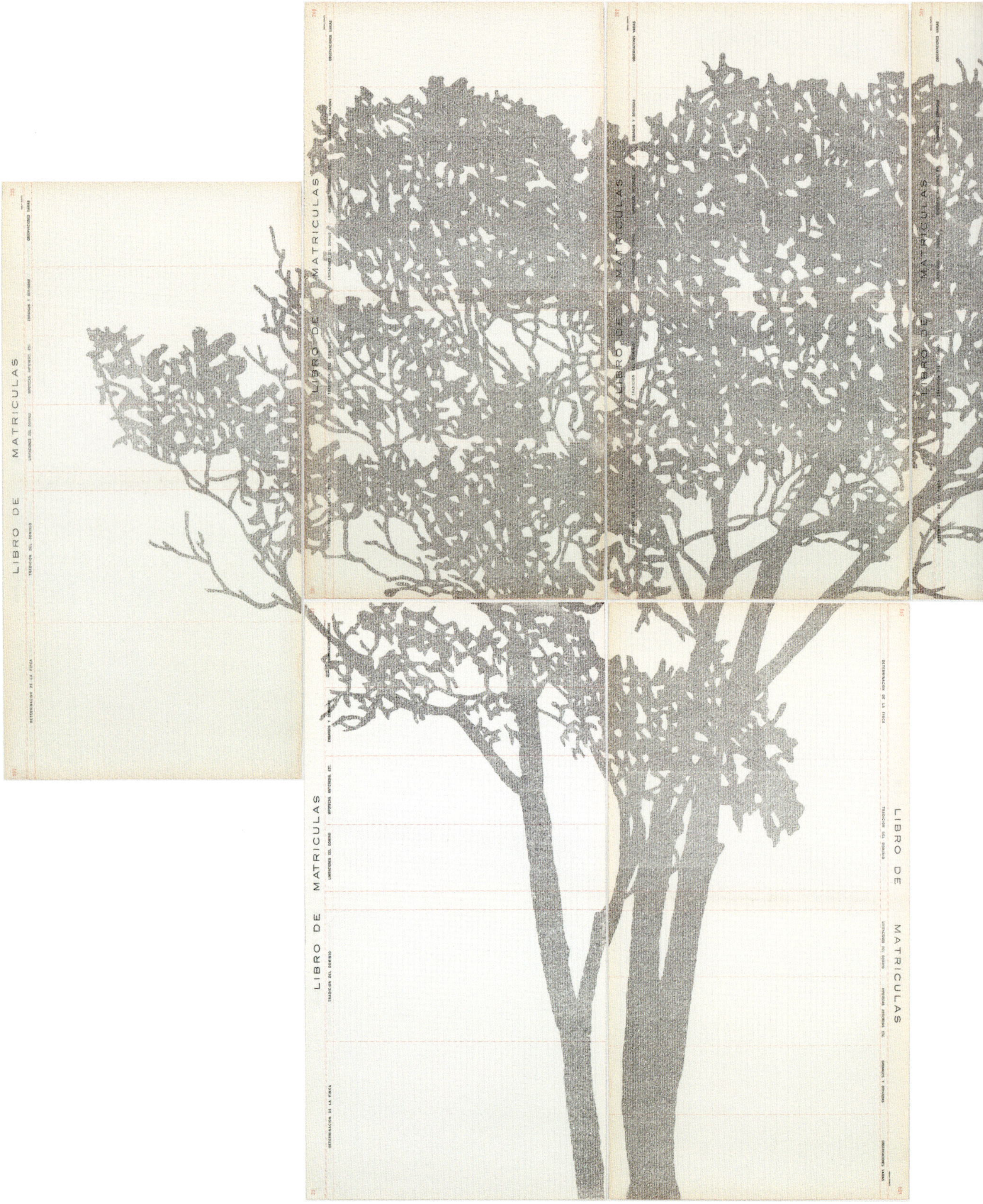
LIBRO DE MATRICULAS
LIBRO DE MATRICULAS
LIBRO DE MATRICULAS
LIBRO DE MATRICULAS
LIBRO DE MATRICULAS
LIBRO DE MATRICULAS

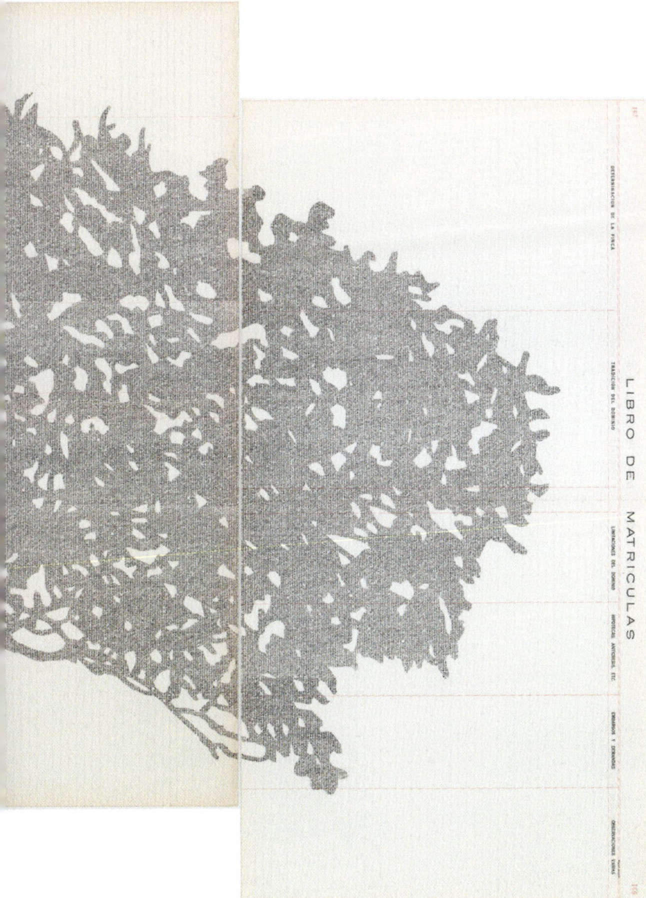

Johanna Calle
Perímetros (Nogal Andino), 2012

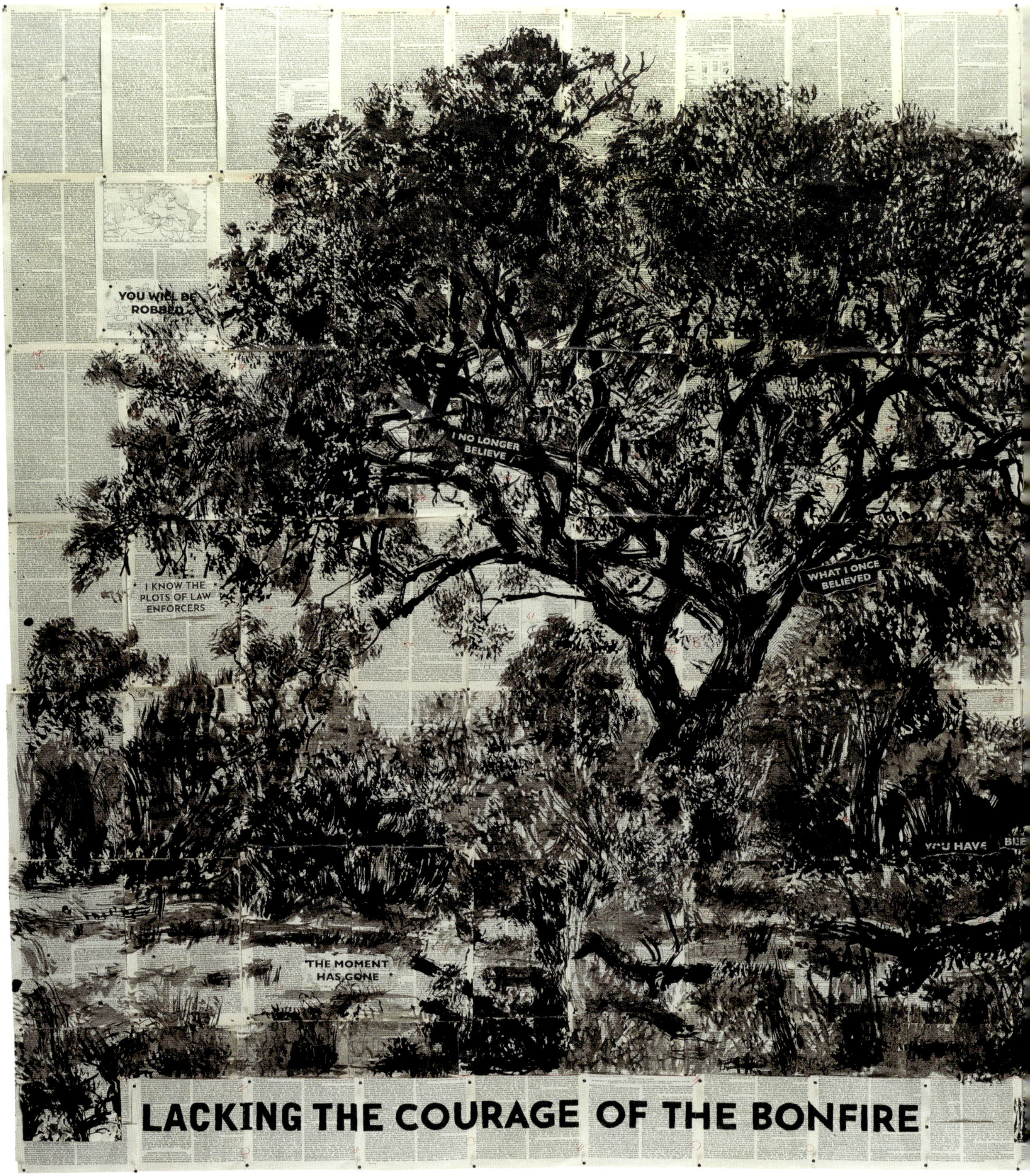
YOU WILL BE ROBBED
I NO LONGER BELIEVE
I KNOW THE PLOTS OF LAW ENFORCERS
WHAT I ONCE BELIEVED
THE MOMENT HAS GONE
LACKING THE COURAGE OF THE BONFIRE

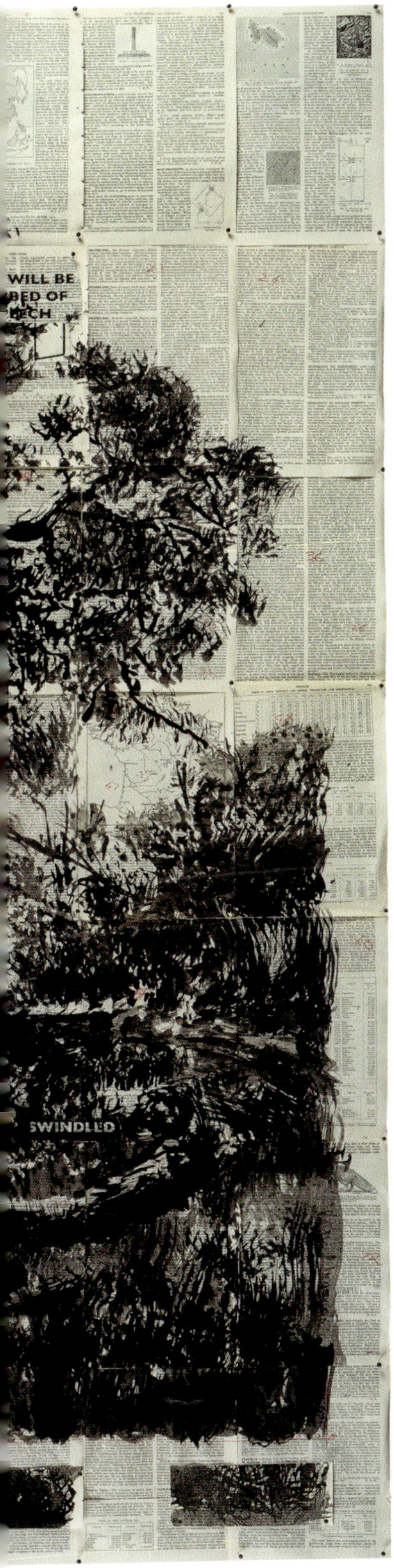

William Kentridge
Untitled (Lacking the Courage of the Bonfire), 2019

Overleaf:
Eva Jospin
Forêt (Forest), 2013

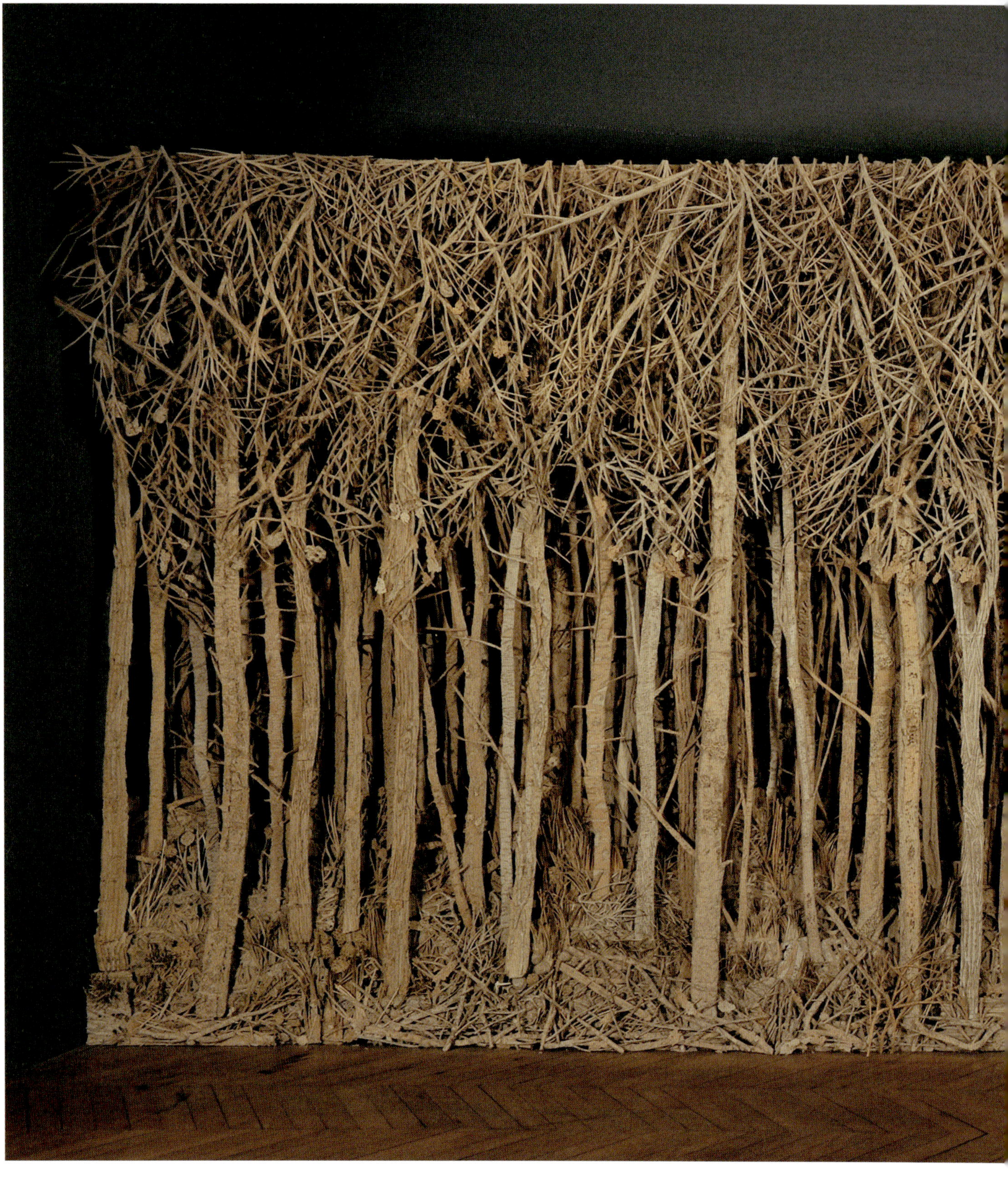

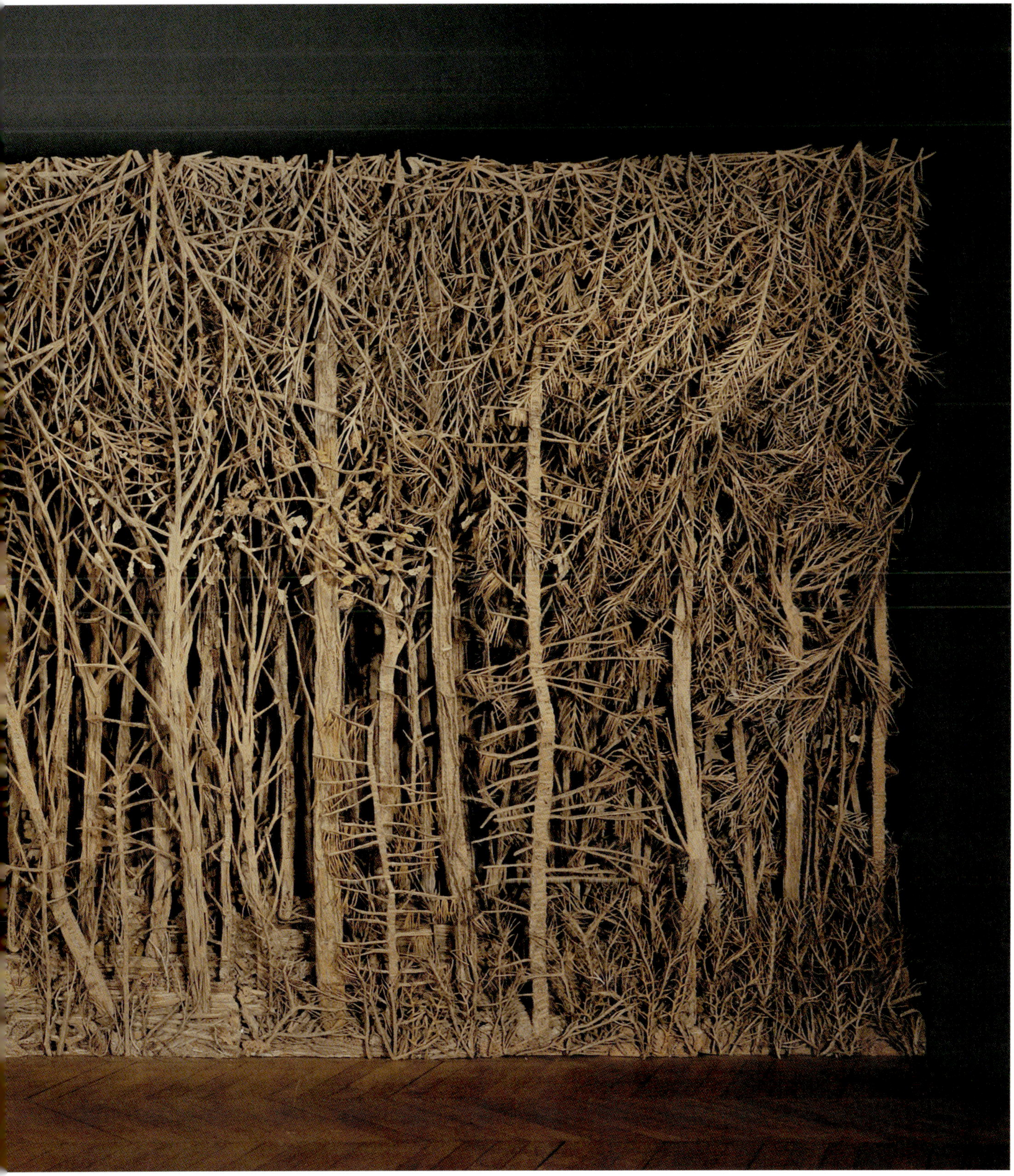

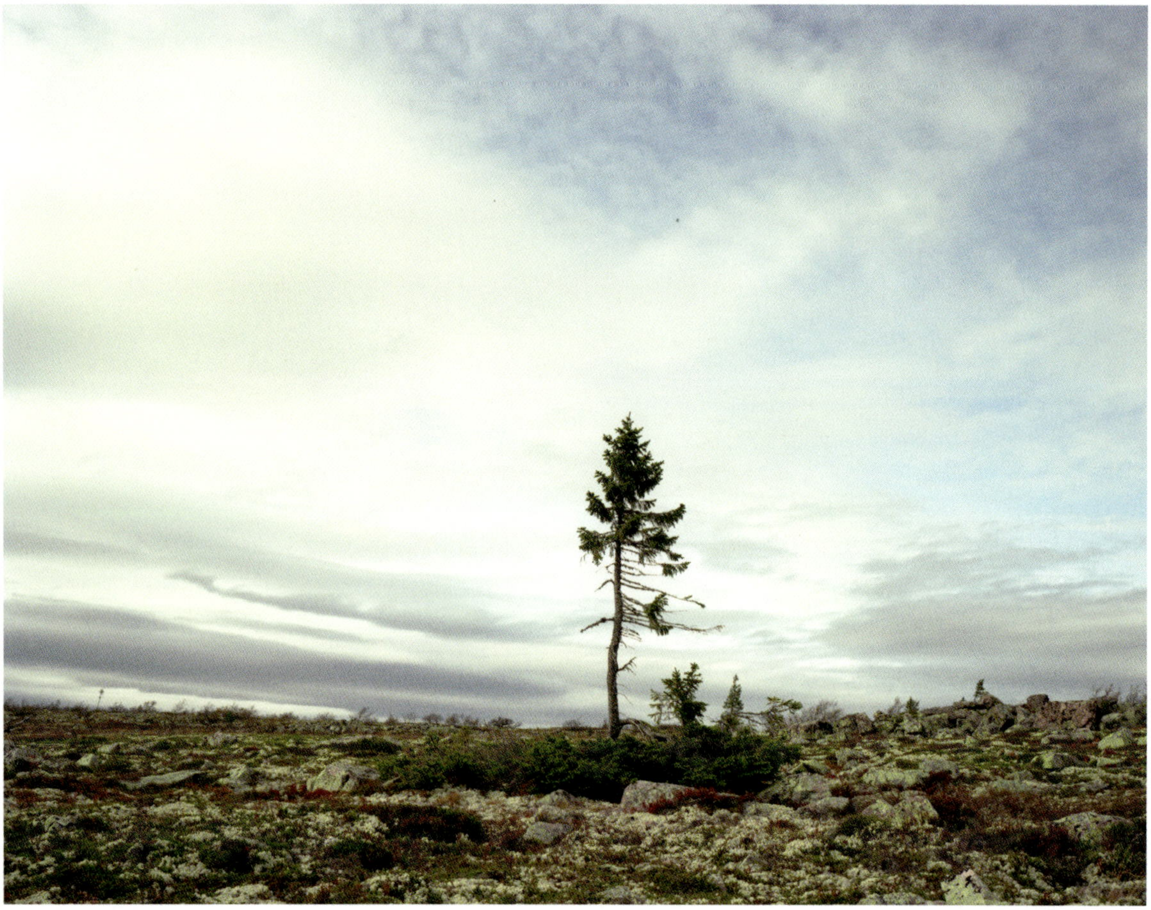

Spruce Gran Picea #0909-11A07 (9,550 years old; Sweden)

Rachel Sussman
Spruce Gran Picea
#0909-11A07 (9,550 years old;
Sweden), 2009

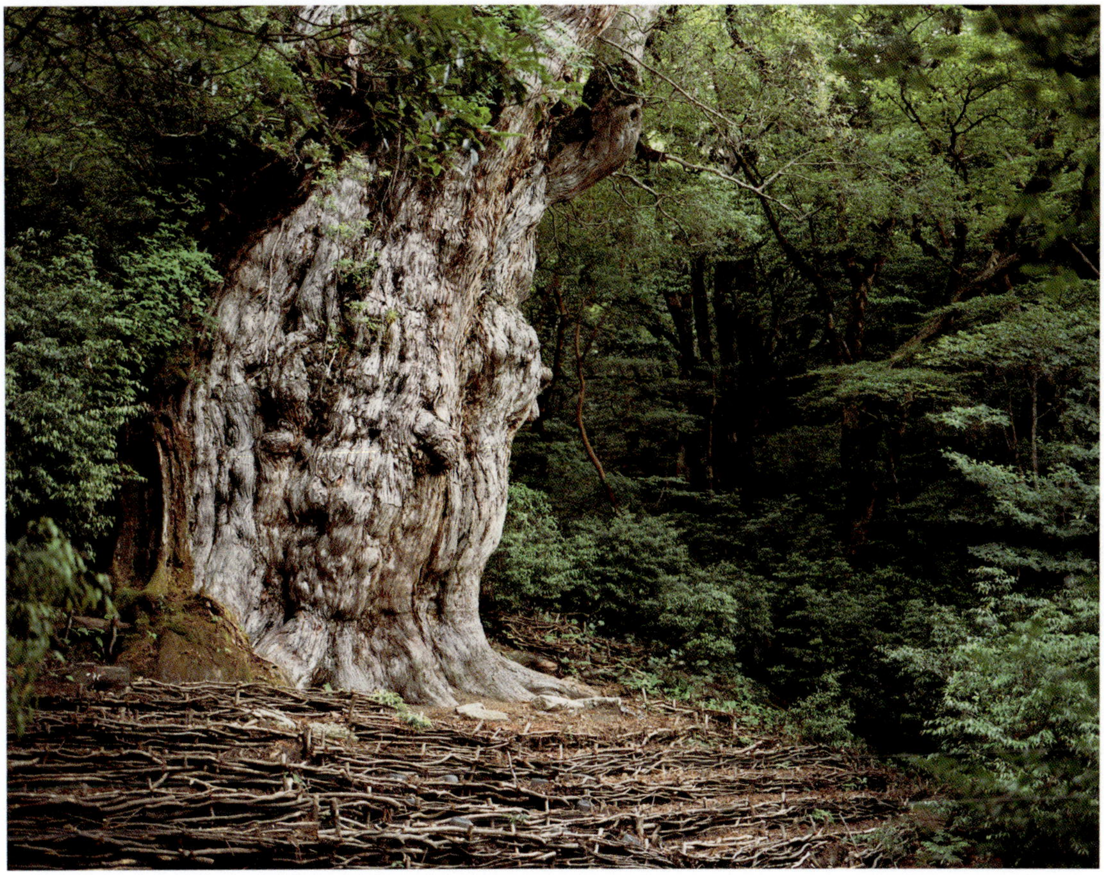

Jomon Sugi, Japanese Cedar #0704-002 (2,180-7,000 years old; Yaku Shima, Japan)

Rachel Sussman
Jomon Sugi, Japanese Cedar #0704-002 (2,180–7,000 years old; Yakushima, Japan), 2004

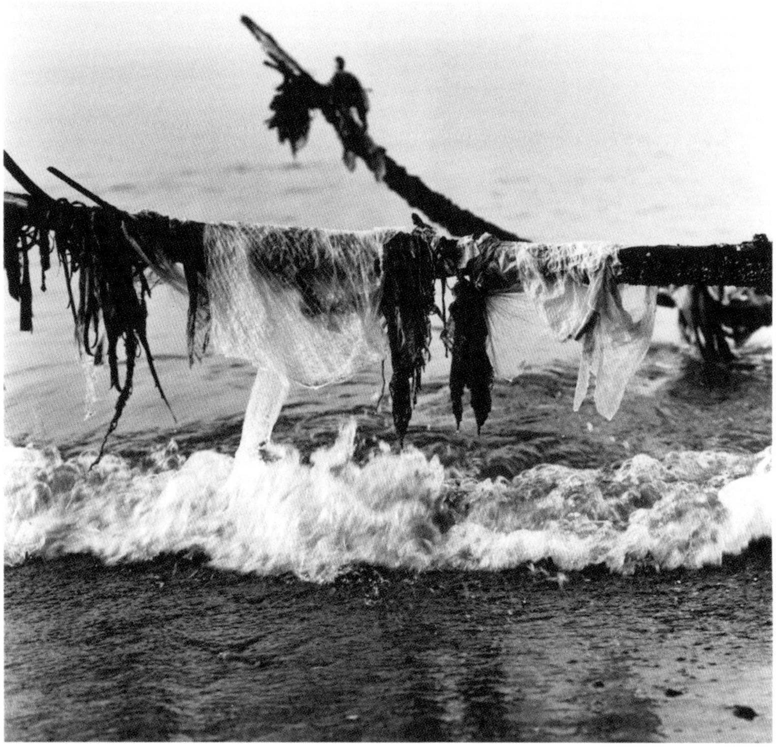

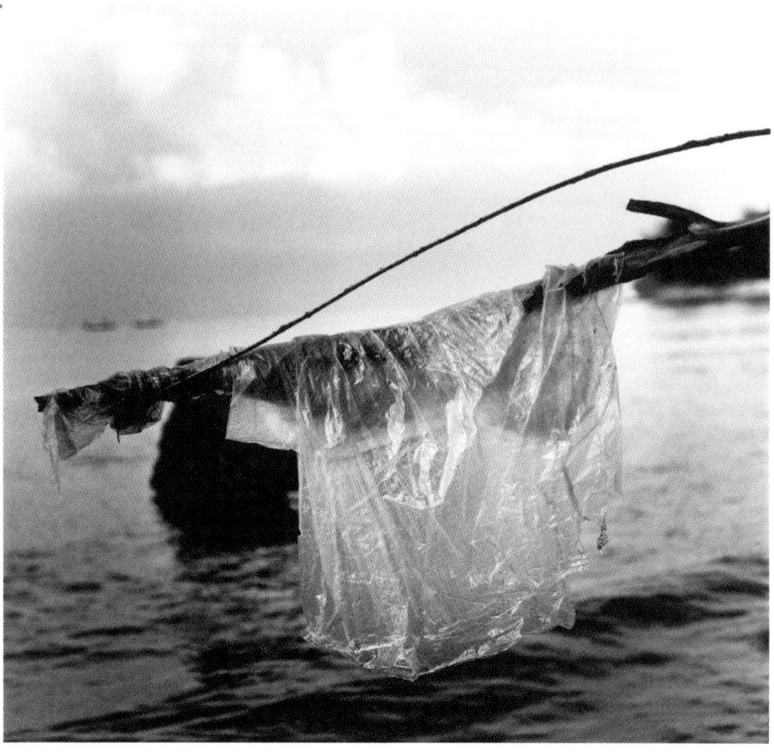

Simryn Gill
Channel #1, 2,
4 and *5*, 2014

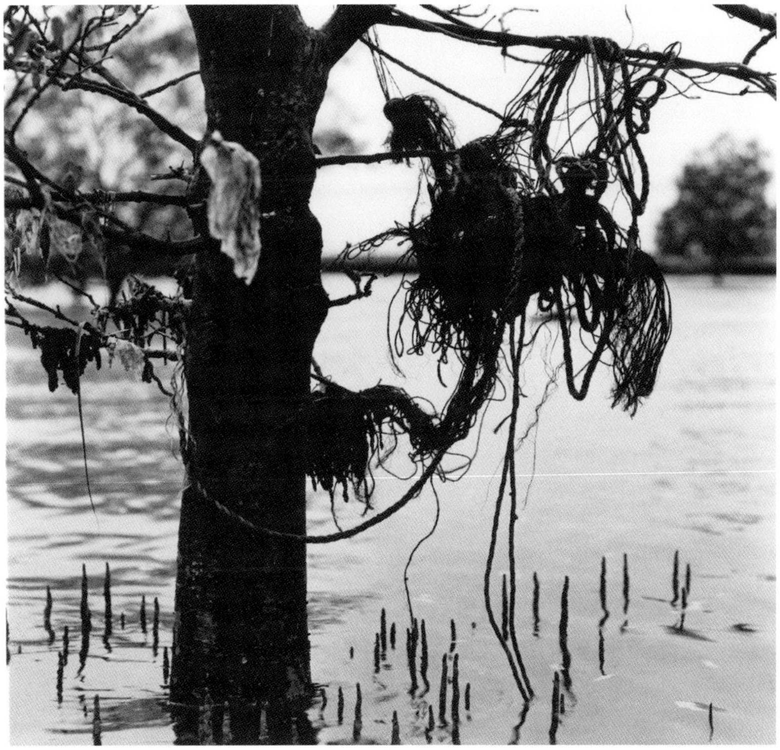

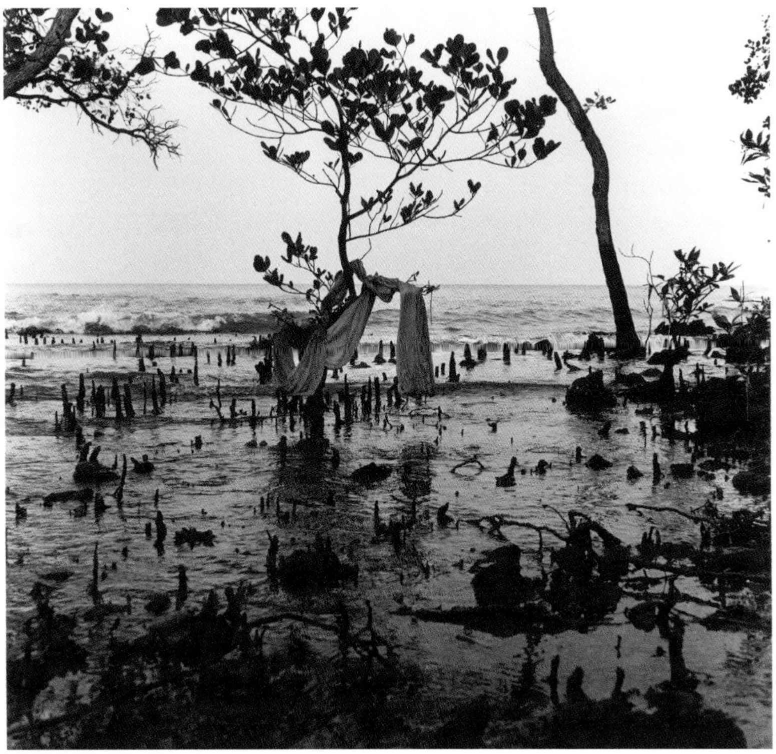

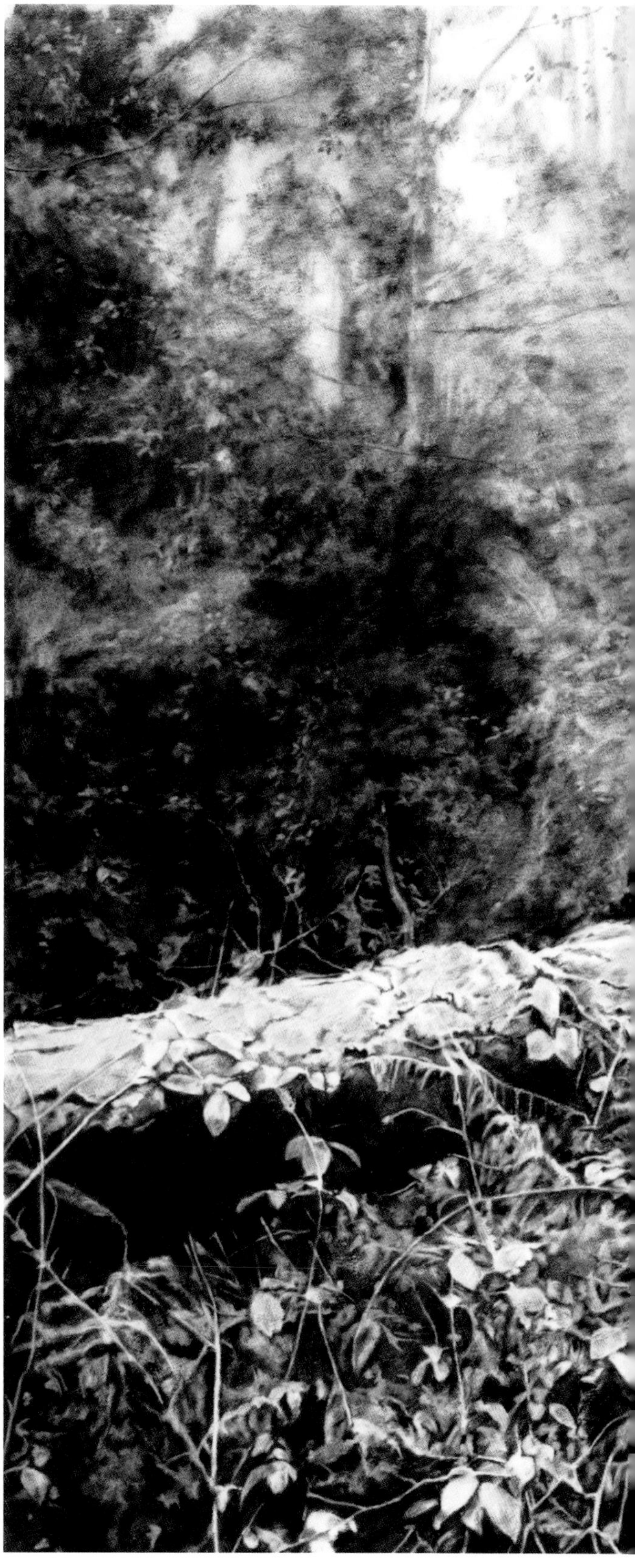

George Shaw
Woodsman 5, 2009

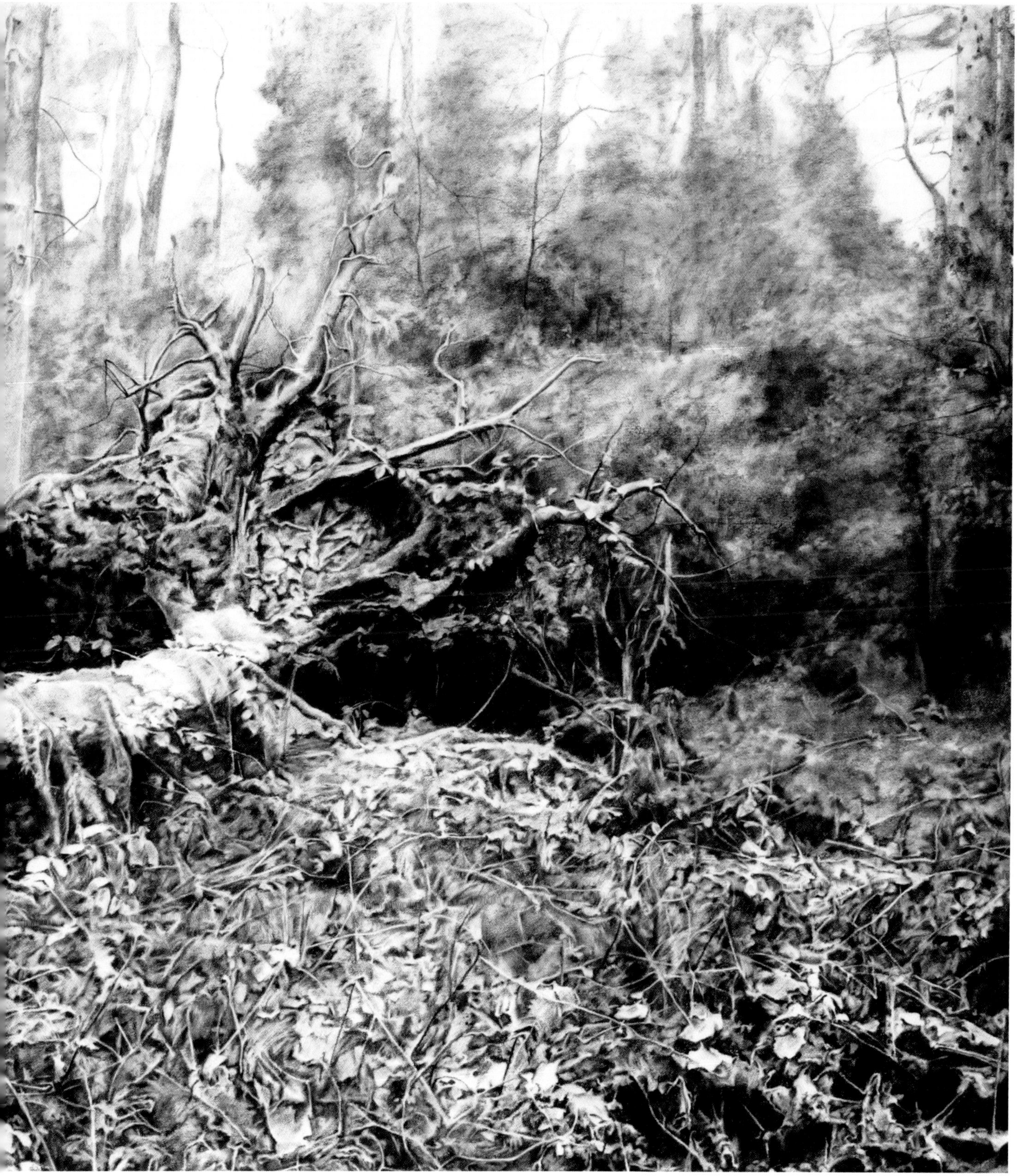

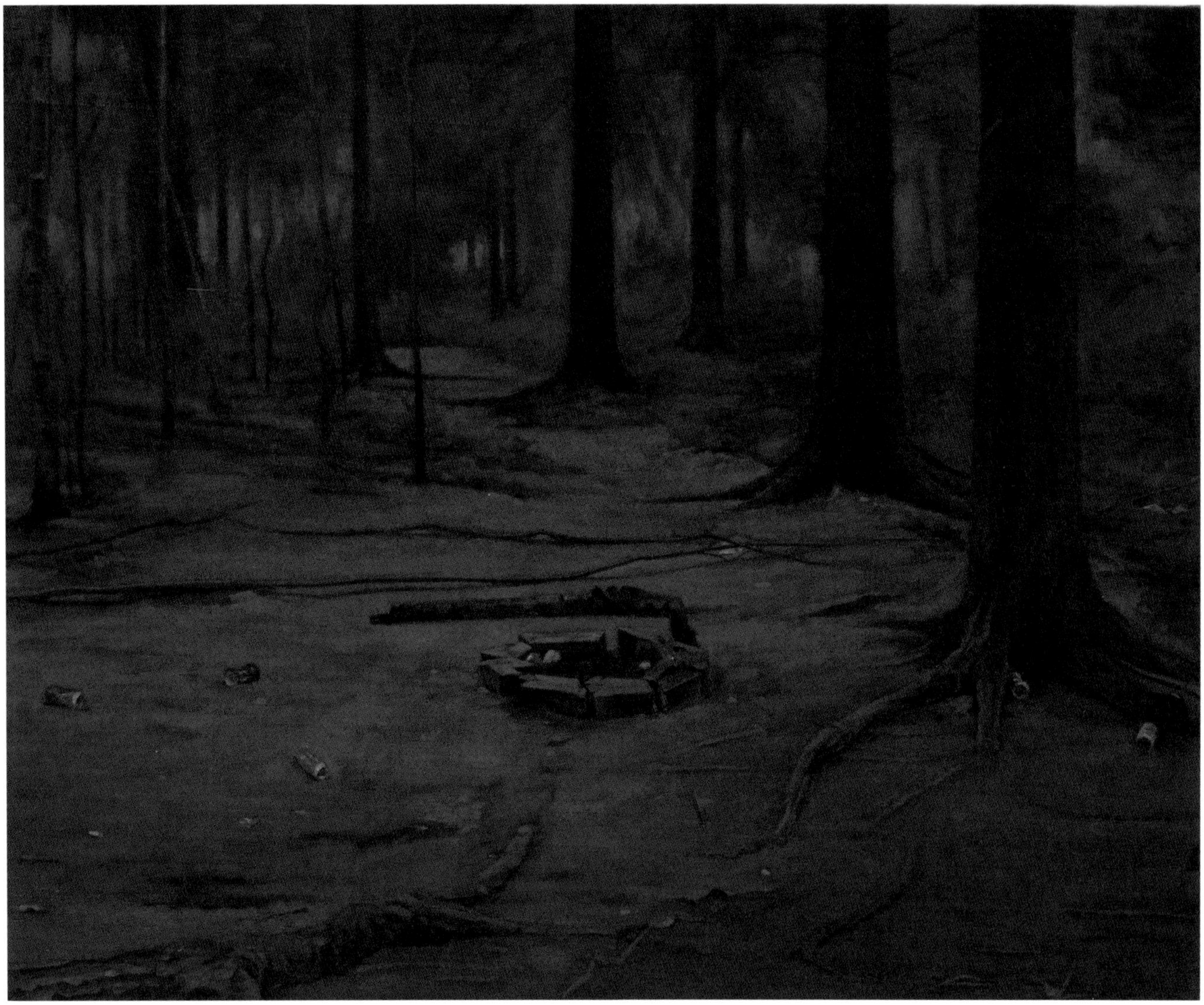

George Shaw
The Heart of the Wood,
2015–16

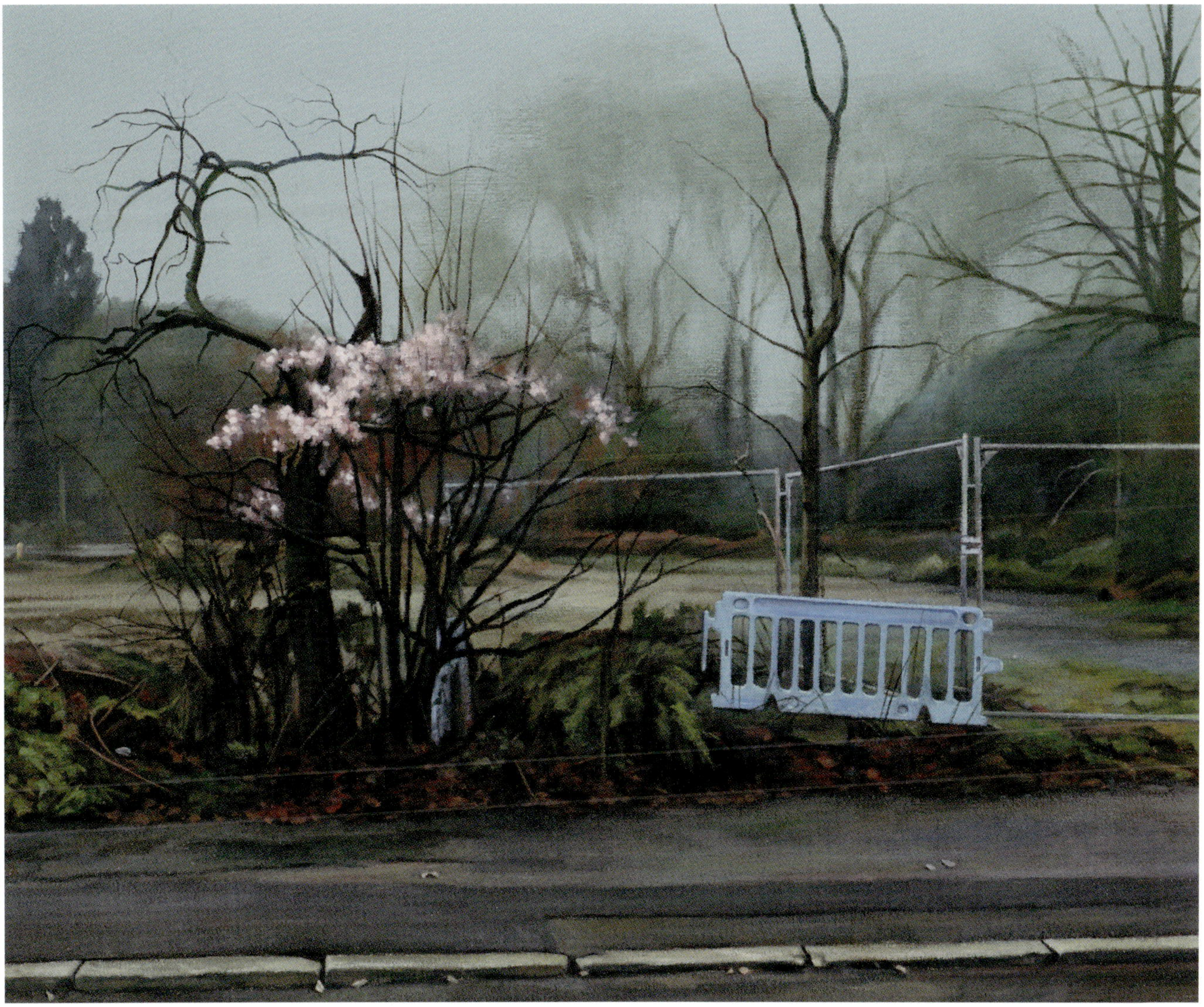

George Shaw
Trespasser (2), 2019

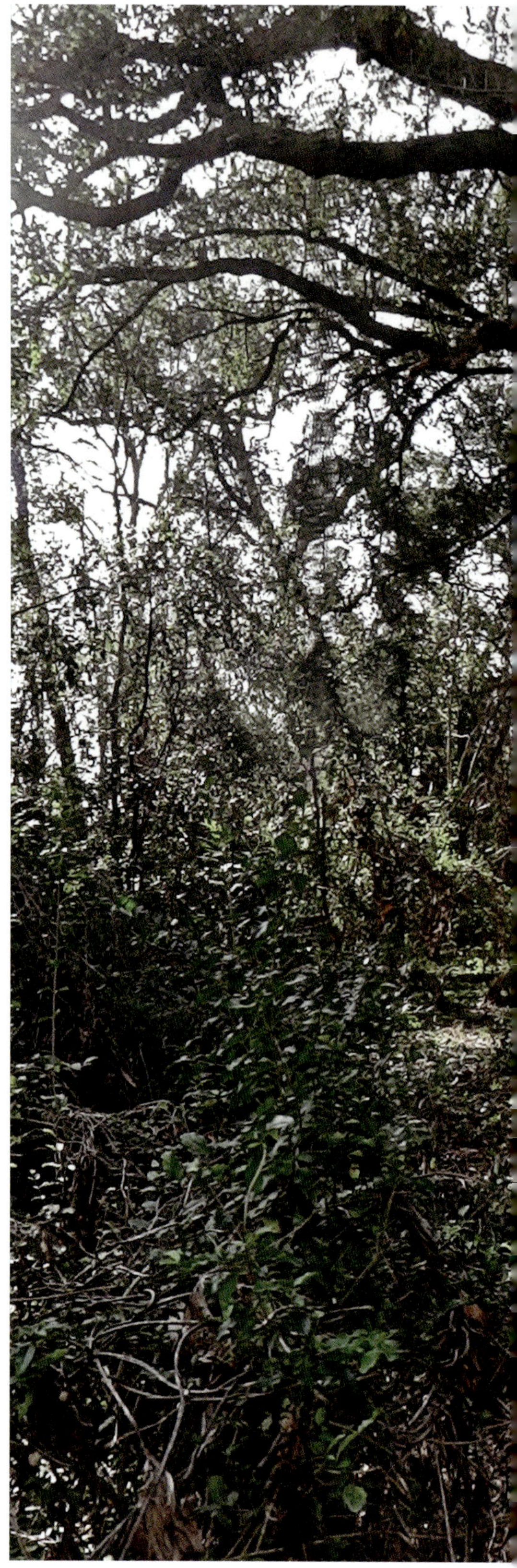

Steve McQueen
Lynching Tree, 2013

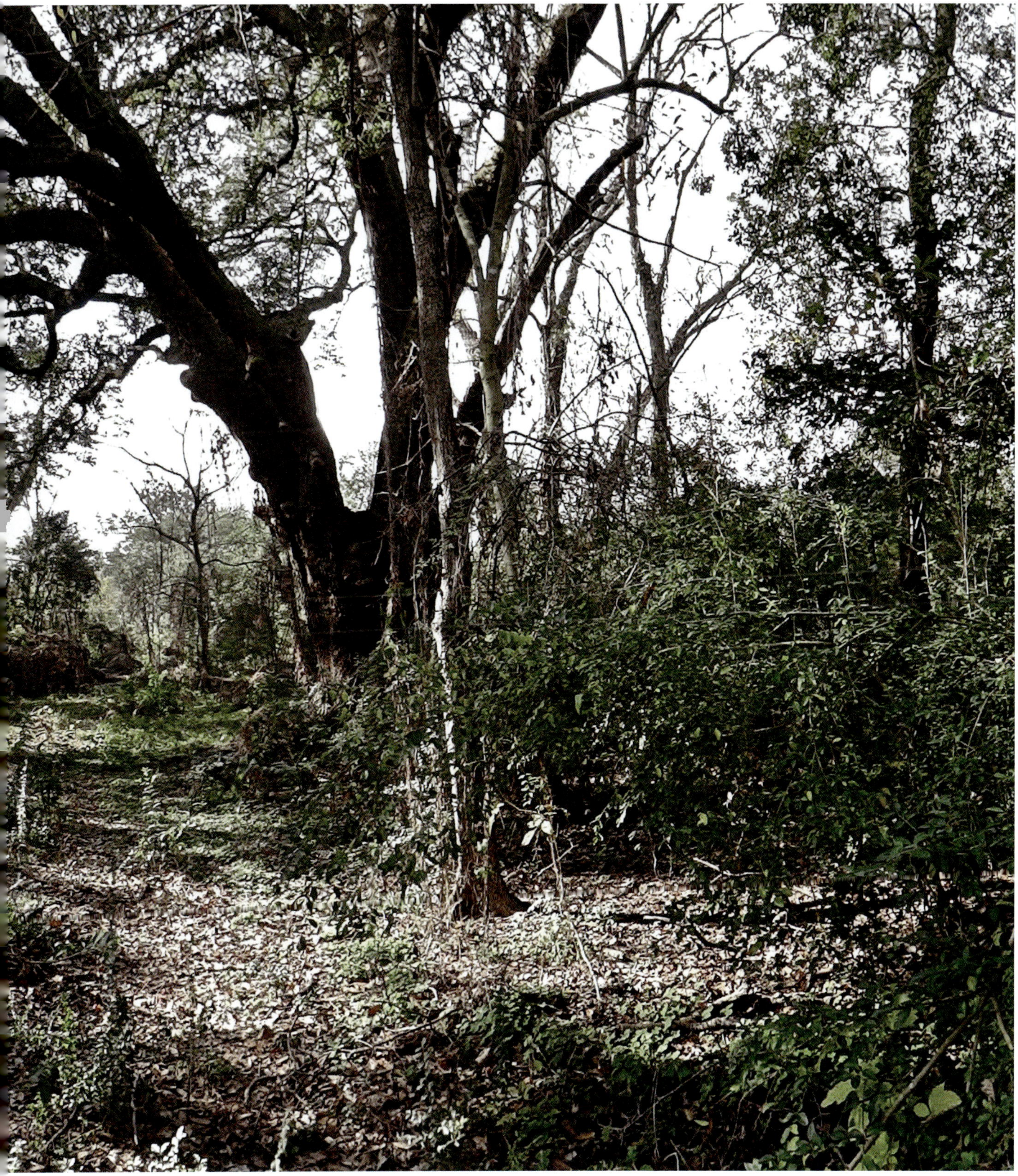

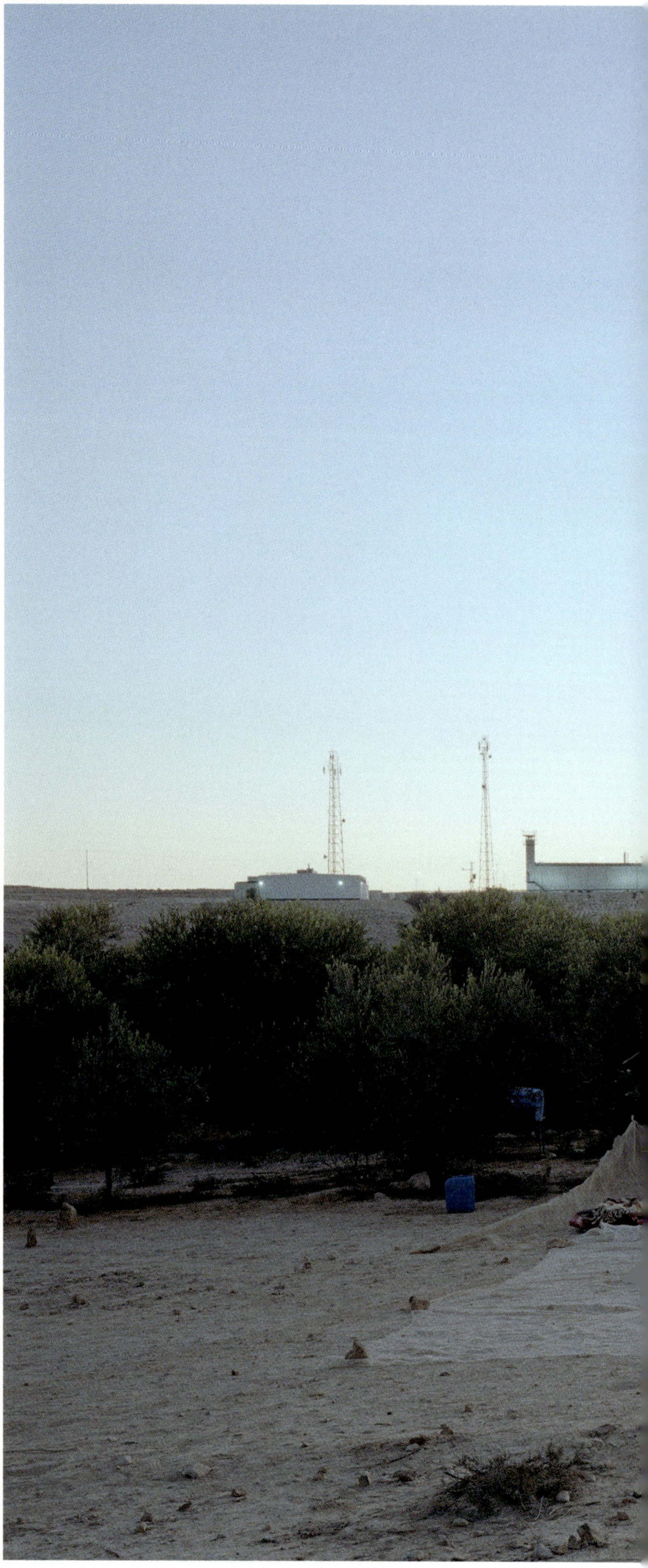

Jeff Wall
Daybreak
(on an olive farm/Negev Desert/Israel), 2011

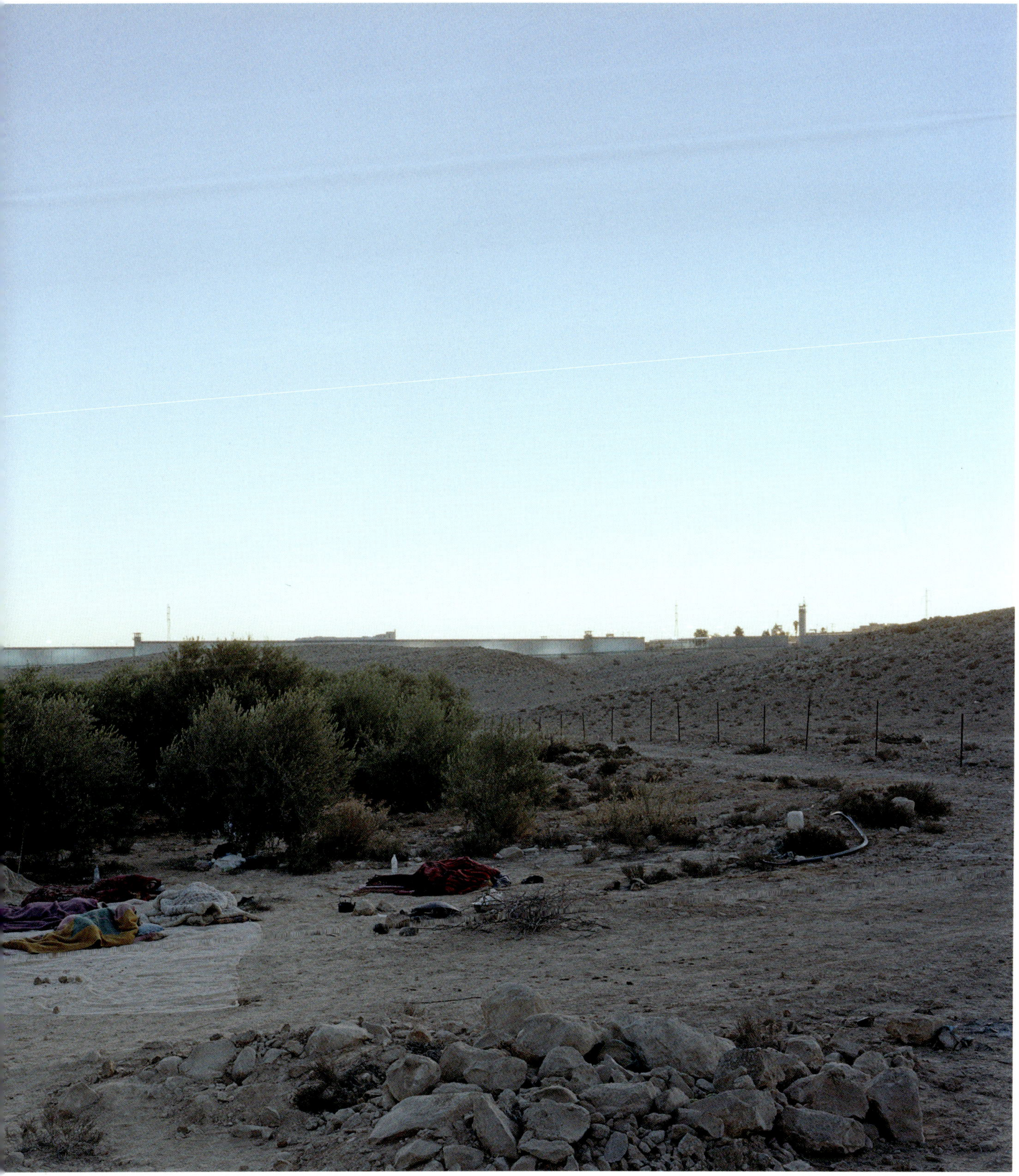

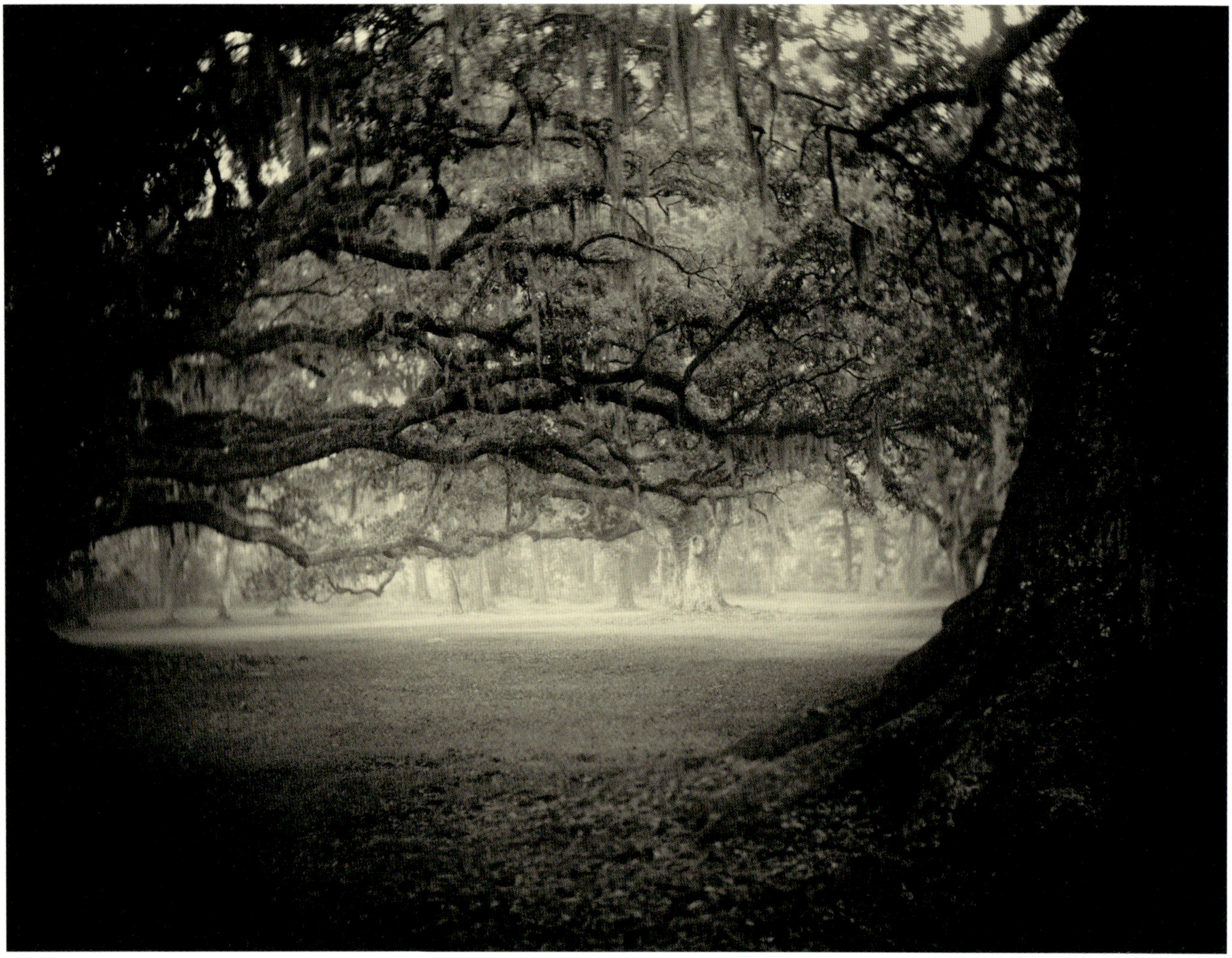

Sally Mann
Deep South, Untitled (Fontainebleau), 1998

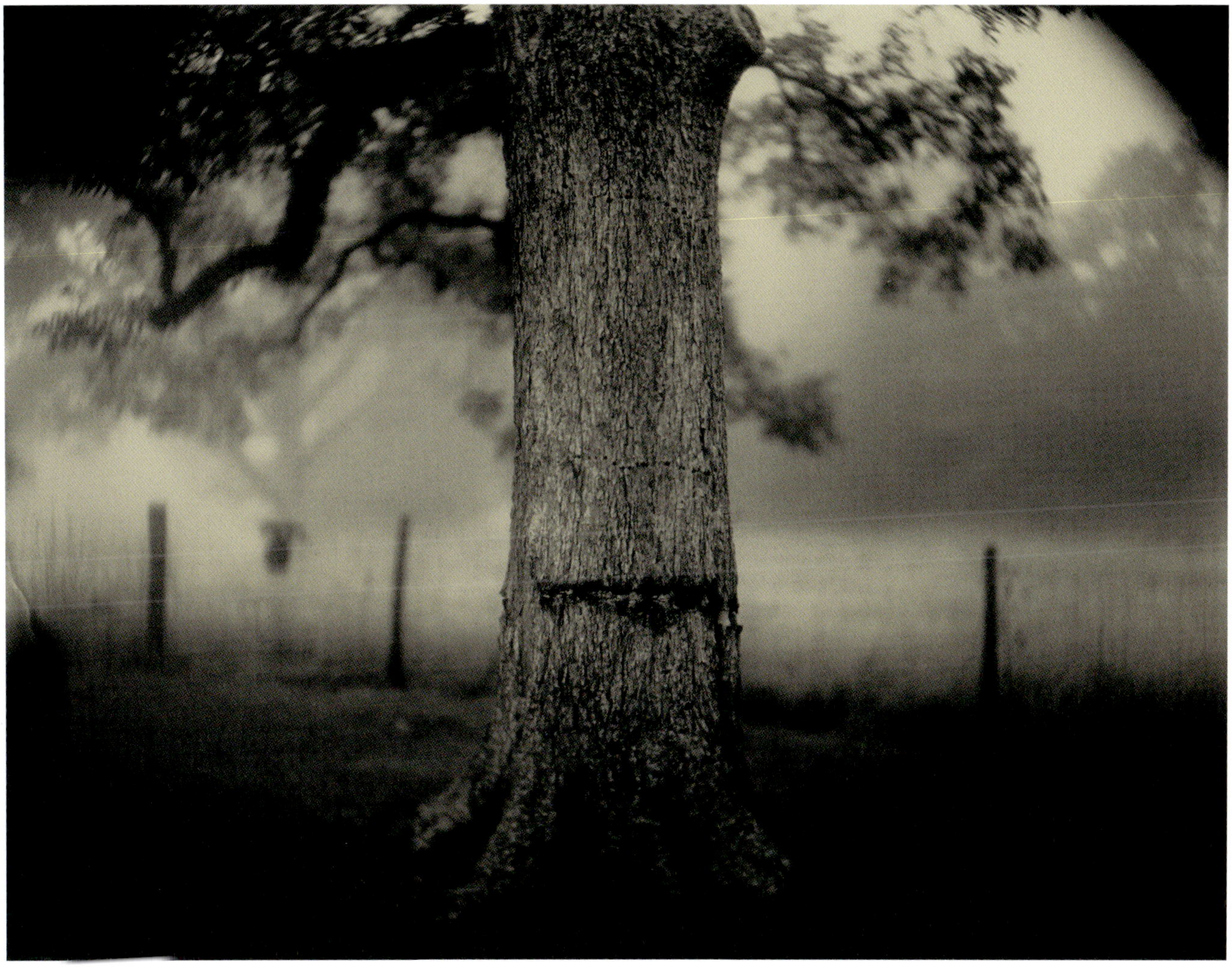

Sally Mann
Deep South, Untitled
(Scarred Tree), 1998

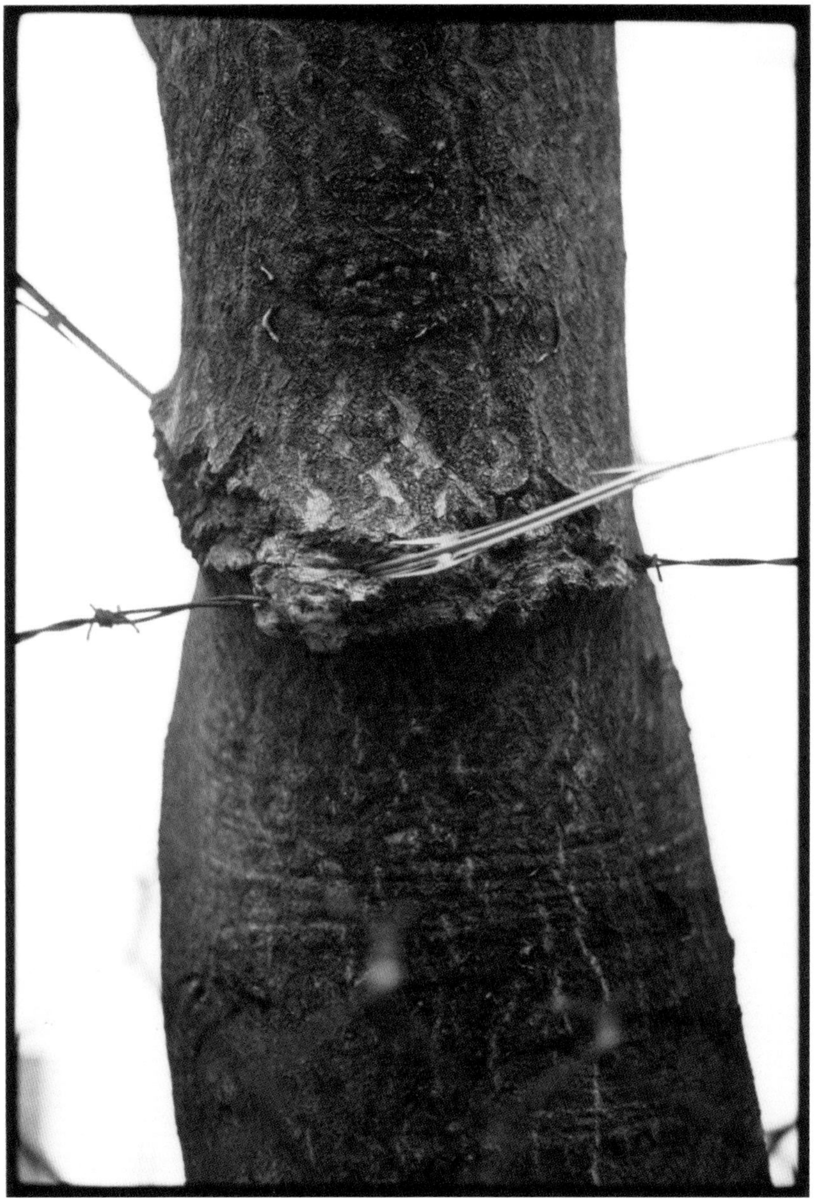

Zoe Leonard
Untitled, 2000

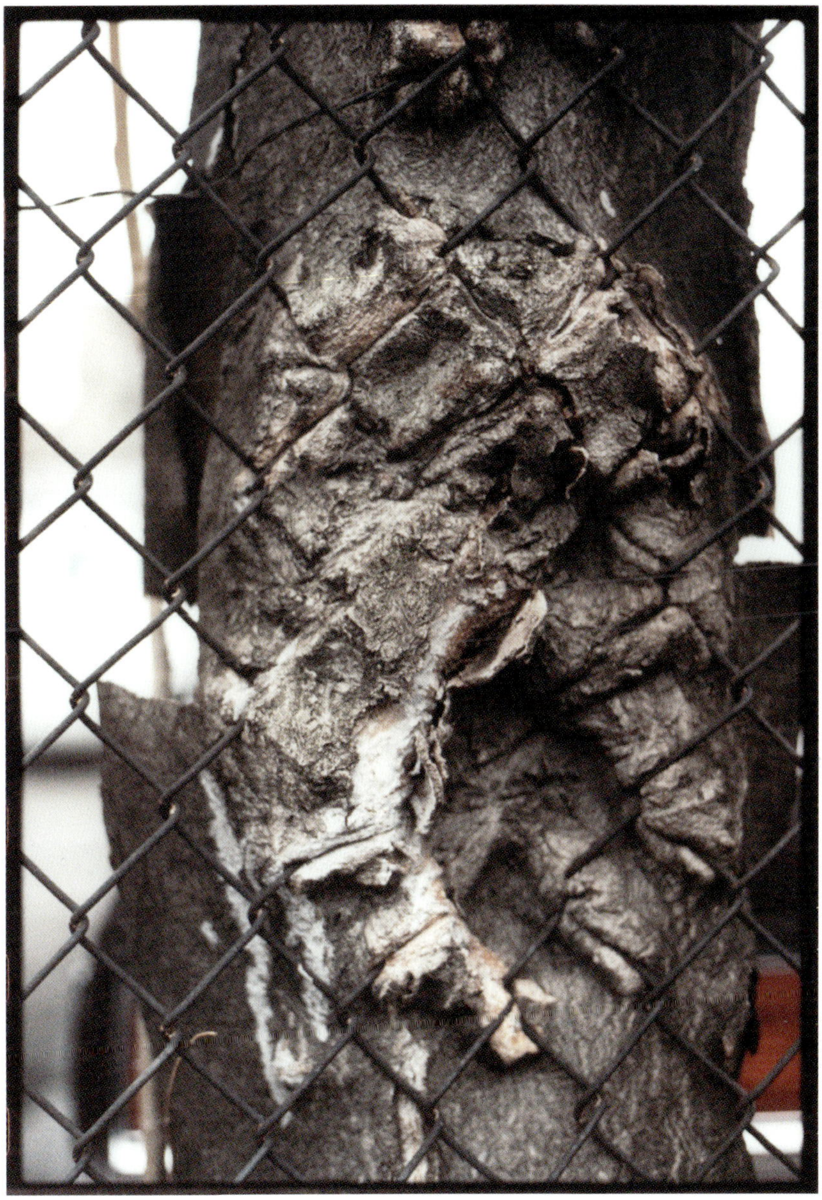

Zoe Leonard
Untitled, 2000

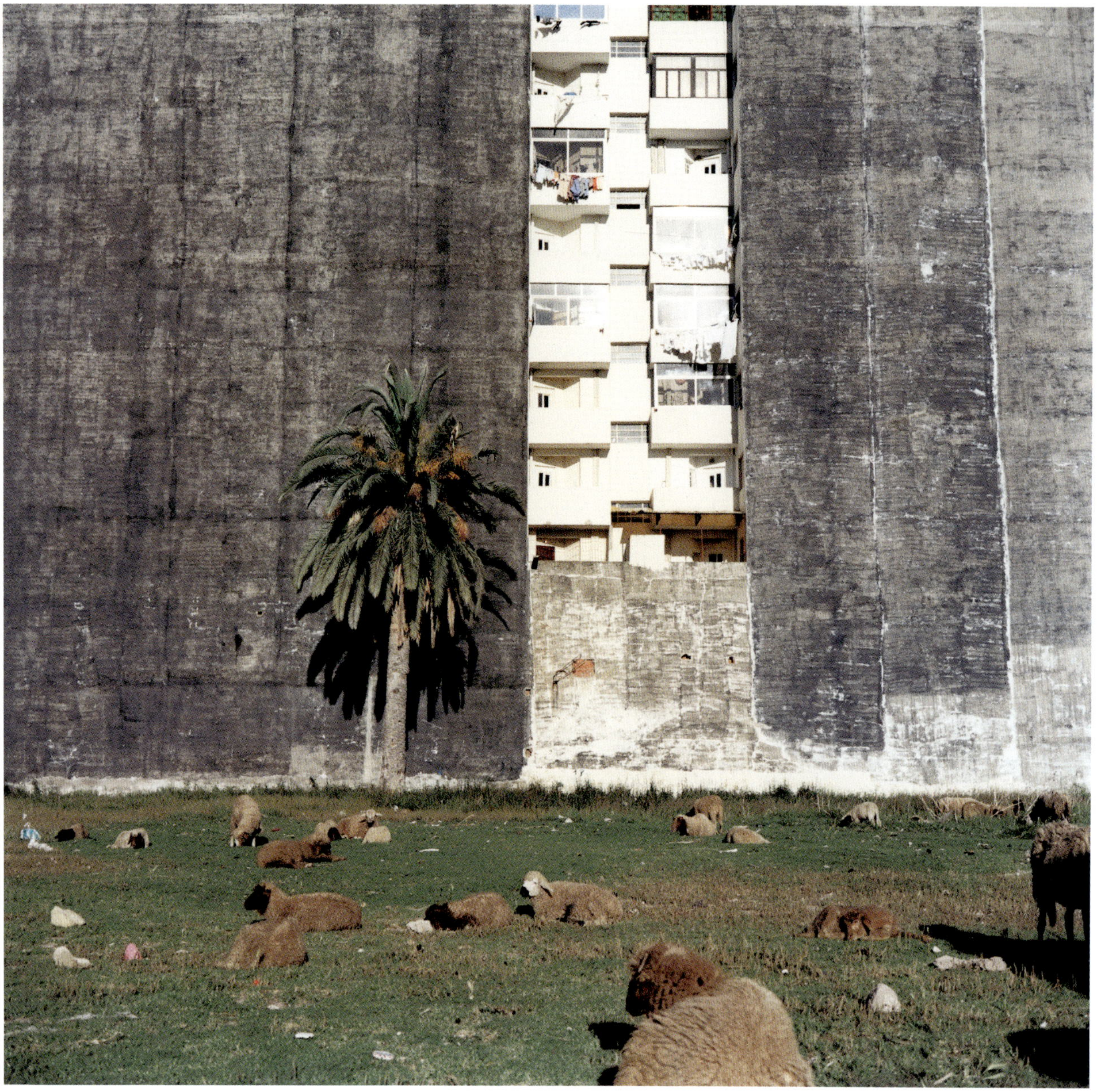

Yto Barrada
Terrain Vague – Tanger
(Vacant Lot – Tangier), 2001

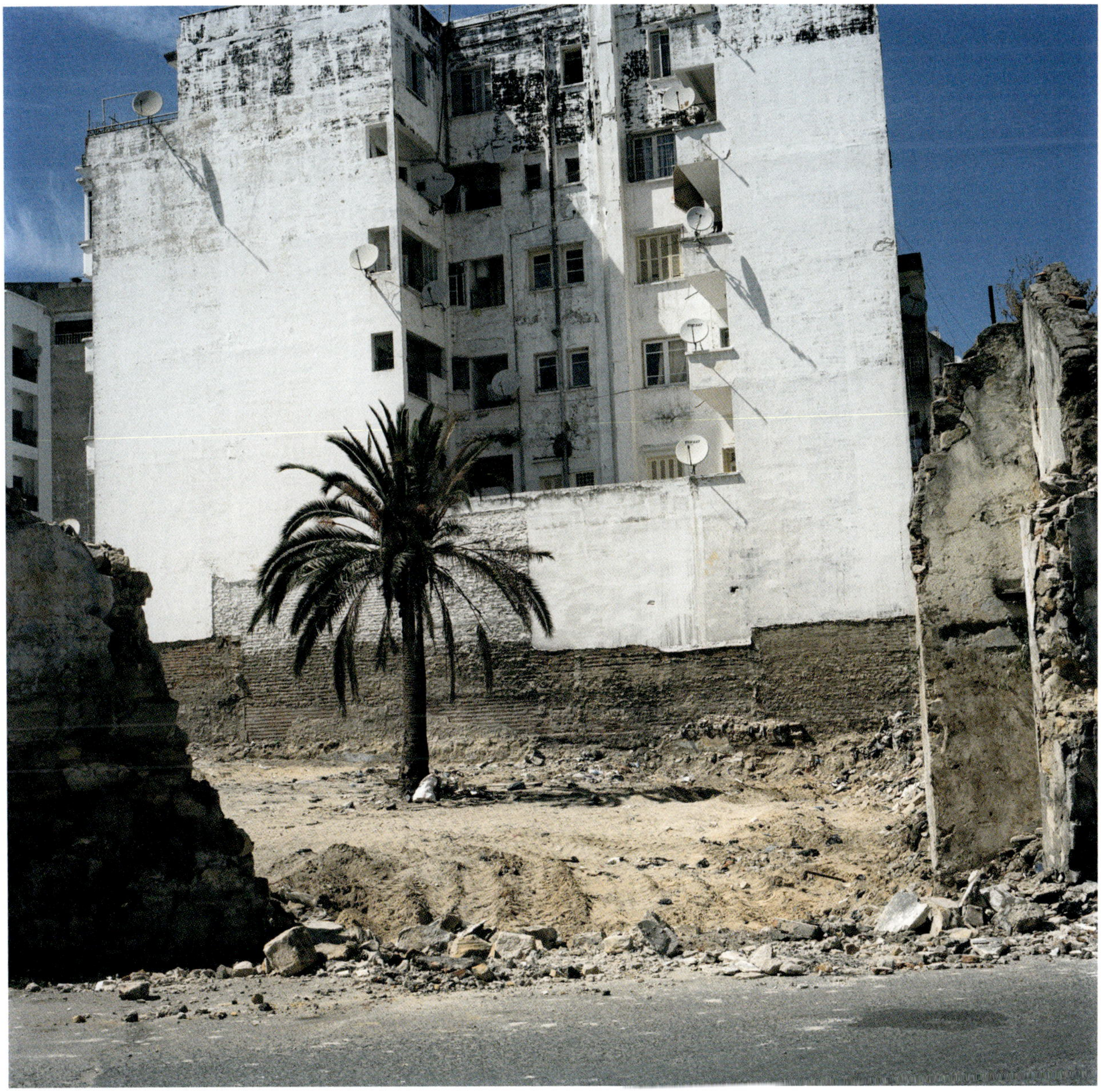

Yto Barrada
Terrain Vague No. 2
(Vacant Lot No. 2), 2009

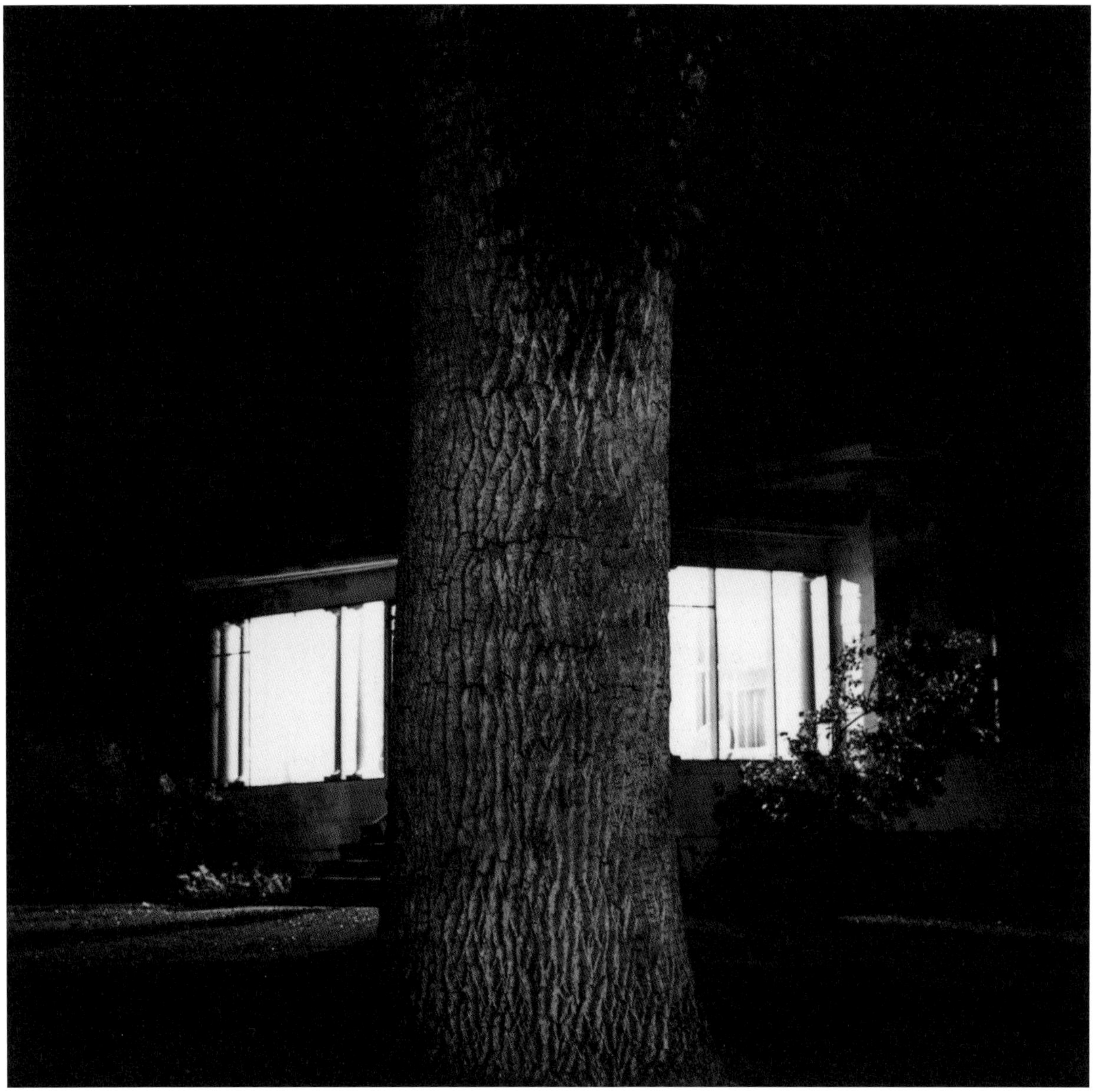

Robert Adams
Above Boulder, Colorado, c.1979

Robert Adams
Ontario, California, 1983

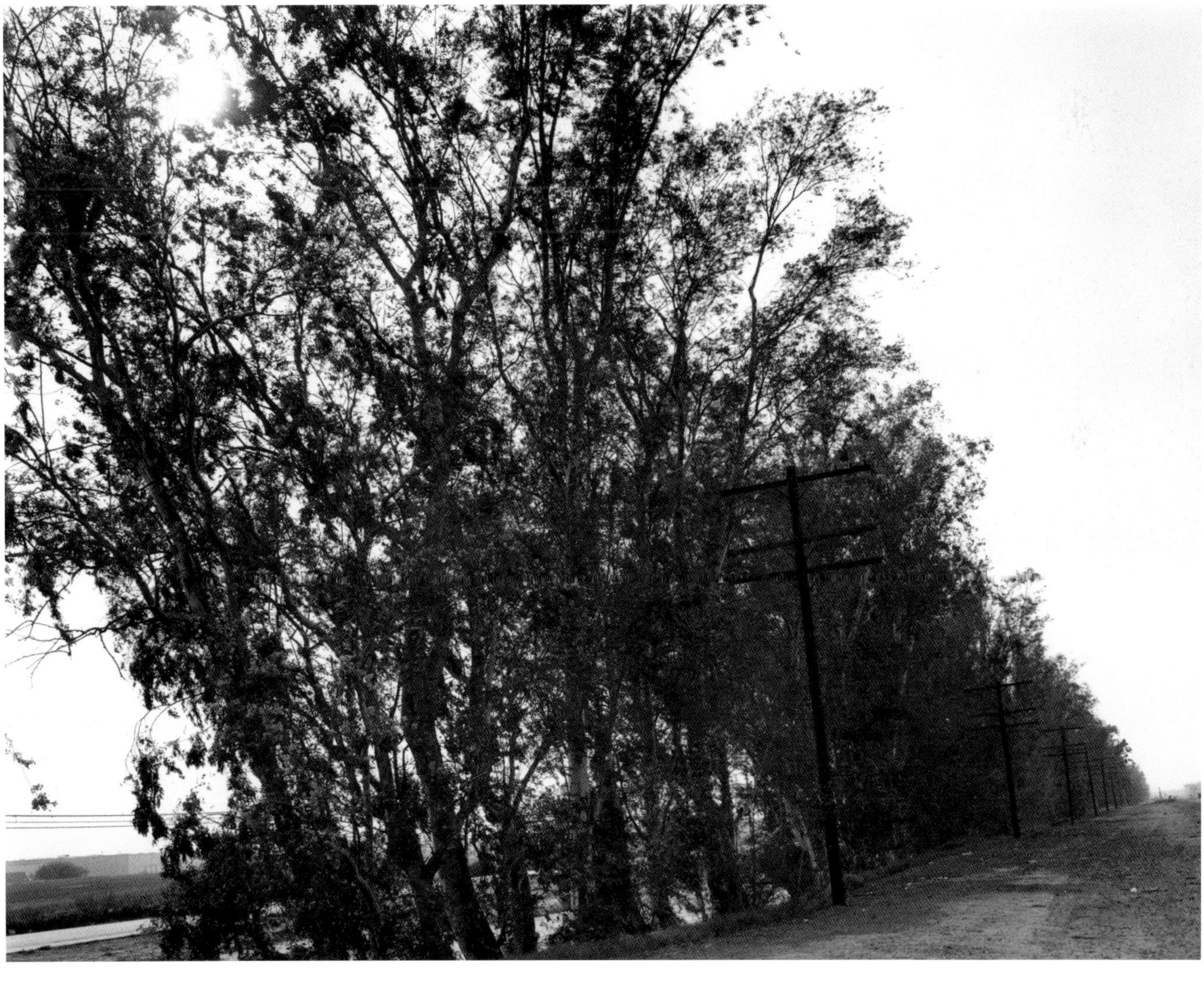

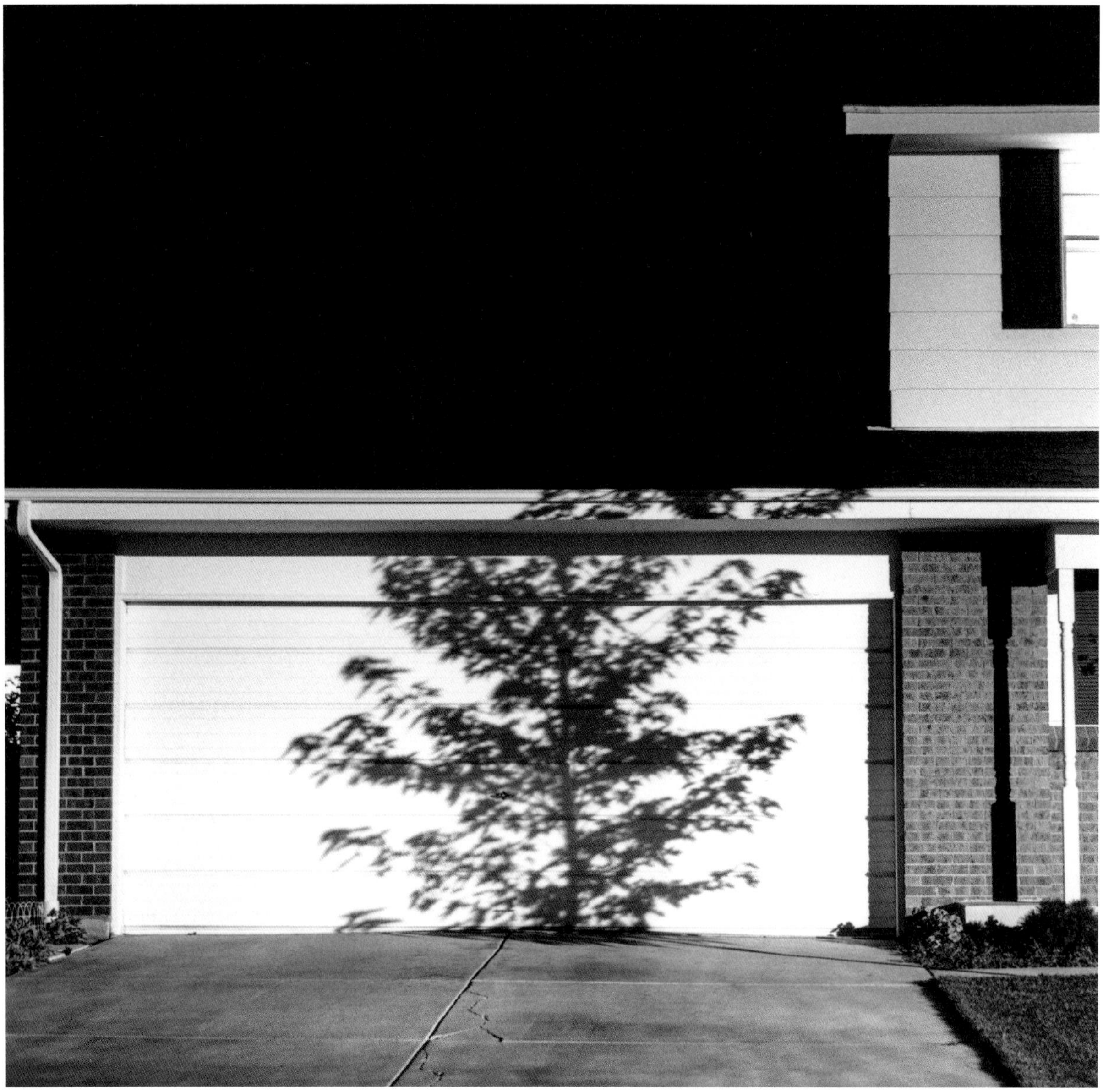

Robert Adams
Longmont, Colorado, 1976

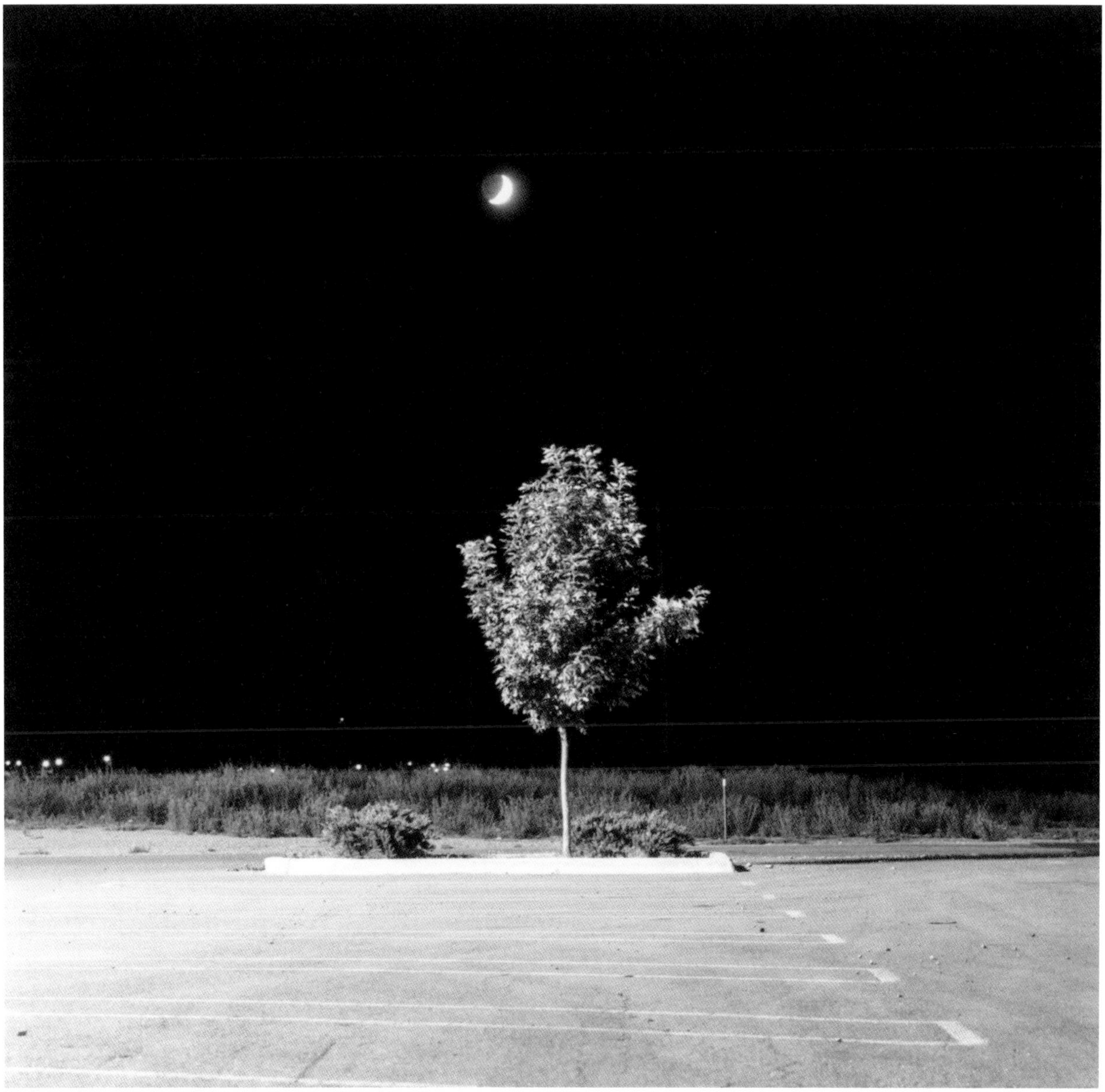

Robert Adams
Fort Collins, Colorado, 1976

'The spectacle of the tragic death of something nobler than ourselves is the sublime shock which can inaugurate radical transformation. In this epoch, a tree standing self-consciously alone in the city would, better than any other monument or form of propaganda, evoke the environmental tragedy which implicates our economy, our culture of cities, and our social order.'

— Jeff Wall

ROBERT ADAMS

pp. 140–43

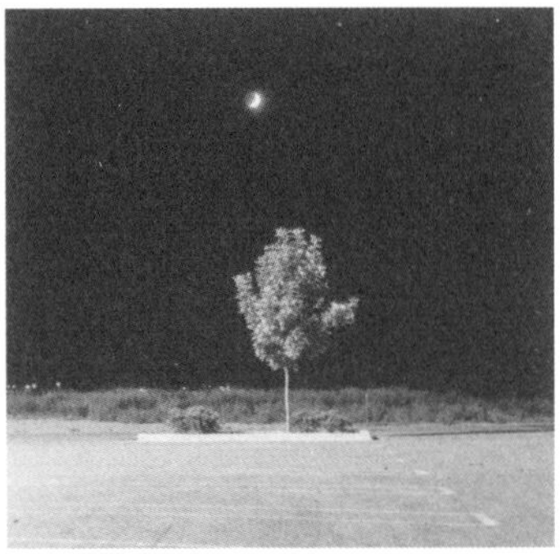

Fort Collins, Colorado, 1976

For Robert Adams, becoming a photographer was wrapped up in an 'intense emotional response to the landscape, and caring about it, and worrying about it'. For the past 50 years, he has been making small-scale, black-and-white photographs of the American West that capture the beauty and grandeur of the landscape and look squarely at our impact on it. Trees – in urban areas, in forests, on agricultural land – have been one of his most enduring subjects. During the 1970s and 80s, Adams photographed the rapid expansion of cities in central Colorado, a state where he had spent much of his childhood. *Fort Collins, Colorado* (1976), *Longmont, Colorado* (1976) and *Above Boulder, Colorado* (c.1979) all depict lone trees that seem out of place in their newly suburban settings – marooned in nocturnal parking lots, or stranded in crisp front yards. In the 1990s, Adams turned his attention to the wide-scale industrial forestry that was taking place across much of the northwestern United States, decimating ancient woodland. 'The West is gone', Adams has said. 'What did we do with it? What have we traded for this great forest? What did we get in exchange?'.

EIJA-LIISA AHTILA

pp. 74–75

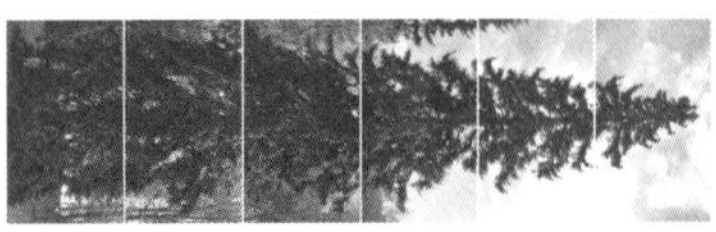

Horizontal - Vaakasuora, 2011

Eija-Liisa Ahtila creates large-scale cinematic installations that often address the relationship between humans and the natural world. With *Horizontal – Vaakasuora* (2011), Ahtila attempts to make a full-scale 'portrait' of a spruce tree. The 30-metre-tall tree – with its branches moving in the wind – was filmed in six separate sections, then assembled horizontally as a single moving image in order to present the spruce as close as possible to its actual size within the confines of a human-built space. The horizontal format references both the wide-screen aspect ratio of the cinematic image and the tradition of landscape painting, drawing attention to the ways in which we look at the world around us. A soundtrack of wind, forest noises and birds chirping immerses the viewer, and yet, with each billowing section of tree slightly out of time with the next, the striking dissonance of this image reminds us of the artifice of an anthropocentric worldview. Ahtila was inspired by the theoretical biologist Jakob von Uexküll's concept of *umwelt*, which describes how all living organisms inhabit separate but simultaneous worlds, different times and spaces, presenting the human perspective as only one of many possibilities.

YTO BARRADA

pp. 138–39

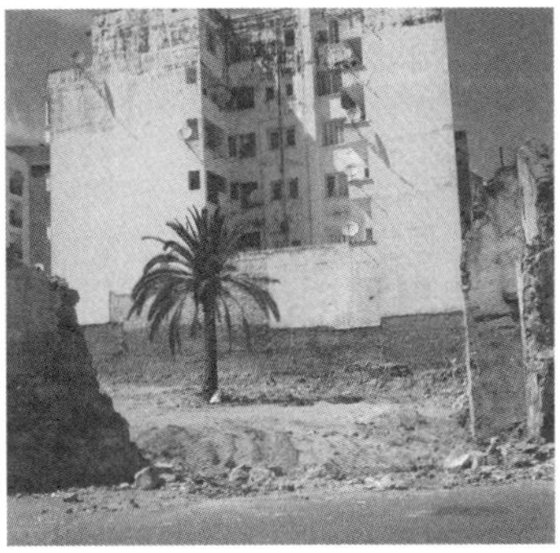

Terrain Vague No. 2 (Vacant Lot No. 2), 2009

Imbued with playfulness and wit, Yto Barrada's practice underlines landscape's entanglement with politics and economics. Over the past decade, Barrada has made a substantial series of cut-out metal sculptures of street signs in the shape of palm trees. Her sculpture *Palm Sign* (2010), a battered metal palm tree adorned with half-blown coloured light bulbs and scratched paint, conjures the down-at-heel modernity of Tangier whilst alluding to Morocco's historical use of imported palm trees to fulfil the exotic expectations of tourists. Barrada's square colour photographs *Terrain Vague – Tanger (Vacant Lot – Tangier)* (2001) and *Terrain Vague No. 2 (Vacant Lot No. 2)* (2009) belong to a series cataloguing vacant lots in Tangier. In both images, a solitary palm tree tenaciously occupies this undetermined urban space, against a background of rectilinear modern apartment buildings. Evidence of former dwellings presumably bulldozed by developers, these lone palms bear witness to the changing face of the city and hint at the off-screen political contests driving this transformation. More explicitly, Barrada's film *Beau Geste* (2009) begins with a voice-over elaborating on this situation: 'A patchwork of vacant lots ring the city, each one is the stage for a power struggle between the shareholders and the space, the city, the developers and the local people, plants and animals. Sometimes a single palm tree bears evidence of the house and walled garden that stood there.' Barrada's photographs depict the scale of this power struggle. From human to plant to animal, these unattended spaces become sites of opportunity, rich transitional zones in which suppressed interests can be realised.

JOHANNA CALLE

pp. 116–17

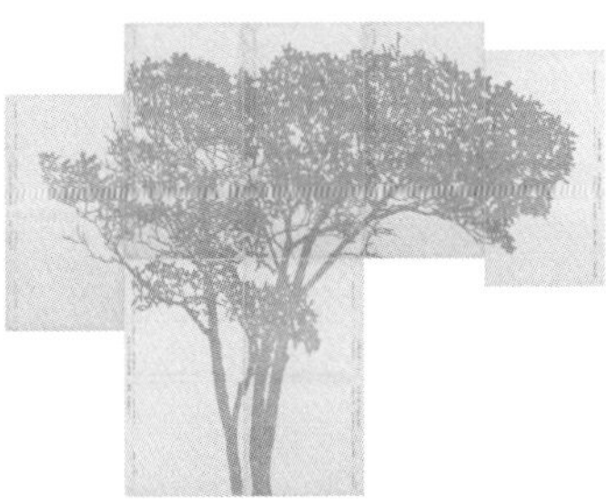

Perímetros (Nogal Andino), 2012

While the subjects that Johanna Calle tackles are often deeply emotive – among them land rights and the violent state of Colombian politics – the materials and processes that she works with are, in her words, deliberately 'austere'. The artist refers to *Perímetros (Nogal Andino)* (2012) as 'a drawing done with a typewriter'. In this work, the silhouette of an Andean walnut – a type of tree that grows on the high planes of Colombia – has been formed from dense typewritten text taken from Colombia's Law of Land Restitution (2011), a law that recognises the rights of people displaced by armed conflict. Calle has typed the text onto blank pages taken from an antique notary book that once recorded changes in land ownership. Like much of Calle's work, this drawing questions the power and authority of the written word over oral traditions. The silhouette of the Andean walnut refers to the historic practice of planting trees to delineate areas of land.

GILLIAN CARNEGIE

pp. 99–101

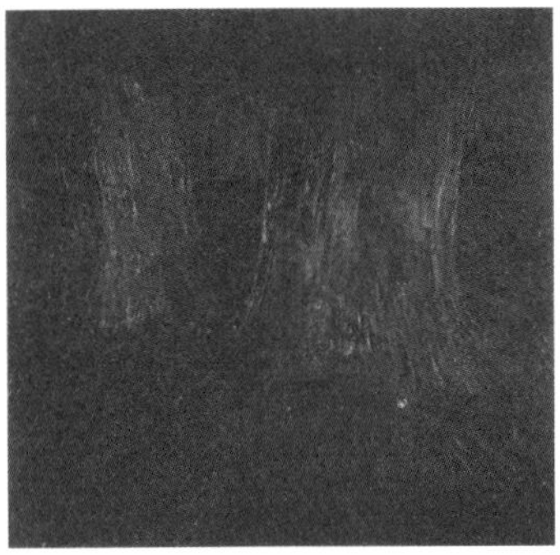

Black Square, 2003

Gillian Carnegie pushes the boundaries of traditional figurative painting, notably whilst depicting what could be viewed as mundane landscape and still life motifs. She often returns to the same subjects repeatedly, basing her paintings on photographs she takes. Part of a series of monochrome landscapes begun in 2000, Carnegie's *Black Square* (2003) features textured paint both matt and glossy, only fully revealing the image under particular lighting conditions or in relation to the viewing angle. In this way, the artist responds to the challenge of depicting a night scene by emphasising the materiality of oil paint. The thick impasto allows *Black Square* (a title borrowed from Kazimir Malevich's landmark Suprematist abstraction) to be seen as an object, rather than purely an image, and the use of a single colour accentuates the fact that the image has literally been sculpted. In *Green and Silver* (2005) and *Section* (2015), the artist paints the tree as a subject in varying degrees of abstraction, often against a sombre background of concrete or subdued tones.

For Carnegie, the exercise is both to paint an image of a tree, and to manipulate the paint to become an image itself. She thus questions the historical dichotomy between matter and image, between abstraction and representation, underlining the constructed character of all images.

TACITA DEAN

pp. 102–03

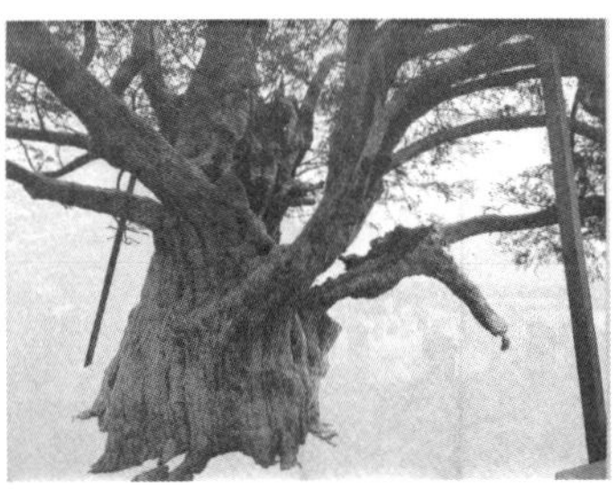

Crowhurst II, 2007

This monumental photograph is one that the artist took of the 'Crowhurst yew', which – at over 4,000 years old – is one of the oldest living trees in the UK. Dean has painted around the branches of the yew with white gouache, so that everything but the aged tree and its crutch-like supports is obscured. *Crowhurst II* (2007) is one of a series of 'painted trees' that the artist began in 2005. Like much of Dean's work, this series – which includes postcard- as well as near-life-size depictions of trees – was informed by chance and coincidence. Prompted by her discovery of a collection of postcards of France's forest of Fontainebleau while travelling in Japan, Dean began researching the oldest living trees in the UK. One, an 800-year-old oak, stood not far from her childhood home in Kent. Another, the yew pictured here, shared its name with Donald Crowhurst, an ill-fated amateur sailor who entered a round-the-world yacht race in 1968, never to return. Crowhurst is the subject of a number of Dean's earlier works, including *Disappearance at Sea* (1996) and *Teignmouth Electron* (2000).

PETER DOIG

pp. 50–51

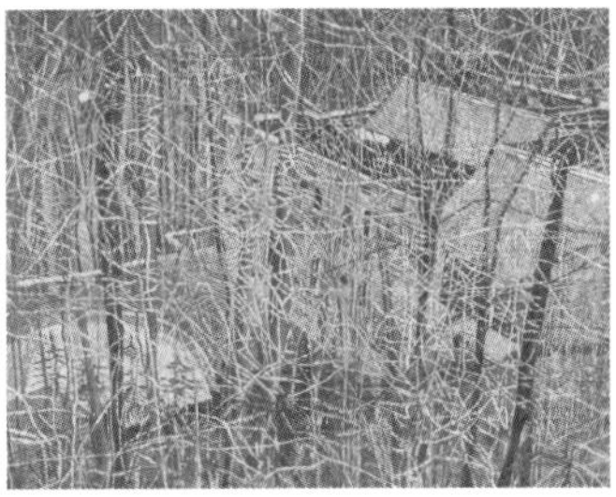

The Architect's Home in the Ravine, 1991

While trees populate many of his landscapes, Peter Doig intended *The Architect's Home in the Ravine* (1991) to be about 'the act of looking through'; through trees, branches, snow, into the painting. To view its subject – the modernist house of architect Eberhard Zeidler in Toronto (Canada) – people must peer through a curtain of trees veiled in a mesh of frosted twigs. The buildings, walled garden and pond that emerge from behind this privacy screen are conjured from patches of colour, glimmers of human habitation applied after the trees were painted. Doig based the painting on his own black-and-white photograph of the house, together with what he calls 'abstractions of memories' of both this and another modernist building glimpsed through impene-trable woodland. The second building – one of Le Corbusier's utopian Unité d'Habitation housing blocks, situated in Briey-en-Forêt (France) – became the subject of Doig's subsequent *Concrete Cabin* paintings (1992–96). His initial encounter with this derelict structure was unnerving: 'I can remember the terror of the pitch black, with the densest trees around. When you do finally see the light of a house it's incredibly welcoming.' Doig transplants the brilliantly coloured panels of Le Corbusier's building into his vision of Zeidler's house. The large size of the painting is 'about the idea of getting absorbed, so you physically get lost.'

JIMMIE DURHAM

p. 83

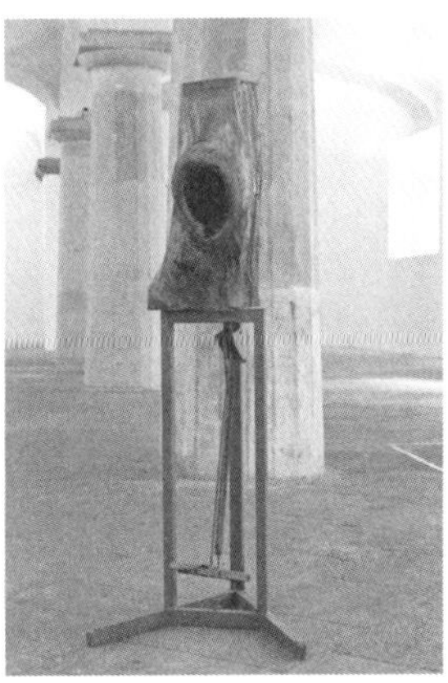

It should work, 2012

Jimmie Durham's art is serious and political, humorous and humane. A poet, performer, essayist and visual artist, he is an 'interventionist' and gatherer of stray objects. Wood, in its various forms – sticks, branches, logs, construction lumber and entire tree trunks – has been a collaborator in his sculptural assemblages and installations throughout his working life. In 1994, on relocating to Europe from North America, one of his first actions was to find a pole, cut from a sapling tree, and use it to mark the centre of the world (in Brussels). During a visit to São Paulo in 2010, Durham discovered a massive block of rosewood in a flea market – a rare relic of Brazil's destroyed hardwood forests, it was 'like finding a giant diamond' and inspired him to work with ancient, salvaged wood. Each piece was given a text and would 'try to talk [...] not about its history or predicament, but about something unexpected.' In Italy, Durham was given two large dead olive trees. The partially carved section of trunk in *It should work* (2012) is from one of these. Mounted on an inoperable piece of old industrial machinery, a pedestal with a pedal, its knothole mouth appears to scream. Or perhaps it is shouting an ambiguous message.

KIRSTEN EVERBERG

pp. 66–67

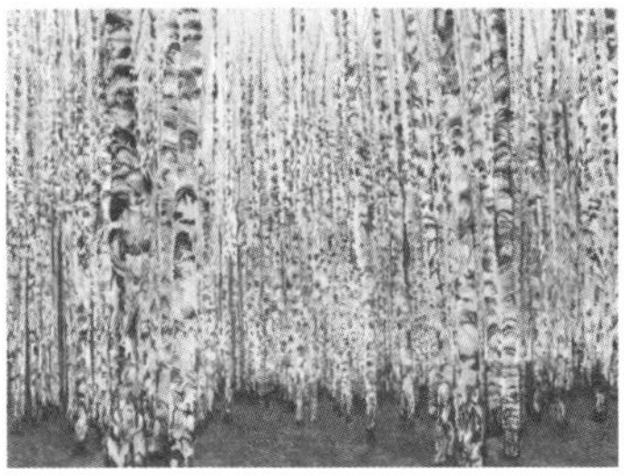

White Birch Grove, South (After Tarkovsky), 2008

Kirsten Everberg makes paintings of both plush interior settings and landscapes that explore space as image. Often portraying dense woodland settings from films, her landscapes question how we construct time through visual language, and how cinema frames places in relation to narrative and memory. Everberg's 2008 painting *White Birch Grove, South (After Tarkovsky)* was made in response to the Russian filmmaker Andrei Tarkovsky's first feature film, *Ivan's Childhood* (1962), a lyrical and fragmentary exploration of the human cost of war. Rather than working from production stills, Everberg projected the black-and-white film onto the panel surface, further mediating the image of the original landscape. An impenetrable grove of birch trees in bluish whites and grays populates the entire image, repeated in such a way that belies the viewer's sense of perspective, creating a kind of *mise en abyme*. The artist's combination of oil and enamel paint exaggerates this tension between surface and background, the photographic and the painterly. Viewed from a distance, the large-scale work hangs almost as a life-size window in the gallery; up close, the trees dissolve into glossy pools of abstraction.

ANYA GALLACCIO

p. 89

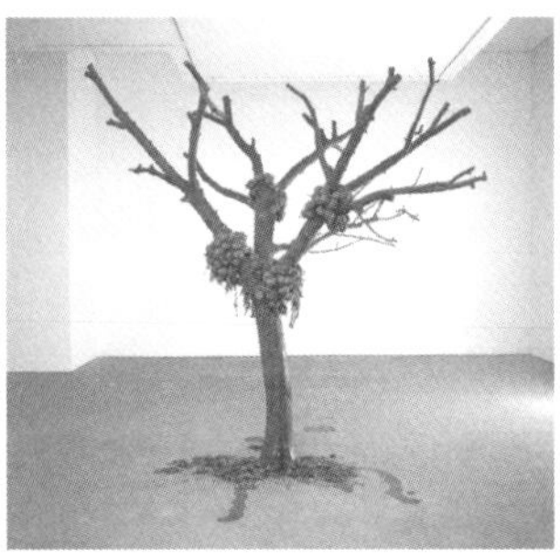

because I could not stop, 2002

Anya Gallaccio describes herself as a pragmatist rather than a romantic. A self-confessed 'city-girl', she nonetheless conceives of the natural world as a farmer might – never losing sight of the relationship of plants and trees to industry and economics. 'We think of forests as a wilderness, as sublime places', she comments, 'we don't think of going for a walk in a tree factory'. For *because I could not stop* (2002), the artist made a bronze cast of a living but condemned apple tree. 'The apple is a fruit that needs human intervention (pruning, grafting and so on) to perform at its best', explains Gallaccio. Apple trees are of interest to her partly because of the way they function as sculptural objects, already 'constructed', 'designed' and 'sculpted' by the labour of the gardener. Strung across the bronze boughs of this tree are swags of ceramic apples, a fruit laden with conflicting cultural associations – from health and wellbeing to original sin. In an early version of this work, the apples were real, and would rot and fall over the course of the exhibition. The scorched floor that this version sits on adds to a sense of ill-defined unease – a reminder, perhaps, of the vulnerability, and combustibility, of wood.

SIMRYN GILL

pp. 124–25

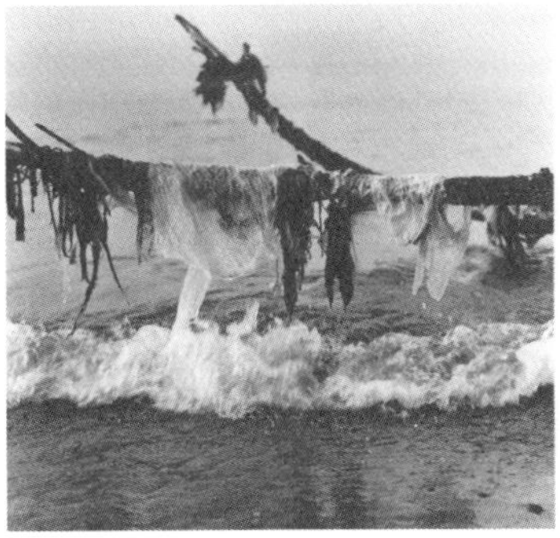

Simryn Gill
Channel #1, 2014

Simryn Gill's practice is a growing collection of record-keeping works responding to the places where she lives. Gill grew up in Port Dickson, a town on the Malaysian coast of the Straits of Malacca, one of the busiest shipping lanes in the world. Mangroves used to thrive along the shoreline in this part of the tropics, growing in symbiosis with the ocean's tide and its saline sediments. Since 1993, Gill has been documenting the landscape, objects and buildings in and around Port Dickson, using different media from installations to photographs. The 29 near-square-format photographs from her *Channel* series record migratory beach debris tangled into the branches of remnants of the region's once iconic mangrove forests. Large ships approaching the industrial port town can be distinguished in the background of some of these images. Through this series, Gill looks at a small stand of mangrove trees, which have become repositories of the waste thrown into the sea: plastic, clothing and fishing paraphernalia.

RODNEY GRAHAM

pp. 72–73

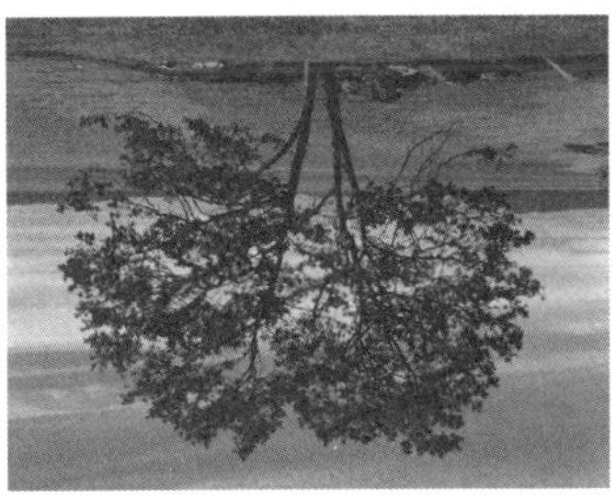

Gary Oak, Galiano Island, 2012

In 1979, Canadian artist Rodney Graham constructed a walk-in camera obscura opposite a standalone tree on his uncle's ranch. When visitors entered the structure, they saw a ghostly, inverted image of the tree on the far wall. Ten years later, Graham made his first 'inverted tree' photograph. He has continued to take them in different places across the world since. *Gary Oak, Galiano Island* (2012) was taken in British Columbia, Canada, where the artist lives. 'I was interested in the image of the inverted tree from a symbolic perspective, and from an empirical one', Graham comments; '– upside down is the way we actually "see" things before the brain intervenes, and the way things appear on the ground glass on the back of the field camera.' With this series, which was partly inspired by Robert Smithson's *Upside Down Trees* photographs, Graham deliberately subverts familiar landscape traditions in art by – almost literally – turning them on their head. The photographs in this series also function as a kind of portraiture, and are intentionally unsettling. 'It's always disturbing to look at something upside down', the artist notes.

SHI GUOWEI

pp. 58–61

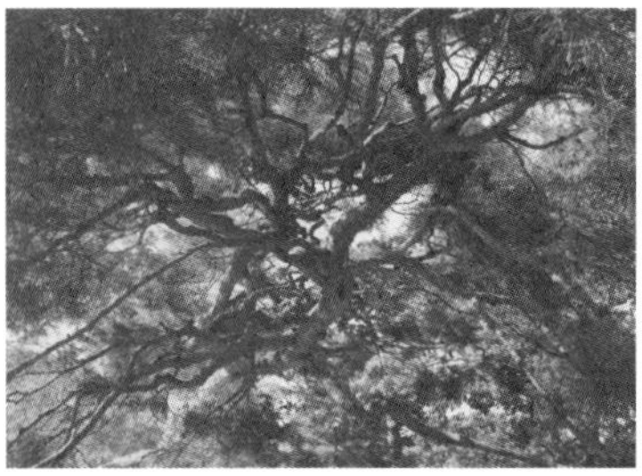

Pine, 2016

To create his works, Shi Guowei borrows a hundred-year-old technique of manually pigment-toning black-and-white photographs. The result sits in the frontier between photography and painting, and remarkably conveys nature's most subtle atmospheric qualities. Guowei's work presents specific components of a landscape from wide-angle perspectives. He photographs a scene from different angles and merges them into one cohesive image of a meadow, rock, forest or solitary tree. After chemically developing the print, he carefully paints onto the photographic paper using water-based ink. The artist is not concerned with depicting a purely descriptive representation of the natural world and instead relies on his own memory to colour his 'photo-paintings'. In *Pine* (2016) and *Kyoto* (2019) foliage and branches fill the entire frame, destabilising the viewer's sense of depth and preventing the establishment of a single vantage point. This strange perspective creates a surreal image, suffused with nostalgia and reminiscent of the sublime. The works resonate with traditional Chinese landscape painting where the natural is almost mystical, deployed to illustrate inner worlds and abstract emotions.

HUGH HAYDEN

pp. 84–85

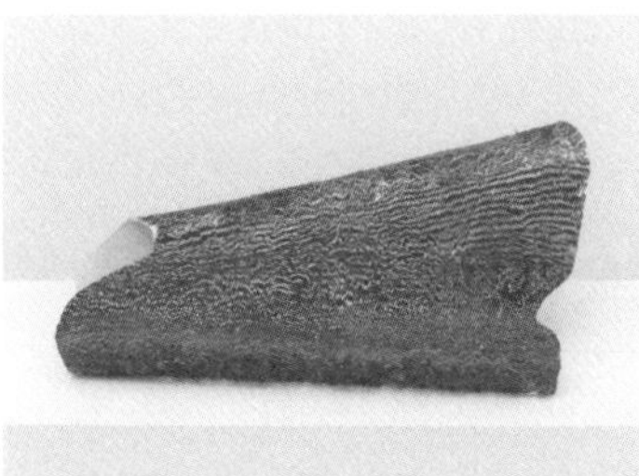

Zelig 3 / Untitled (trunk), 2014

Hugh Hayden's *trompe l'oeil* sculpture of a mossy log takes its name from Woody Allen's 1983 film in which Allen's character suffers from 'chameleon disorder', unconsciously mirroring the traits and appearances of those around him. The log gives itself away with its thin canvas skin visible around its hollow core. Its bark has in fact been painstakingly reconstructed by the artist using adolescent peacock feathers sourced from deceased pet birds purchased online. Hayden has worked extensively with trees as both material and subject matter – using Christmas fir trees salvaged on Park Avenue, New York, and the persevering mesquite trees, native to the southwestern US and Mexico, but widely considered by Texans as an undesirable invasive species. For Hayden, raised in Texas and trained as an architect, nature is rich with signifiers of aspiration and adaptation, ready to be reconfigured. The unlikely camouflage of a bird – like the peacock – explores the idea of blending into the natural landscape as a metaphor for assimilation into or rejection from greater social ecosystems. As Hayden has said: 'There's this blur between the social and the natural environment. I think of feathers like pixels, in a way.'

EVA JOSPIN

pp. 120–21

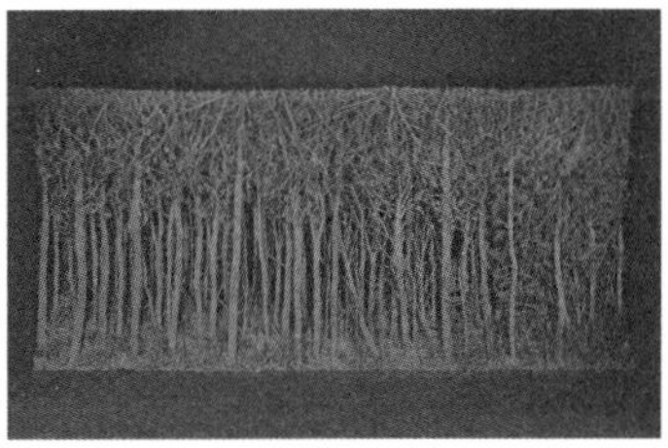

Forêt (Forest), 2013

Eva Jospin turns cardboard back into the forests from which it originates. Having started out as a maker of small-scale collages and sculpture, she began creating monumental installations from sheets of cardboard after moving to a more spacious studio. Her initial impulse was practical; wanting to produce larger-scale work and lacking the means to do so, she made use of the stacks of corrugated cardboard packaging that had accumulated after the move. As a medium for sculpture, cardboard is a difficult, intransigent material to work with; it is fragile, easily damaged and resists precision. Using an array of scalpels, power drills and sanders, Jospin slices through the flat outer boards and the fluted corrugations sandwiched between them, carving out apparently solid trees, engraving fissures, grooves and delicate veins, and hollowing out shadowy voids. In her thickets and tangles of undergrowth, Jospin achieves a mass of textures and an extraordinary illusion of depth. Informed by literature and mythology, Gothic architecture and Renaissance paintings and gardens, her highly detailed forest sculptures represent a sort of magic realism. As Jospin puts it: 'My forest is entirely cerebral. It is not figurative. It reflects human concerns; the idea of losing or finding oneself, our connections with childhood, fairy tales, ancient fears.'

KAZUO KADONAGA

pp. 80–81

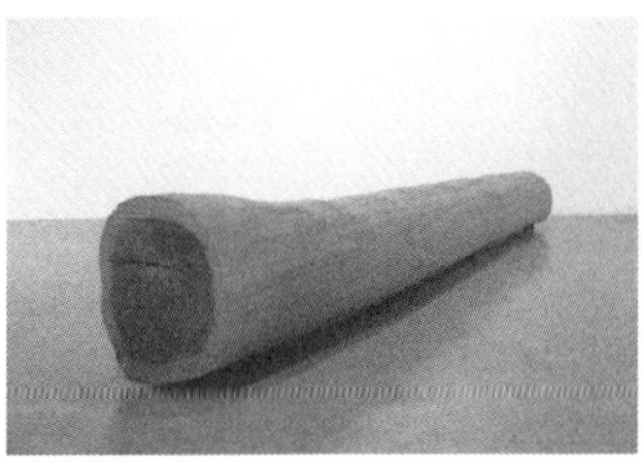

Wood No. 5 CH, 1984

Kazuo Kadonaga's art-making processes developed from a deep connection to both forestry and industrial techniques. His family owned cedar forests and ran a lumber mill in Ishikawa (Japan). In his visits to the forest, Kadonaga selected the trees that would become sculptures. For Kadonaga, wood is both material and subject, continuing a Japanese tradition of revealing the innate essence of the artwork's medium to guide the creation, rather than the western tendency of creating the form from the material. For *Wood No. 5 CH* (1984), the artist stripped the bark from a cedar log and sliced it lengthwise into approximately 800 paper-thin sheets, using the same machine employed to produce the thin wood sheets used in plywood and veneers. The wood slices were then industrially dried and glued back together with precise care, restoring the original log form. The result is a four-metre long intricate sculpture that, over time, continues to perform organic processes: like a living tree, the work is susceptible to its environment, swelling in humidity or shrinking in dryness, and sometimes producing small cracking or splintering sounds.

WILLIAM KENTRIDGE

pp. 118–19

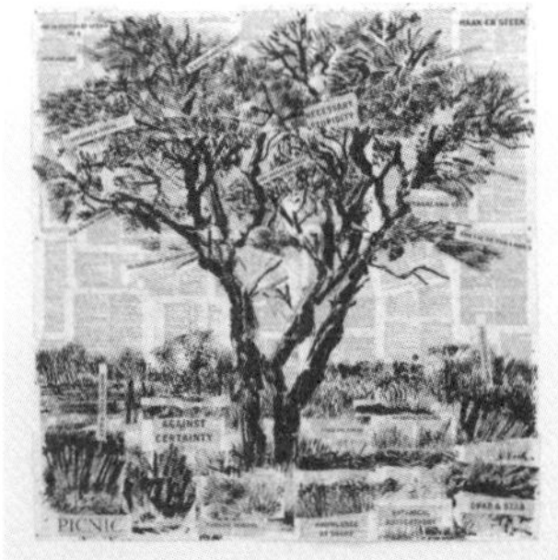

Untitled (Lacking the Courage of the Bonfire), 2019

Trees recur throughout William Kentridge's work as markers of South Africa's political landscape; they exist as containers of histories both colonial and mythical. The tree acts as a stand-in for both knowledge itself – its use as paper for books, its literal branches – and the act of knowing, as a witness to painful memories played out across the terrain. *Untitled (Lacking the Courage of the Bonfire)* was made during the research process for Kentridge's 2019 opera *Waiting for the Sibyl*, performed at the Teatro dell'Opera in Rome. A large tree is painted in calligraphic brushwork onto the pages of old encyclopedias, pieced together as a whole after the drawing has been completed. The tree's burgeoning branches shelter various collaged phrases: 'You will be robbed of speech', 'I know the plots of law enforcers', 'You have been swindled.' Kentridge has used the pages of mass-produced books as material for his drawings of trees for around 20 years, evoking the violence inherent in Western practices of scholarly classification and their corollary notion of universal knowledge. Kentridge's fragments of speech – often taken from conversations overheard in public space – gesture towards a more personal and unknowable history, one shared by trees as symbolic carriers of history within themselves.

TOBA KHEDOORI

pp. 62–65

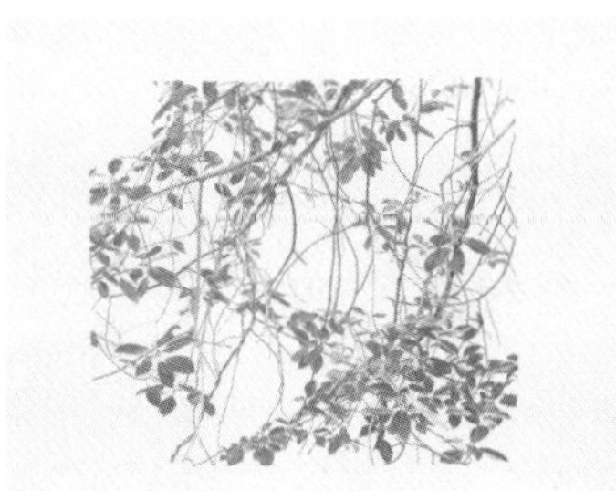

Untitled, 2018

Toba Khedoori is best known for her intricately detailed drawings and paintings on large sheets of waxed paper, in which she isolates objects, architectural elements, natural forms and landscapes against an expanse of white. Executed in oil paint, *Untitled* (2018) depicts a tangled network of branches, tendrils and leaves surrounded by a field of empty space, as if floating in a void. The abstraction that results from the withholding of information and context contrasts with the painstaking realism of the artist's precise rendering, creating an unsettlingly ambiguous image; by omitting a central trunk from her picture, for example, the artist leaves us wondering whether the branches even belong to the same tree. In an untitled drawing in coloured pencil from 2008, a solitary tree – a silhouette of leafless branches – is doubled, as if to indicate the reflexive structure of roots that we know to be the invisible other half of every tree. In this way, Khedoori's composition becomes decentred, uprooted from perspective – inviting a different way of looking at a picture.

LUISA LAMBRI

pp. 52–53

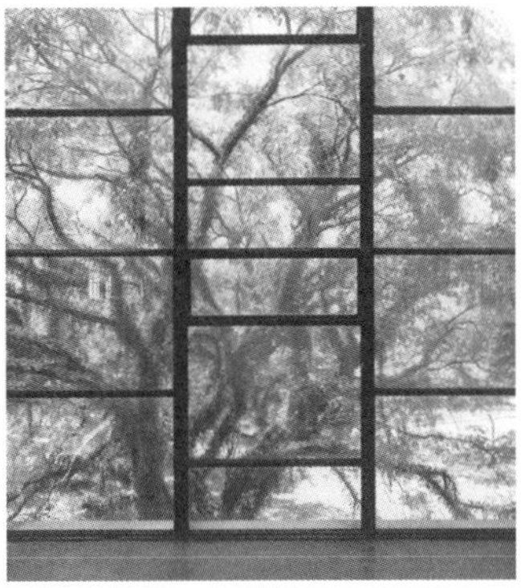

Untitled (Palácio da Indústria, #01), 2003

Luisa Lambri's photographs of architectural interiors question 'the relationship that we have to the world we have constructed around us'. Rather than documenting entire buildings, she turns her gaze on unnoticed details. *Untitled (Palácio da Indústria, #01)* (2003) portrays part of an upper-floor window in the Ciccillo Matarazzo Pavilion, home of the São Paulo Biennial. Designed by Brazilian modernist architect Oscar Niemeyer, the vast building is famous for its curvaceous internal walkways. But Lambri chooses to concentrate on the meandering branches of a tree, viewed through the strict orthogonal grid of the window's glazing bars. The opposing rhythms of nature and artifice echo Niemeyer's dialogue between the building and its surrounding park. The room's austerity, mirrored in shard-like reflections, is softened by thousands of epiphytes: non-parasitic air plants that clothe the tree's branches and filter the light. In her 2007 evocation of American architect John Lautner's Sheats-Goldstein Residence, a space-age house in the Hollywood Hills, Lambri looks upwards, focusing on a skylight canopied by an overhanging eucalyptus tree. Remarking that Lautner's way of working with skylights brings 'outside and inside together at the same time', she says she did nothing more than photograph the light.

MYOUNG HO LEE

pp. 106–07

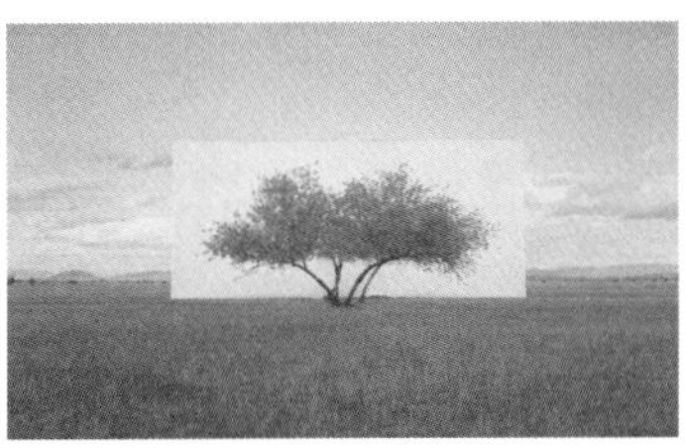

Tree... #2, 2012

South Korean artist Myoung Ho Lee began photographing trees because they are 'something you see every day, but we often overlook them; we forget their value and just pass by'. Since 2004 he has focused attention on individual trees in the landscape by treating them like studio portraits, dissociating them from their immediate context and spotlighting their true shapes and forms. Lee selects his subjects for their personalities and patiently observes them through different seasons and at varying times of day before deciding how to portray them. Then, in a complex performance-like process involving heavy machinery and skilled production crews, he isolates a chosen tree from its background by installing an expanse of white canvas behind it. Though evidence of this elaborate mechanical intervention is removed during retouching, the backdrop retains traces of the hoisting operation. The tree's actual habitat – in this case, the Mongolian steppe – appears as a natural frame around the canvas.

ZOE LEONARD
pp. 136–37

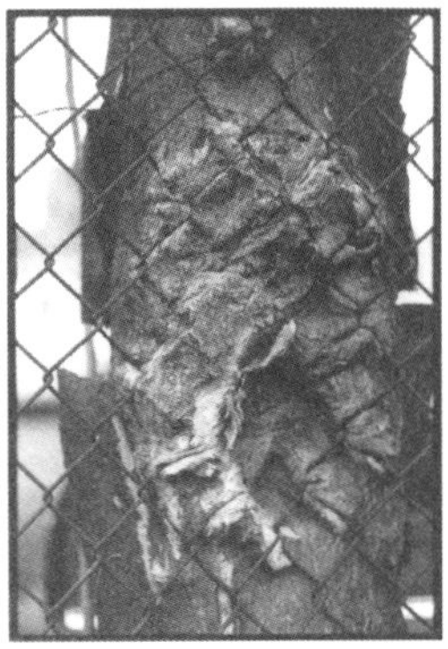

Untitled, 2000

In an untitled series from the 1990s and 2000s, Zoe Leonard portrays New York City trees that have grown enmeshed with the chain-link fences and iron railings surrounding them. These photographs range from black-and-white wide and medium shots to coloured close-ups of different trees across the city. For the artist, these works are really about us – not so much about nature as an entity separate from us, but more about who we are and how we behave in nature. They reflect our bizarre relationship to other living things – this impulse to contain them or use them, but to keep us separate from them, while simultaneously seeking their presence in our cities. Despite these inhospitable conditions, trees survive and even thrive in urban environments – their trunks and roots bursting from sidewalks, making their way through metal enclosures. Leonard's photographs of trees reflect her wider interest in disregarded subjectivities and struggles against various types of social and economic oppression.

ROBERT LONGO
pp. 68–69

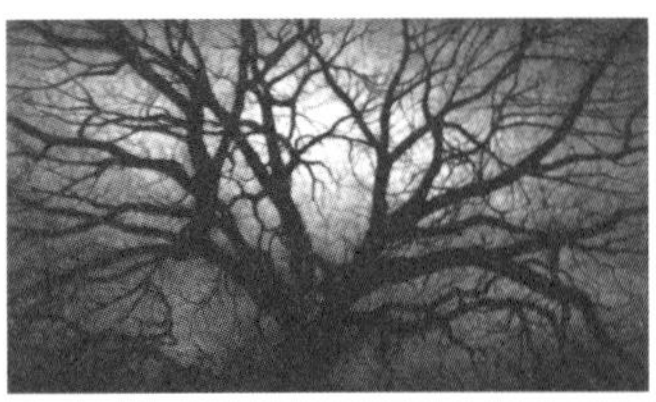

Untitled (Sleepy Hollow), 2014

A decade ago, as part of a cycle of work entitled *The Mysteries*, Robert Longo began making a series of colossal drawings of dark forests shot through with shafts of light or suffused with mist. As with his other epic charcoal drawings, these hauntingly atmospheric images appear at first to be photographs. Close up, the illusion unravels and they fragment into abstractions. Longo, who characterises his art as existing somewhere between representation and abstraction, considers abstract expressionism a vital part of his American heritage. In 2013–14, he translated 12 abstract expressionist paintings, including masterpieces by Lee Krasner, Jackson Pollock and Mark Rothko, into black-and-white drawings. *Untitled (Sleepy Hollow)* (2014), completed shortly afterwards, is both a portrait of a particular tree and a meditation on ramification and fractal growth patterns; the way branches fork and divide. Part of a series collectively named *Axis Mundi* after the cosmic tree symbolising the centre of the world, it derives from photographs he took in a park shortly before suffering a stroke, fused with images of his brain taken during his recovery. Its title alludes to America's first ghost story, Washington Irving's 'The Legend of Sleepy Hollow' (1820), which features a headless horseman and is full of gothic 'twilight superstitions'. In using 'the archaic, primitive medium of charcoal' (a carbonised form of wood), Longo's overarching aim is to 'slow down the way we consume images and the realities they convey.'

SALLY MANN

pp. 134–35

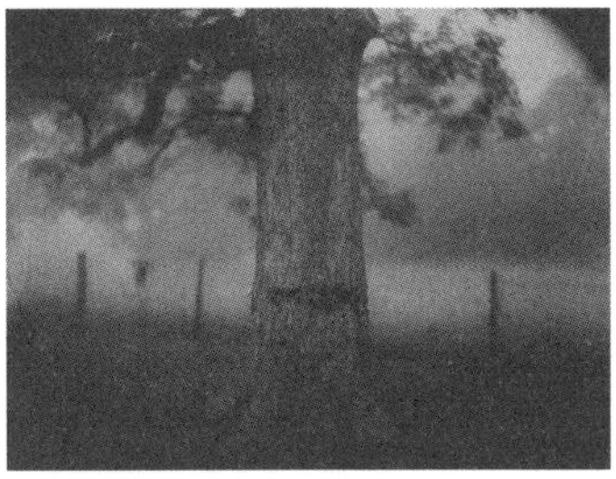

Deep South, Untitled (Scarred Tree), 1998

Since the early 1970s, Sally Mann has made photographs of the land and people around her home in rural Virginia. From 1984 to 1994, she focused on her children until she found that 'the kids seem to be receding into the landscape; I have been ambushed by my backgrounds.' Then, in 1998, she set out to photograph America's Deep South, in Louisiana and Mississippi. Using her car as a mobile darkroom, Mann worked with bulky large-format plate cameras and experimented with the complicated wet-plate collodion process practiced by nineteenth-century photographers. She welcomed accidental flaws – scratches, drips and streaks caused by specks of dust in the emulsion – and chose to use damaged lenses that make the light appear refulgent. Her intensely personal explorations of the romantic southern landscape evoke 'the indelible marks that slavery left on the world surrounding me.' The moss-draped live oaks pictured in *Deep South, Untitled (Fontainebleau)* (1998) once gave shelter to enslaved African Americans on a sugar cane plantation in Louisiana. More obviously unsettling, *Deep South, Untitled (Scarred Tree)* (1998) – coincidentally shot near the site of a Mississippi slave market – portrays a tree with a severed limb that has survived partial strangulation by barbed wire; though healed, the wound seems still to bleed.

STEVE MCQUEEN

pp. 130–31

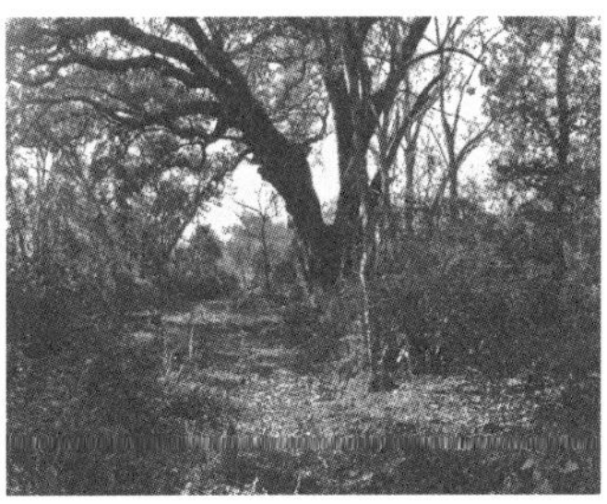

Lynching Tree, 2013

Steve McQueen's colour photograph *Lynching Tree* was taken while the artist and director was filming his Academy Award-winning film *12 Years a Slave* (2013). It depicts a poplar tree on the outskirts of New Orleans, Louisiana, once used as a gallows on which African-American slaves were hanged and then buried beneath it. The tree features in the film during a scene in which two runaway slaves are hanged. Without its title, the image appears banal, almost bucolic – it could be any tree, devoid of historical or localised significance. Whilst no human figures feature in the landscape, *Lynching Tree* becomes an evidence-bearer of the brutal racial violence embedded within this site. McQueen's artwork asks us to look beyond the mundane surface of this scene, and instead to consider the landscape as an archive scarred by terrorism – a living archive of trees and minerals as witnesses. In doing so, it refuses to allow us to forget all the other trees and seemingly innocent places across the southern states of America that also played a part in slavery's bloody legacy.

JEAN-LUC MYLAYNE

pp. 76–77

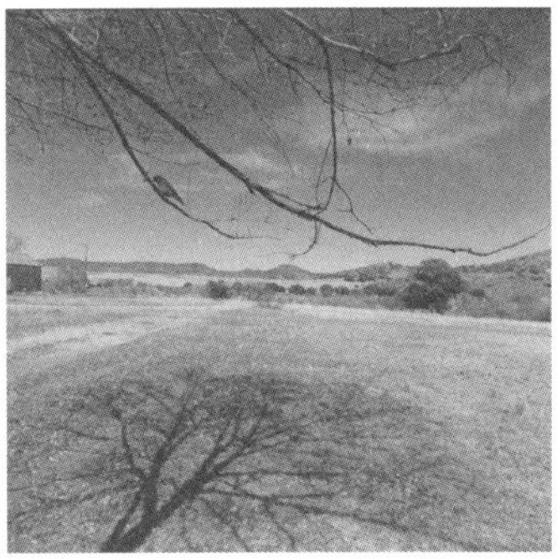

No. 304, Mars Avril 2005, 2005

Jean-Luc Mylayne uses a combination of different lenses, stacked one on top of the other, to create his large-scale, formally surprising photographs. This enables him to achieve multiple points of focus within a single image. One of the effects of this technique is that looking at his work is an active event: your attention is constantly being snagged, and your gaze sent in new directions. Mylayne has been taking photographs of common garden birds since 1976, when both he and his partner Mylène gave up their house and worldly goods to dedicate themselves to the task. As well as technical ingenuity, his photographs are the result of time and patience. Having chosen the exact location of his shot, Mylayne waits for as long as it takes for the desired bird to enter the frame. This might take anything from one to three months – a duration recorded in the title of each image. The settings that Mylayne chooses for his photographs demand as much attention as his feathered subjects. In *No. 284, Février Mars 2004* (2004), the tree and the woodcutting tools in the background are captured in sharp focus, while the bird in the foreground is an exquisite blur. In *No. 304, Mars Avril 2005* (2005), our view of the agricultural landscape beyond is framed – top and bottom – by the sweeping branches of a mostly leafless tree, and its shadow-counterpart.

MARIELE NEUDECKER

pp. 96–97

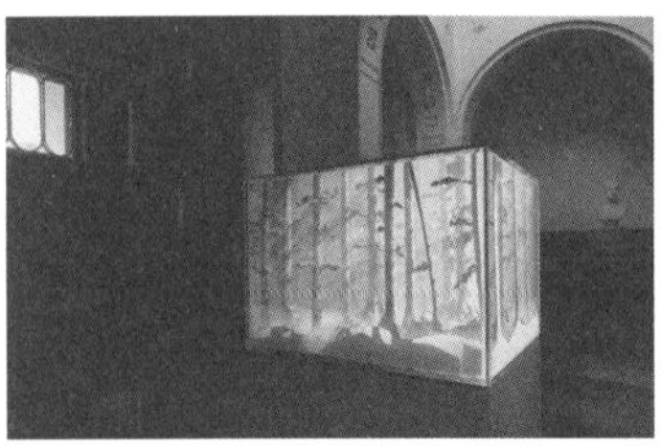

And Then the World Changed Colour: Breathing Yellow, 2019

As part of her investigations into the experience of landscape in art and life, Mariele Neudecker has filled rooms with life-size casts of trees, produced full-scale models of tracts of wild woodland, and included trees, alive and dead, in her films. Forests are a recurrent theme in many of her 'tank works', water-filled vitrines that contain three-dimensional micro worlds devoid of people but possessing a distinct sense of someone having been there before you. The earliest of these, made in the early 1990s, are recreations of nineteenth-century Romantic paintings; visions of the northern European sublime. They imagine what such landscapes would look like if you could see them from all sides, from different angles, under very gradually changing atmospheric conditions. *And Then the World Changed Colour: Breathing Yellow* (2019), Neudecker's most recent tank work, was commissioned to accompany an exhibition of paintings by Harald Sohlberg (1869–1935) at Dulwich Picture Gallery, where it was sited in the mausoleum with its amber-tinted windows. The sculpture takes a detail of pines from one of Sohlberg's landscapes and creates a segment of dense forest saturated with a strange, sulphurous light. Describing this as a space where 'the real and imaginary collide,' Neudecker wanted to evoke 'an immersive experience, as well as a detached one: you are both inside the forest and clearly outside of it; you inhabit the space in your mind and are physically distanced by artifice, glass and refraction'.

VIRGINIA OVERTON

pp. 4, 86–87

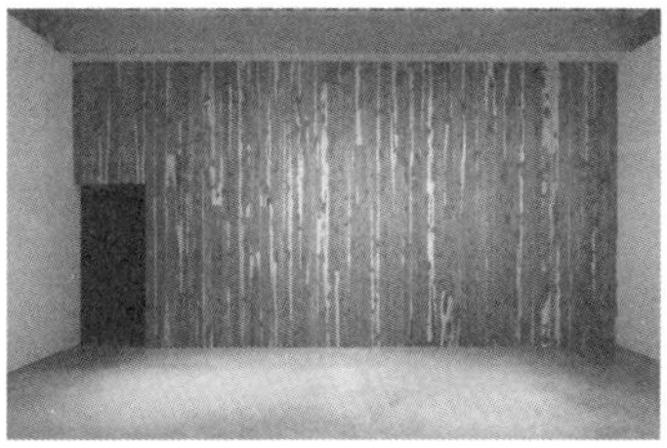

Untitled (Juniperus virginiana), 2016

For Virginia Overton, the qualities of materials are more important than their intended use, or what they might be 'traded or bought for in a hardware store or lumber mill'. For *Untitled (Juniperus virginiana)* (2020), Overton has lined one of the gallery walls with planks of aromatic red cedar sourced from the woods that surround her family's farm in rural Tennessee. The impact of this work is olfactory as well as visual – the planed cedar, sumptuously coloured and full of detail, fills the gallery space with its distinctive scent. For two separate works, both *Untitled* (2014), the artist has paired a plank of the same red cedar, this time with its bark intact, with a 'plank' of marbleised mirror. The patterned surface of the mirror echoes the striated surface of the wood, and vice versa. Although Overton often works with found or salvaged materials, she doesn't consider her sculptures readymades. Much of her work engages with its environment. This is the case for the tree-shaped weathervane *Untitled (Juniper)* (2014), which channels and responds to the force of the wind.

ROXY PAINE

pp. 91–95

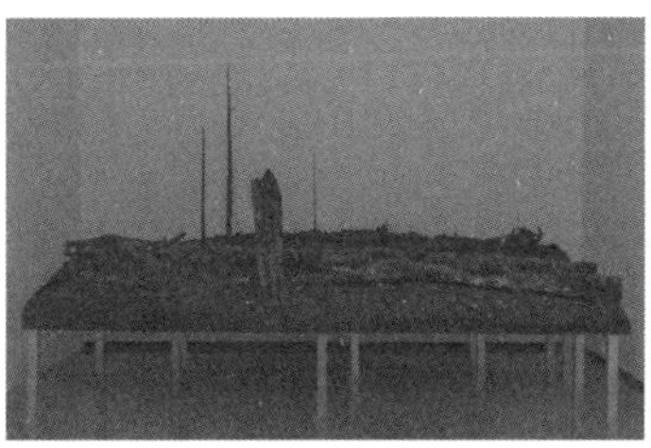

Desolation Row, 2016

In paradoxical acts of displacement, Roxy Paine uses wood to emulate metal and plastic and makes tree-like 'dendroid' sculptures out of stainless steel. Constructed from industrial piping, his dendroids are arboreal imposters that inhabit outdoor spaces alongside actual trees and in smaller versions fit comfortably indoors. Some are fused, coupled together to form arches or, like *Rotoplasm* (2012), are conjoined, the branches of one segueing into those of the other. Paine is 'interested in looking at how a living entity, a creation of nature, can be seen to translate into an industrial entity, a creation of humans'. His work is the continual exploration of how the process of translation, and the attempts to that translation, can never be fully completed or resolved. With *Desolation Row* (2016), a scene of ecological devastation is presented as a compressed vista of burned-down forest. The once majestic trees, now consumed by fire, are painted fibreglass; the fallen timber replicates the charred and blackened surface of torched wood while the glowing, randomised diodes become smouldering embers that might reignite anywhere at any moment. Earth and ash combine in a barren expanse of scorched, undulating forest floor, and skeletal standing trees lead the eye to further eruptions of live fire on the far horizon. Reflecting on this apocalyptic aftermath, Paine asks: 'Is this fire manmade? Is it because of how we have altered the planet? Is it just a natural fire?'

GIUSEPPE PENONE

pp. 78–79

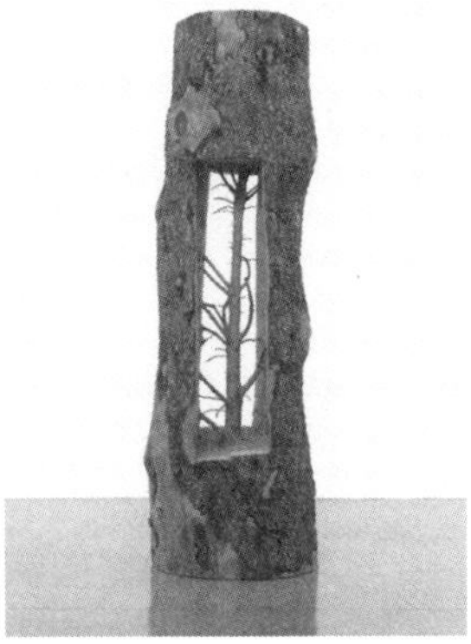

Albero Porta – Cedro (Door Tree – Cedar), 2012

For Giuseppe Penone, trees are 'perfect sculptures'. 'What fascinates me about trees is their structure', he comments, 'the tree is a being that memorialises the feats of its own existence in its very form'. Trees first appeared in Penone's sculptural work in 1968. For *Tree of 12 Metres* (1980–82), the artist has carved two industrially planed pieces of timber in a way that reveals the once-living trees within them. *Albero Porta – Cedro (Door Tree – Cedar)* (2012), carved from a large, untreated trunk, is concerned with time and the process of ageing; visible at the base of the cavity are rings that chart the tree's growth. The same concentric circles or 'growth rings' make up Penone's large-scale wall-drawing *Propagazione* (1995–2019), at the centre of which is the artist's thumbprint. 'If you observe the lines that make up the pattern of your skin, you notice that the surface is similar to the bark of a tree, ripples in water, the veins within a stone', he comments. As well as working with wood, the artist often makes sculptures using bronze, a material that he considers almost 'vegetal'. *Soffio di Foglie* (1982) (in English, 'breath of leaves') features a bronze cast of the shape that his body made in a pile of leaves – now suspended between the trunks of six saplings.

ABEL RODRÍGUEZ

pp. 114–15

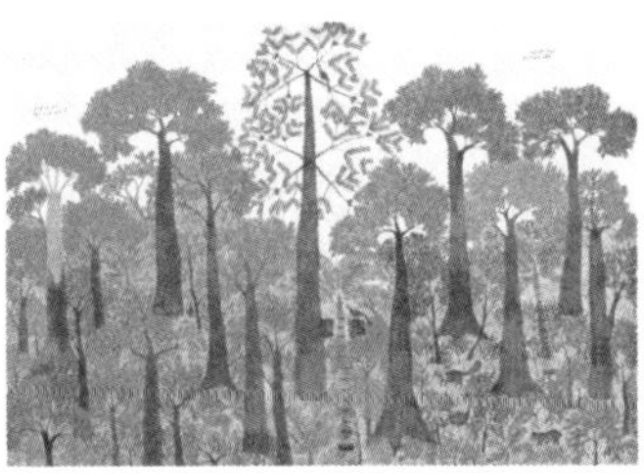

Terraza Alta II, 2018

Abel Rodríguez is a member of the Nonuya, an indigenous group of the Colombian Amazon region. Growing up, Rodríguez benefited from stories and teachings about the rainforest passed down from generation to generation. He learned about plants to such an extent that he is able to identify hundreds of species of tropical forest flora. In 2002, after moving to urban Bogotá, Rodríguez documented his plant knowledge, creating botanical paintings of the Amazon's flora from memory. Deceptively simple, these works convey incredibly precise information about plants' anatomical features, the distribution of branches and leaves, types of bark, flowers and fruits, seasonal changes and even intricate ecological relationships between species. Rodríguez has also been working collaboratively with his son, Wilson Rodríguez, on a series of drawings including *Terraza Baja* (2018). These works not only demonstrate an exceptional understanding of tree architecture, ecological dynamics and the effects of climate change, but also the ability to perceive the world from a non-anthropocentric perspective.

UGO RONDINONE

p. 105

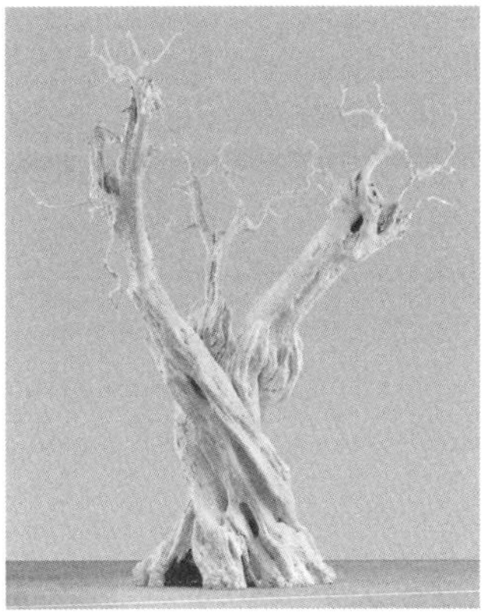

Wind Moon, 2011

Trees have always been a presence and a recurring symbol in Ugo Rondinone's art. They are the subject of the monumental landscape drawings inspired by German Romanticism that he began in 1989 and the material for sculptural installations that followed a few years later. Later still, in 2006, Rondinone became the owner of a grove of ancient olive trees on land in Basilicata in southern Italy, the area his parents and ancestors were from. He selected six of these living trees, all aged between 1,500 and 2,000 years old, and, without harming them in any way, took moulds of them where they stood. These were then cast in aluminium and painted white. Usually exhibited in the open air, often in busy urban contexts, the sculptures' wild gesticulations are both theatrical and comical in their exuberant expressiveness. Their strange forms, the result of centuries of exposure to prevailing winds, are exaggerated by their whiteness and the fact they have lost their leaves and crowns, which Rondinone did not include in the moulds. What interests him is that 'once they are cast bare naked they become a memorial of condensed time […] Time can be experienced as a lived abstraction, where the shape is formed by this accumulation of time and wind force.'

GEORGE SHAW

pp. 126–29

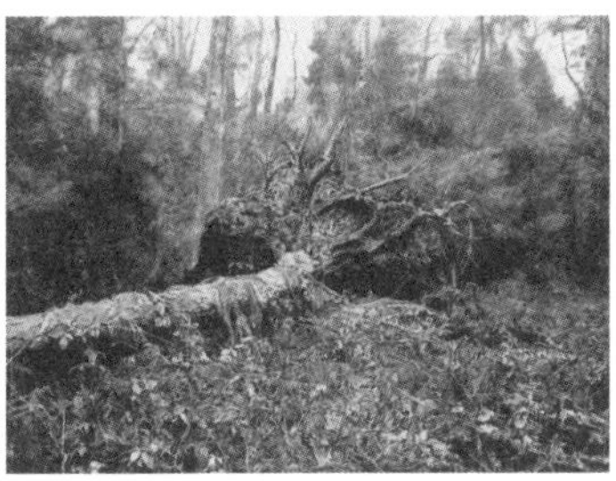

Woodsman 5, 2009

George Shaw grew up on a post-war council estate on the edge of Coventry (UK). Tile Hill estate and the woods that lie just beyond it have been the main subjects of Shaw's paintings for the past 20 years. Speaking of the relationship between the estate and the woods, Shaw states: 'I don't think it's ever left me, that sense of possibility and familiarity and possible danger lurking out there somewhere beyond.' Shaw made *Heart of the Wood* (2015–16) during a two-and-a-half-year residency at the National Gallery, London. During that time, he became fascinated by the woodland setting of many of the paintings in the collection. In Shaw's unpeopled, enigmatic painting we can see traces of modern-day bacchanalia. *Woodsman 5* (2009) is one of six monumental drawings of fallen trees that the artist made shortly after the death of his father; the series takes its name from a local pub that had recently been demolished.

ROBERT SMITHSON

p. 71

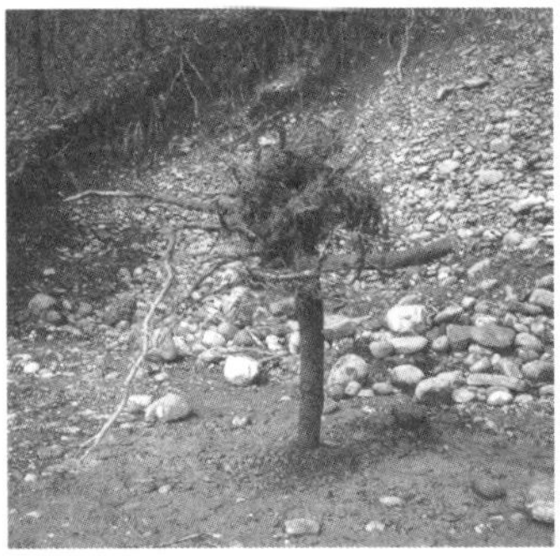

Upside Down Tree I, 1969

Robert Smithson is best known for his 'earthworks' – interventions in the natural landscape that were often large in scale, such as *Spiral Jetty* (1970) at Great Salt Lake, Utah. In 1969 Smithson made and photographed a series of three *Upside Down Trees* as he travelled from New York to the Yucatan peninsula (Mexico) via Florida. On this trip Smithson also produced his *Yucatan Mirror Displacements (1–9)* series, where he placed and photographed multiple square mirrors in the landscape; in the *Upside Down Trees*, the artist's 'planting' of uprooted trees represents a more violent form of reversal. The macabre spectacle of the zombie-like inverted tree, parading a tangled mass of dead roots in place of branches, makes explicit the often parasitic relationship of art and culture to the natural world. In his essay 'Incidents of Mirror Travel in the Yucatan' (1969), Smithson suggests that the upside-down trees could also be seen as 'totems of rootlessness'.

JENNIFER STEINKAMP

pp. 108–11

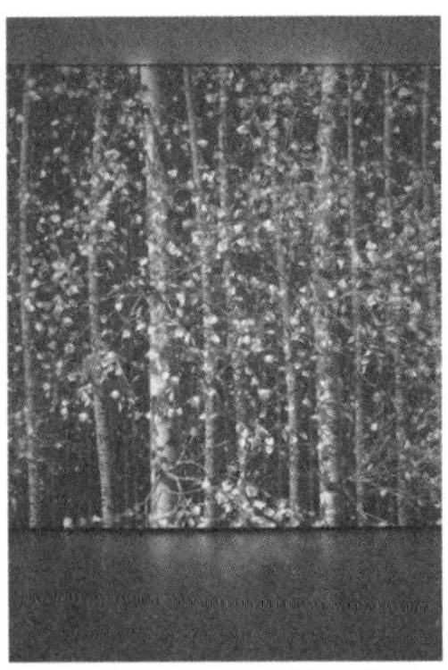

Blind Eye, 1, 2018

In a number of immersive video installations made over the past two decades, Jennifer Steinkamp has made use of three-dimensional animation to portray organic subjects such as trees and flowers. Steinkamp's projections interact with architecture to blend illusionary landscape with physical space, and typically extend from floor to ceiling. *Eye Catching* (2003), first shown at the 2003 Istanbul Biennial, saw three computer-animated serpentine trees projected onto the walls and reflected in the water of the Yerebatan Cistern in response to the ancient Medusa sculptures housed in the sixth-century building. In her cinemascope-proportioned animated video, *Blind Eye, 1* (2018), Steinkamp presents a life-size grove of birch trees that sway and billow as if blown by wind. With the removal of the horizon line, the densely packed, computer-generated forest appears to exist in a state between hyperrealism and a more hand-drawn quality up close. The trees' leaves grow, colour and fall, collapsing the changing of the seasons into a three-minute loop which seamlessly repeats. The artist was struck by how the knot scars left on the trunk after branches have fallen can appear like singular eyes, referencing a kind of monocular vision.

THOMAS STRUTH

pp. 54–57

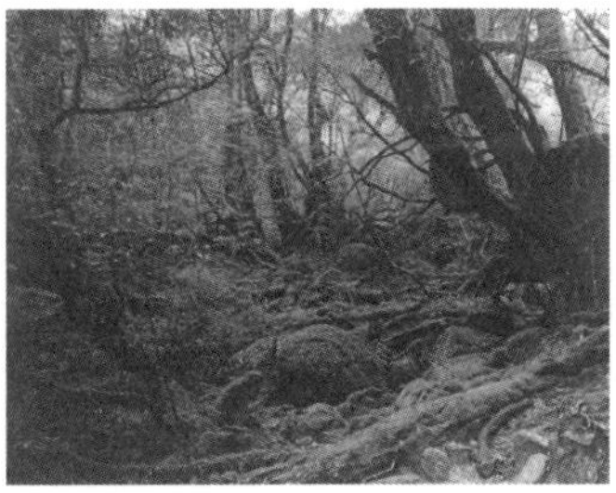

Paradise 13, Yakushima, Japan 1999, 1999

For his series *New Pictures from Paradise* (1998–2007), Thomas Struth took photographs in forests and jungles around the world – from Australia and Japan to China and the United States. 'I wanted to make pictures which were very full', Struth explains, 'and the forest seemed the ideal subject-matter.' All of the photographs in this series share the same decentralised composition. There is no single focus point, and no clearly defined foreground or background. Instead, our eyes are encouraged to roam across the image – taking in and getting lost in the wealth of detail. 'One can spend a lot of time in front of these pictures and remain helpless in terms of knowing how to deal with them,' Struth has said. For him, this is precisely the point. He hopes that, in front of these photographs, you might let go of your 'usual faculties and analytical tools' and 'surrender to just looking'.

RACHEL SUSSMAN

pp. 23, 122–23

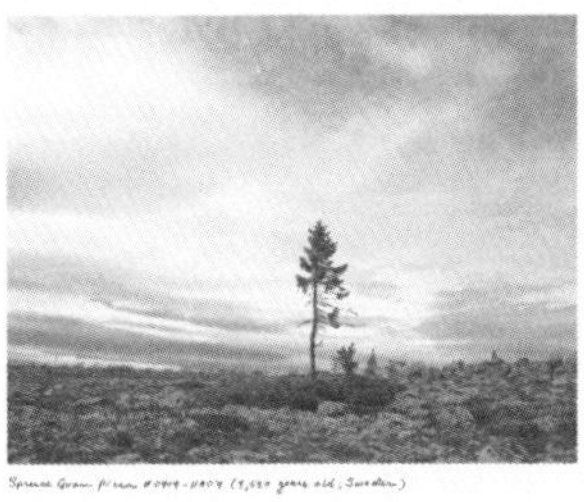

Spruce Gran Picea #0909-11A07 (9,550 years old; Sweden), 2009

Rachel Sussman spent a decade collaborating with scientists to find and photograph the oldest continuously living forms on earth. Travelling to every continent, she searched for ancient organisms clocking in at a minimum age of 2,000 years. The resulting series, *The Oldest Living Things in the World*, includes over 125 large-scale colour photographs. Trees are Sussman's most prevalent subjects, including Jomon Sugi, a supposedly 7,000-year-old tree on the island of Yakushima (Japan). In a nod to scientific field notes, the artist uses handwriting to label each photograph, carefully inscribing the name of the species represented, a catalogue number, its estimated age and location. A meditation on deep time and long-term thinking, Sussman's project alludes to the subjective nature of time while exposing the precarious circumstances that all life forms endure in the face of the climate crisis. Some specimens – notably Old Tjikko, a 9,550-year-old Norway spruce in Dalarna (Sweden) – are living archives of our warming climate, exhibiting unusual new growth habits as temperatures rise. Others have evolved over thousands of years to survive and ultimately thrive in incredibly inhospitable environments, but their longevity is now threatened by human civilisation. Throughout sub-Saharan Africa, vast underground forests have developed in response to a fire-prone landscape by growing beneath the soil and yet, despite their remarkable resilience and ability to adapt, many are routinely destroyed by roadwork or agriculture.

PASCALE MARTHINE TAYOU

p. 112

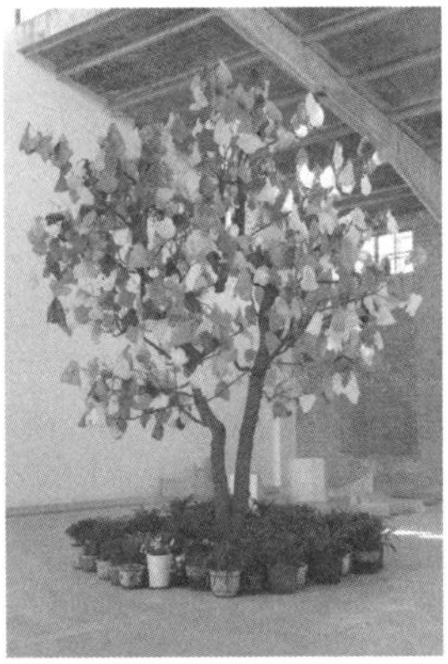

Plastic Tree B, 2010

Pascale Marthine Tayou's sculptures and installations often juxtapose low-cost or disposable materials, traditional relics and organic elements. Trees have been a recurring motif in his work since the early 2000s; these sculptures often bear traces of human presence, including consumer debris as well as references to histories and myths. Tayou's *The Mikado Tree* (2010), a large aluminium and concrete tree trunk covered with multicoloured foliage made from tangled wooden sticks, hints at the history of the 'Pick up Sticks' game ('Mikado' in French), believed to have originated from China in the fifth century AD and subsequently spread through Asia, Europe, and ultimately America. The sculpture playfully comments on the cross-pollination of cultures and civilizations, and how nature fuses with the artificial in contemporary life. Part of his varied series of *Plastic Tree* sculptures, *Plastic Tree B* (2020) presents a dead tree festooned with brightly coloured plastic bags that evoke a kind of droopy, kitsch leafage. Transforming its negligible and everyday materials so that they appear scintillant and aestheticised, Tayou's sculpture ambivalently evokes the seductive appeal of consumer culture whilst simultaneously alluding to its destructive impact on the natural environment.

JEFF WALL

pp. 132–33

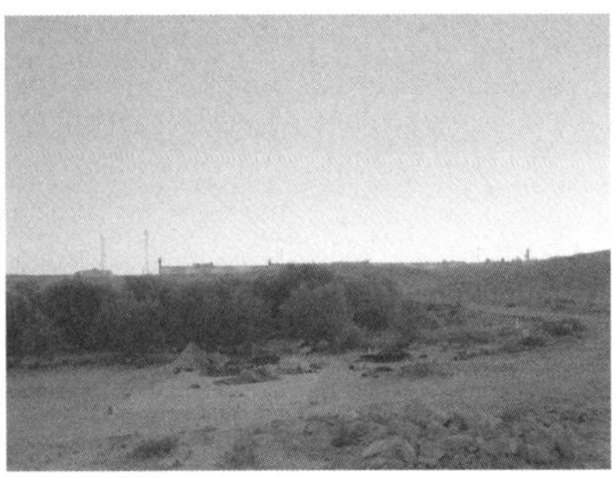

Daybreak
(on an olive farm/Negev/Desert/Israel),
2011

Daybreak (on an olive farm/Negev Desert/Israel) (2011) depicts Bedouin workers asleep next to the olive grove that they work in by day. The building behind them is one of Israel's largest prisons. Jeff Wall first encountered this scene – or one just like it – during a trip to Israel in 2010, returning at harvest time the following year to photograph it. One of the things that interested Wall about this scene was what it said about freedom – while the workers are free to sleep under the open sky, thousands of people are incarcerated just half a mile away. As with other images by Wall, which often involve staging and collaboration with those being depicted, the photograph both is and is not documentary. As Wall notes, 'the tableau form, like a magic substance, both records with great fidelity and transforms the thing to which it is being true into another thing: a picture'.

Nous les arbres (Trees)
Fondation Cartier pour l'art contemporain, Paris, France
12 July 2019–5 January 2020

Into the Woods: Trees in Photography/ Trees in Illustration
Victoria and Albert Museum, London
18 November 2017–22 April 2018

Verschwindende Vermächtnisse: Die Welt als Wald (Disappearing Legacies: The World as a Forest)
CeNak (Center of Natural History, University of Hamburg), Hamburg, Germany
10 November 2017–29 March 2018

About Trees
Zentrum Paul Klee, Bern, Switzerland
17 October 2015–24 January 2016

In Focus: The Tree
J. Paul Getty Museum, Los Angeles, USA
8 February–3 July 2011

Some Trees
Neuer Aachener Kunstverein, Aachen, Germany
16 January–27 March 2005

The Magic of Trees
Fondation Beyeler, Basel, Switzerland
21 November 1998–5 April 1999

The Tree of Life: New Images of an Ancient Symbol
A Hayward Touring exhibition, organised by Southbank Centre, London
March 1989–November 1990

All dimensions are given in centimetres, and are height × width × depth.

Robert Adams
Fort Collins, Colorado, 1976
Gelatin silver print
12.7 × 12.7
Private collection, San Francisco
p. 143

Longmont, Colorado, 1976
Gelatin silver print
17.78 × 17.78
Private collection, San Francisco
p. 142

Above Boulder, Colorado, c.1979
Gelatin silver print
22.9 × 28.6
Courtesy the artist, Matthew Marks Gallery and Fraenkel Gallery
p. 140

Ontario, California, 1983
Gelatin silver print
12.7 × 12.7
Courtesy the artist, Matthew Marks Gallery and Fraenkel Gallery
p. 141

Driftwood Stump. Clatsop Beach, Clatsop County, Oregon, c.1991
Gelatin silver print
23 × 28
Courtesy the artist, Matthew Marks Gallery and Fraenkel Gallery

Eija-Liisa Ahtila
Horizontal – Vaakasuora, 2011
6-channel projected installation with 5.1 audio
6 min, no dialogue
Courtesy the artist and Marian Goodman Gallery, London
pp. 74–75

Yto Barrada
Terrain Vague – Tanger (Vacant Lot – Tangier), 2001
Chromogenic print
60 × 60
Courtesy Pace Gallery, Sfeir-Semler Gallery, Hamburg, Beirut, and Galerie Polaris, Paris
p. 138

Terrain Vague No. 2 (Vacant Lot No. 2), 2009
Chromogenic print
100 × 100
Courtesy Pace Gallery, Sfeir-Semler Gallery, Hamburg, Beirut,and Galerie Polaris, Paris
p. 139

Johanna Calle
Perímetros (Nogal Andino), 2012
Typed text on vintage notarial ledger
166 × 207
Archivos Pérez & Calle
pp. 116–17

Gillian Carnegie
Black Square, 2003
Oil on canvas
191 × 191
Private collection
p. 99

Green and Silver, 2005
Oil on canvas
231 × 160
Courtesy Galerie Gisela Capitain, Cologne
p. 100

Section, 2015
Oil on canvas
51 × 45.5
Courtesy Galerie Gisela Capitain, Cologne
p. 101

Tacita Dean
Crowhurst II, 2007
Gouache on photograph
297 × 380.5
De Pont museum, Tilburg, Netherlands
pp. 102–03

Peter Doig
The Architect's Home in the Ravine, 1991
Oil on canvas
200 × 275
Private collection
pp. 50–51

Jimmie Durham
It should work, 2012
Industrial machine, olive tree knot
165 × 75 × 70
Private collection, Derbyshire
p. 83

Kirsten Everberg
White Birch Grove, South (After Tarkovsky), 2008
Oil and enamel on canvas on panel
182.9 × 243.8
Hammer Museum, Los Angeles. Purchase
pp. 66–67

Anya Gallaccio
because I could not stop, 2002
Direct-cast bronze, ceramic, rope
280 × 200 × 150
Private collection

Simryn Gill
Channel #1, 2014
Photograph, gelatin silver print on paper
31.9 × 31.6
Tate: Purchased with funds provided by Tate Members, Tate Patrons and Tate International Council 2018
p. 124 (top)

Channel #2, 2014
Photograph, gelatin silver print on paper
31.9 × 31.6
Tate: Purchased with funds provided by Tate Members, Tate Patrons and Tate International Council 2018
p. 124 (bottom)

Channel #3, 2014
Photograph, gelatin silver print on paper
31.9 × 31.6
Tate: Purchased with funds provided by Tate Members, Tate Patrons and Tate International Council 2018

Channel #4, 2014
Photograph, gelatin silver print on paper
31.9 × 31.6

Tate: Purchased with funds provided by Tate Members, Tate Patrons and Tate International Council 2018
p. 125 (top)

Channel #5, 2014
Photograph, gelatin silver print on paper
31.9 × 31.6
Tate: Purchased with funds provided by Tate Members, Tate Patrons and Tate International Council 2018
p. 125 (bottom)

Channel #6, 2014
Photograph, gelatin silver print on paper
31.9 × 31.6
Tate: Purchased with funds provided by Tate Members, Tate Patrons and Tate International Council 2018

Channel #7, 2014
Photograph, gelatin silver print on paper
31.9 × 31.6
Tate: Purchased with funds provided by Tate Members, Tate Patrons and Tate International Council 2018

Channel #8, 2014
Photograph, gelatin silver print on paper
31.9 × 31.6
Tate: Purchased with funds provided by Tate Members, Tate Patrons and Tate International Council 2018

Channel #9, 2014
Photograph, gelatin silver print on paper
31.9 × 31.6
Tate: Purchased with funds provided by Tate Members, Tate Patrons and Tate International Council 2018

Rodney Graham
Gary Oak, Galiano Island, 2012
Transmounted C-print
186.3 × 234.8 × 5
Courtesy the artist and Hauser & Wirth
pp. 72–73

Shi Guowei
Pine, 2016
Painting on photograph
142 × 190.3
Courtesy the artist and Magician Space
pp. 60–61

Kyoto, 2019
Painting on photograph
148.5 × 139.2
Courtesy the artist and Magician Space

Hugh Hayden
Zelig 3 / Untitled (trunk), 2014
Adolescent peacock feathers on reinforced canvas
35.56 × 50.8 × 27.94
Courtesy Lisson Gallery
pp. 84–85

Eva Jospin
Forêt Palatine, 2019–20
Wood and cardboard
540 × 680 × 70
Courtesy the artist

Kazuo Kadonaga
Wood No. 5 CH, 1984
Cedar
56.5 × 471.8 × 45.7
Courtesy the artist and Nonaka-Hill
pp. 80–81

William Kentridge
Untitled (Lacking the Courage of the Bonfire), 2019
Indian ink on found pages
174 × 200
Courtesy private collection/ Goodman Gallery
pp. 118–19

Toba Khedoori
Untitled, 2008
Coloured pencil on paper
162.6 × 129.5
Kravis Collection
p. 65

Untitled (branches 1), 2011–12
Oil on linen
80.6 × 105.1
Private collection. Courtesy David Zwirner
p. 64

Untitled, 2018
Oil, graphite and wax on paper
243.8 × 335
Private collection
pp. 62–63

Luisa Lambri
Untitled (Palácio da Indústria #01), 2003
Lambda print mounted on acrylic
72 × 62.5
Collection Smeets
p. 52

Untitled (Sheats-Goldstein House #06), 2007
Laserchrome print
98 × 79.5
PAAF Collection
p. 53

Myoung Ho Lee
Tree... #2, 2012
Ink on paper
104 × 152
Courtesy Myoung Ho Lee and Gallery Hyundai
pp. 106–07

Zoe Leonard
Untitled, 2000
C-print
25.4 × 20.3
Courtesy the artist, Galerie Gisela Capitain, Cologne and Hauser & Wirth
p. 136

Untitled, 2000
C-print
25.4 × 20.3
Courtesy the artist, Galerie Gisela Capitain, Cologne and Hauser & Wirth
p. 137

Untitled, 2000
C-print
25.4 × 20.3
Courtesy the artist, Galerie Gisela Capitain, Cologne and Hauser & Wirth

Untitled, 2000
C-print
25.4 × 20.3
Courtesy the artist, Galerie Gisela Capitain, Cologne and Hauser & Wirth

Untitled, 2000
C-print
25.4 × 20.3
Courtesy the artist, Galerie

Gisela Capitain, Cologne and Hauser & Wirth

Robert Longo
Untitled (Sleepy Hollow), 2014
Charcoal on mounted paper
177.8 × 304.8
Courtesy Galerie Thaddaeus Ropac, London • Paris • Salzburg
pp. 68–69

Sally Mann
Deep South, Untitled (Fontainebleau), 1998
Gelatin silver print - tea-toned
101.6 × 127
Courtesy Gagosian
p. 134

Deep South, Untitled (Scarred Tree), 1998
Gelatin silver print - tea-toned
101.6 × 127
Courtesy Gagosian
p. 135

Steve McQueen
Lynching Tree, 2013
Light box with transparency
85 × 105 × 13
ISelf Collection
pp. 130–31

Jean-Luc Mylayne
No. 284, Février Mars 2004, 2004
C-print
182.9 × 182.9
Courtesy Sprüth Magers
p. 76

No. 304, Mars Avril 2005, 2005
C-print
123 × 123
Courtesy Sprüth Magers
p. 77

Mariele Neudecker
And Then the World Changed Colour: Breathing Yellow, 2019
Mixed media including water, acrylic, salt, fibreglass, spotlight
64 × 57 × 165
Courtesy the artist and Galeria Pedro Cera, Lisbon

Virginia Overton
Untitled, 2014
Eastern red cedar and marbleised mirror
180.3 × 29.2 × 2.5
Private collection

Untitled, 2014
Eastern red cedar and marbleised mirror
162.9 × 31.3 × 32.5
Courtesy the artist and White Cube

Untitled (Juniper), 2014
Mild steel, gold leaf and paint
288 × 106 × 113
Courtesy the artist and White Cube
p. 4

Untitled (Juniperus virginiana), 2020
Eastern red cedar
Dimensions variable
Courtesy the artist and White Cube

Roxy Paine
Rotoplasm, 2012
Stainless steel and enamel
165.1 × 121.9 × 61
Private collection, Tennessee
p. 91

Desolation Row, 2016
Fibreglass, polyester clear resin, ash, earth, rubber, wax, epoxy, light-emitting diodes, oil paint, stainless steel, aluminium and wood
274.3 × 415.3 × 247.7
Courtesy the artist and Kasmin Gallery, New York
pp. 92–95

Giuseppe Penone
Tree of 12 Metres, 1980–82
Wood
600 × 50 × 50
Tate: Purchased 1989
p. 79

Soffio di Foglie, 1982
Wood, bronze
410 × 300 × 180
Kunstmuseum Liechtenstein, Vaduz

Propagazione, 1995–2020
Pencil on paper and wall drawing
Dimensions variable
Courtesy the artist, Gagosian, Rome, and Marian Goodman Gallery, London

Albero Porta – Cedro/ Door Tree – Cedar, 2012
Cedar
316 × 105 × 105
Courtesy the artist, Gagosian, Rome, and Marian Goodman Gallery, London
p. 78

Abel Rodríguez
El Árbol de la Vida y Abundancia (Tree of Life and Abundance), 2018
Acrylic on paper
107 × 107
Courtesy FLORA ars+natura, Bogotá, Colombia

Terraza Alta II, 2018
Acrylic and ink on paper
70 × 100
Courtesy the artist and Instituto de Visión
pp. 114–15

Abel Rodríguez and Wilson Rodríguez
Terraza Baja, 2018
Acrylic on paper
70 × 100
Courtesy the artists and Instituto de Visión

Ugo Rondinone
White Moon, 2011
Cast aluminium, white enamel
600 × 416
Courtesy the artist and Sadie Coles HQ

George Shaw
Woodsman 5, 2009
Charcoal on paper
152.5 × 198
Private collection
pp. 126–27

The Heart of the Wood, 2015–16
Humbrol enamel on canvas
46 × 55
Courtesy Anthony Wilkinson Gallery, London
p. 128

Trespasser (2), 2019
Humbrol enamel on canvas
46 × 55
Private collection
p. 129

Robert Smithson
Upside Down Tree I, 1969
Alfred, New York, USA, 1969
Exhibition print from 35mm slide
22.9 × 22.9
Photograph by Robert Smithson
Holt/Smithson Foundation
p. 71

Upside Down Tree II, 1969
Captiva Island, Florida, USA, 1969
Exhibition print from 35mm slide
55.9 × 55.9
Photograph by Robert Smithson
Holt/Smithson Foundation

Upside Down Tree III, 1969
Yaxchilan, Yucatan, Mexico, 1969
Exhibition printfrom 35mm slide
22.9 × 22.9
Photograph by Robert Smithson
Holt/Smithson Foundation

Jennifer Steinkamp
Blind Eye, 1, 2018
Video installation
2min 77sec
Courtesy greengrassi, London, Lehmann Maupin, New York and Hong Kong
pp. 108–11

Thomas Struth
Paradise 11, Xi Shuang Banna, Yunnan Province, China 1999, 1999
Chromogenic print
181.3 × 232.8 × 6
Courtesy Thomas Struth and Marian Goodman Gallery
pp. 56–57

Paradise 13, Yakushima, Japan 1999, 1999
Chromogenic print
172.2 × 214.5 × 6
Courtesy Thomas Struth and Galerie Max Hetzler, Berlin, Paris, London
pp. 54–55

Rachel Sussman
Jomon Sugi, Japanese Cedar #0704-002 (2,180–7,000 years old; Yakushima, Japan), 2004
Archival print
111.8 × 137.2
Courtesy the artist
p. 123

Underground Forest #0707-1333 (13,000 years old; Pretoria, South Africa) DECEASED, 2007
Archival print
111.8 × 137.2
Courtesy the artist
p. 23

Spruce Gran Picea #0909-11A07 (9,550 years old; Sweden), 2009
Archival print
111.8 × 137.2
Courtesy the artist
p. 122

Pascale Marthine Tayou
Plastic Tree B, 2020
Tree, plastic bags, plants, flowers, pots and soil
Dimensions variable
Courtesy the artist and GALLERIA CONTINUA, San Gimignano/Beijing/Les Moulins/Habana

Jeff Wall
Daybreak (on an olive farm/Negev Desert/Israel), 2011
Colour photograph
242.9 × 318.6
Courtesy the artist and White Cube
pp. 132–33

Christo
Wrapped Tree, 1966
White birch tree, jute fabric, polyethylene and rope
1000 × 81
p. 12

Anya Gallaccio
because I could not stop, 2002
Installation view, Ikon, Birmingham, 2003
Direct-cast bronze, ceramic, rope
280 × 200 × 150
p. 89

Rodney Graham
Camera Obscura, 1979
Cardboard, plant material, chromogenic print, paint, wood, acrylic sheet
Dimensions variable
p. 17

Shi Guowei
Kyoto, 2017
Painting on photograph
148.5 × 139.2
pp. 58–59

Eva Jospin
Forêt (Forest), 2013
Installation view, *Carte blanche à Eva Jospin*, Manufacture des Gobelins, Paris, 2013
Wood and cardboard
900 × 400
pp. 120–21

Gordon Matta-Clark
Tree Dance, 1971
16mm film, black and white, silent
9min 41sec
p. 32

Ana Mendieta
Tree of Life, 1976
Colour photograph
p. 31

Piet Mondrian
Flowering Apple Tree, 1912
Oil on canvas
78.5 × 107.5
p. 10

Mariele Neudecker
And Then the World Changed Colour: Breathing Yellow, 2019
Installation view, Dulwich Picture Gallery, London, 2019
Mixed media including water, acrylic, salt, fibreglass, spotlight
64 × 57 × 165
Commissioned by Dulwich Picture Gallery, London
With thanks to Dulwich Picture Gallery, curator Kathleen Soriano and Arts Council of England
pp. 96–97

Virginia Overton
Untitled (Juniperus virginiana), 2016
Installation view, *Descent*, Institute of Contemporary Art, University of Pennsylvania, Philadelphia, 2016
Eastern red cedar
417.2 × 790.8
pp. 86–87

Giuseppe Penone
Albero di 8 metri (8-Metre Tree), 2000
Cedar wood
2 elements, 402 × 58 × 59; 401 × 58 × 59
p. 15

Continuerà a crescere tranne che in quel punto (It Will Continue to Grow Except at That Point), 1968–2003
Tree (Ailanthus altissima), bronze
Natural dimensions
p. 30

Ugo Rondinone
Wind Moon, 2011
Cast aluminium, white enamel
520 × 600 × 460
p. 105

Robert Smithson
Dead Tree, 1969
Installation view, *Prospect 69*, Kunsthalle Düsseldorf, Germany, 1969
Tree, mirrors
p. 13

Pascale Marthine Tayou
Plastic Tree B, 2010
Installation view, *REM(A)INDERS*, Galleria Continua/Beijing, 2010
Wild pear tree, plastic bags, Chinese pot, plants, flowers, soil
Dimensions variable
p. 112

Unknown
Fresco from Villa Livia, Museo Nazionale Romano, Palazzo Massimo, Rome, c.30–c.20 BC
p. 29

ACKNOWLEDGEMENTS

This exhibition would not have been possible without the collaboration of the participating artists, their studios and galleries, to whom we are greatly indebted.

We are also grateful to the following individuals and organisations for their collaboration and support:

Viola Ammenti, Marian Goodman Gallery
Thalassa Balanis, Lisson Gallery
Florian Berktold, Hauser & Wirth
Melissa Birle, Sotheby's
Elena Brugnano, Galerie Gisela Capitain
Johanna Calle and Julio Pérez
Elizabeth Callinicos, Goodman Gallery
Margherita Ciocci, Pace Gallery
Markéta Condeixa, Galeria Pedro Cera
Stephanie Daniel, David Zwirner
Poppy Fairfax, Hauser & Wirth
Regina Fiorito, Galerie Gisela Capitain
Martin Fryer
Hannah Gruy, White Cube
Robin Hemmer, Kunstmuseum Liechtenstein
Mattias Herold, Studio Rondinone
Max Edouard Hetzler, Galerie Max Hetzler
Greg Hilty, Lisson Gallery
Patrick Kammann, Galerie Sfeir-Semler
Kazuo Kadonaga
Melissa Lazarov, Gagosian
Julia Lee, Studio Rondinone
Lisa Le Feuvre, Holt/Smithson Foundation
Ludmilla Lencsés, Sprüth Magers
Leo Lichen, Magician Space
Élodie Maincent, GALLERIA CONTINUA
Pepi Marchetti Franchi, Gagosian
Portland McCormick, Hammer Museum
Stuart Mitchell, Studio Rondinone
Clare Morris, Thomas Dane Gallery
Anne Caroline Müller, Atelier Thomas Struth
Marie Mur, Atelier Eva Jospin
Hannah Murray, Tate
Mariska Nietzman, Kasmin Gallery
Rodney Nonaka-Hill, Nonaka-Hill
Takayoshi Nonaka-Hill, Nonaka-Hill
Anatol Orient, Anderson O'Day Fine Art
Gary Owen
Charlotte Panis, Regen Projects
Ilppo Pohjola, Crystal Eye
Hella Pohl, Galerie Thaddaeus Ropac
Samantha Rees, Kasmin Gallery
Florian Rehn, Galerie Max Hetzler
Maria Schnyder, De Pont museum
Claire Smith, White Cube
Yookyung Sohn, Gallery Hyundai
Jo Stella-Sawicka, Goodman Gallery
Brandon Studer, Studio Rondinone
Xunzhi Sun, Magician Space
Putri Tan, Gagosian
Roger Tatley, Marian Goodman Gallery
Pascale Marthine Tayou
Ted Turner, Matthew Marks Gallery
Bernard Utudjian, Galerie Polaris
Anthony Wilkinson, Anthony Wilkinson Gallery

LENDERS

Eija-Liisa Ahtila
Anthony Wilkinson Gallery
Archivos Pérez & Calle
Yto Barrada
Collection Smeets
David Zwirner
De Pont Museum
Gagosian
Galeria Pedro Cera
Galerie Gisela Capitain, Cologne
Galerie Max Hetzler
Gallery Hyundai
Goodman Gallery
greengrassi
Hammer Museum
Hauser & Wirth
Hugh Hayden
Holt/Smithson Foundation
ISelf Collection
Eva Jospin
Kazuo Kadonaga
Kasmin Gallery
Kravis Collection
Kunstmuseum Liechtenstein
Myoung Ho Lee
Lehmann Maupin
Lisson Gallery
Magician Space
Marian Goodman Gallery
Matthew Marks Gallery
Jean-Luc Mylayne
Mariele Neudecker
Nonaka-Hill
PAAF Collection
Pace Gallery
Giuseppe Penone
Sprüth Magers
Thomas Struth
Rachel Sussman
Tate
White Cube

And those who wish to remain anonymous.

SUPPORTERS

This exhibition has been generously supported by:

Gagosian
Gallery Hyundai
Lisson Gallery
Pace Gallery
Pro Helvetia
Sadie Coles HQ

EXHIBITION CREDITS

Hayward Gallery
Ralph Rugoff, Director
Katie Guggenheim, Assistant Curator
Phoebe Cripps, Assistant Curator, maternity cover
Marie-Charlotte Carrier, Curatorial Assistant
Justine Jean, Curatorial Intern
Carlotta Pierleoni, Curatorial Intern
Miharu Hori, Curatorial Intern
Aoife Leach, General Manager
Imogen Winter, Senior Registrar
Alice Peters, Assistant Registrar
Alison Maun, Exhibition Bookings and Indemnity Coordinator
Juliane Heynert, Installation Manager
William Clifford, Senior Technician
Marcia Ceppo, Operations and Logistics Manager
Matt Arthurs, Philip Gardner, Kate Parrott, Installation Technicians
Rachel Ward, Operations Administrator
Lucy Biddle, Exhibitions Interpretation Manager
Jennifer Hawkins, Administrator
Beatrice Walker, PA to Director
Nancy Brian, Librarian
Leonie Warner, Senior Visitor Experience Manager
Kate Ford, Duty Manager
Emma Bani-Walker, Duty Manager
Gareth Spencer, Duty Manager

Exhibition graphics design by Nina Jua Klein
Lighting by Lightwaves Ltd.

Hayward Gallery Publishing
Alice Nightingale, Art Publisher
Diana Adell, Publishing Project Manager
Alex Glen, Sales Manager

Southbank Centre
Debo Amon, Literature Programmer
Elaine Bedell, Chief Executive
Iona Bell, Marketing Officer
Bea Colley, Literature Programmer
Chris Denton, Executive Director, Audiences
Helen Faulkner, Senior Marketing Manager
Roger Hennigan, Technical Manager
Ted Hodgkinson, Head of Literature and Spoken Word
Andrea Ioannou, Philanthropy Manager
Ellie Mayes, Corporate Development Manager
Filipa Mendes, Senior Press Manager
Marie Ortinau, Education Manager
Amanda Pearlman, Head of Retail and Buying
Ruth Pelopida, Technical Director
Hilary Philpot, Head of Health and Safety
Justin Pledger, Head of Corporate Partnerships
Jessica Santer, Head of Creative Learning
Trish Thomas, Head of Digital Engagement
Hilton Wells, Head of Technical Services, Property Development

COPYRIGHT CREDITS

IMAGE CREDITS

All images are courtesy the artist unless otherwise stated:

Courtesy the artist and White Cube pp. 4 (photo © White Cube [George Darrell]), 86–87 and 159 (top) (photo © Constance Mensh); courtesy the artist p. 12 (photo: Ab de Jager); courtesy Holt/Smithson Foundation pp. 13, 71, 162 (top); courtesy the artist p. 15 (photo © Cathy Carver), 30 (photo © Archivio Penone); collection of the Vancouver Art Gallery, Acquisition Fund, VAG 86.21 a-f p. 17 (photo: Vancouver Art Gallery); Getty Research Institute, Los Angeles (2861-964) p. 40; courtesy Sotheby's pp. 50–51, 149 (top); courtesy the artist and Thomas Dane Gallery p.53; courtesy the artist and Marian Goodman Gallery pp. 56–57, 74–75 and 146 (bottom) (photo: Antti Ruusuvuori); courtesy the artist and Magician Space, Beijing pp. 58–61, 152 (top); courtesy the artist and David Zwirner pp. 62–64, 154 (bottom); courtesy Regen Projects, Los Angeles p. 65 (photo: Douglas M. Parker Studio); courtesy the artist and 1301PE, Los Angeles pp. 66–67 and 150 (top) (photo: Fredrik Nilsen); courtesy GalerieThaddaeus Ropac, London/ Paris/Salzburg pp. 68–69, 156 (bottom); courtesy Hauser & Wirth pp. 73, 151 (bottom); courtesy Sprüth Magers and Gladstone Gallery pp. 76–77, 158 (top); courtesy Gagosian Gallery pp. 78 and 160 (top) (photo © Archivio Penone), 134–35 and 157 (top); p. 79 (photo © Tate); courtesy Nonaka-Hill, Los Angeles pp. 80–81, 153 (bottom); courtesy the artist and Fondazione Morra Greco pp. 83 and 149 (bottom) (photo: Danilo Donzelli); courtesy Lisson Gallery and the artist pp. 84–85 and 152 (bottom) (photos: Mark Waldhauser); courtesy the artist and Kasmin Gallery, New York pp. 91, 92–95 and 159 (bottom) (photos: Christopher Stach); courtesy Pedro Cera and the artist pp. 96–97, 158 (bottom) and cover (photos: Benjamin Jones); courtesy the artist and Cabinet, London pp. 99, 148 (top); courtesy Galerie Gisela Capitain, Cologne pp. 100, 101 (photo: Simon Vogel); courtesy Collection de Pont Museum, Tilburg (NL) pp. 102–03 and 148 (bottom) (photo: Peter Cox); courtesy Studio Rondinone pp. 105 and 161 (top) (photo: Stefan Altenburger); courtesy Myoung Ho Lee and Gallery Hyundai pp. 106–07, 155 (bottom); courtesy greengrassi, London, Lehmann Maupin, New York and Hong Kong pp. 108–11, 162 (bottom) (photo: Jennifer Steinkamp); courtesy the artist and GALLERIA CONTINUA, San Gimignano/Beijing/Les Moulins/ Habana pp. 112 and 164 (top) (photo: Oak Taylor-Smith); courtesy the artist and Instituto de Visión pp. 114–15, 160 (bottom); courtesy Archivos Pérez & Calle pp. 116–17 and 147 (bottom) (photo: O Monsalve); courtesy the artist and Goodman Gallery pp. 118–19, 154 (top) (photo: Thys Dullart); courtesy the artist pp. 120–21, 153 (top) (photo: Rebecca Fanuele); courtesy the artist and Utopia Art Sydney pp. 124–25, 151 (top); courtesy Anthony Wilkinson Gallery, London pp. 126–27 and 161 (bottom) (photo: Peter White), 128–29 (photos: Matthew Hollow); courtesy the artist, Thomas Dane Gallery and Marian Goodman Gallery pp. 130–31, 157 (bottom); courtesy the artist, Galerie Gisela Capitain, Cologne and Hauser & Wirth pp. 136–37, 156 (top); Galerie Polaris Paris pp. 138–39, 147 (top); courtesy the artist, Matthew Marks Gallery and Fraenkel Gallery pp. 140–41; courtesy Fraenkel Gallery, San Francisco pp. 142–43, 146 (top).

Published on the occasion of
the exhibition:

AMONG THE TREES

Hayward Gallery, London
4 March–17 May 2020

Curator: Ralph Rugoff
Assistant Curators: Phoebe Cripps
and Katie Guggenheim
Curatorial Assistant:
Marie-Charlotte Carrier

This exhibition has been made possible by the provision of insurance through the Government Indemnity Scheme. Hayward Gallery would like to thank HM Government for providing Government Indemnity and the Department for Culture, Media and Sport and Arts Council England for arranging the indemnity.

Published in 2020 by
Hayward Gallery Publishing
Southbank Centre
Belvedere Road
London SE1 8XX
UK
www.southbankcentre.co.uk

Art Publisher: Alice Nightingale
Publishing Project Manager: Diana Adell
Sales Manager: Alex Glen
Catalogue designed by Melanie Mues,
Mues Design, London
Printed in Belgium by Graphius

Text on individual artists written by Lucy Biddle (Robert Adams, Johanna Calle, Tacita Dean, Anya Gallaccio, Rodney Graham, Jean-Luc Mylayne, Virginia Overton, Giuseppe Penone, George Shaw, Thomas Struth, Jeff Wall); Marie-Charlotte Carrier (Yto Barrada, Simryn Gill, Shi Guowei, Zoe Leonard, Abel Rodríguez, Rachel Sussman, Pascale Marthine Tayou); Phoebe Cripps (Gillian Carnegie, Kirsten Everberg, Kazuo Kadonaga, William Kentridge, Steve McQueen, Jennifer Steinkamp); Katie Guggenheim (Eija-Liisa Ahtila, Hugh Hayden, Toba Khedoori, Robert Smithson); and Helen Luckett (Peter Doig, Jimmie Durham, Eva Jospin, Luisa Lambri, Myoung Ho Lee, Robert Longo, Sally Mann, Mariele Neudecker, Roxy Paine, Ugo Rondinone).

Matteo Pasquinelli's text originally published in Khadija von Zinnenburg Carroll (ed.), *Botanical Drift: Protagonists of the Invasive Herbarium* (Berlin: Sternberg Press, 2018), pp. 163–74

A catalogue record for this book is available from the British Library.

ISBN 978 1 85332 366 9

Distributed in North America,
Central America and South America by
ARTBOOK | D.A.P.
75 Broad Street, Suite 630
New York, NY 10004
USA
tel: +1 212 627 1999
www.artbook.com

Distributed in the UK and Europe by
Cornerhouse Publications
HOME, 2 Tony Wilson Place
Manchester, M15 4FN
UK
tel: +44 (0)161 212 3466
www.cornerhousepublications.org

Cover: Mariele Neudecker, *And Then the World Changed Colour: Breathing Yellow*, 2019 (detail)

This book is printed on a mix of recycled paper, paper from responsibly managed forests certified by the Forest Stewardship Council, and from forests where no wood is illegally or unethically harvested.

All paper is elemental chlorine free.

FSC
www.fsc.org
MIX
Paper from
responsible sources
FSC® C014767

SOUTHBANK
CENTRE

LOTTERY FUNDED
ARTS COUNCIL ENGLAND
Supported using public funding by
ARTS COUNCIL
ENGLAND